Emotionally Involved

Emotionally Involved

The Impact of Researching Rape

Rebecca Campbell

Routledge   New York   London

Published in 2002 by
Routledge
29 West 35th Street
New York, NY 10001

Published in Great Britain by
Routledge
11 New Fetter Lane
London EC4P 4EE

Routledge is an imprint of the Taylor & Francis Group.

Library of Congress Cataloging-in-Publication Data
Campbell, Rebecca, 1969–
    Emotionally involved : the impact of researching rape /
    Rebecca Campbell.
       p.   cm.
    Includes bibliographical references and index.
    ISBN 0-415-92591-6   —   ISBN 0-415-92594-0 (pbk.)
    1. Rape—Research.   2. Rape—Psychological aspects.
    3. Research teams—Psychology.
    4. Research teams—Attitudes.
    I. Title.
  HV6558 .C36   2001
  362.883'07'2—dc21   2001019661

10 9   8   7   6   5   4   3   2   1

For Delores
and
For Eric

contents

acknowledgments

I n its development, this writing project was known among my family, friends, and colleagues simply as "the book." "The book" developed its own personality, occupying space in all of our lives as if it were a real member of the cast. It became such a fixture around the house that I wouldn't have been surprised if it had started receiving credit card offers in the mail or other correspondence. "The book" was a temperamental roommate—it had good days and bad days, but generally preferred not to be disturbed. "The book" needed to be fed, watered, and walked, and occasionally sent on vacation. Sometimes "the book" craved company and companionship; at other times it was satisfied only with solitude. For all those who alternately tolerated and supported "the book" and its quirkiness, I thank you.

The UIC Women & Violence Project was funded by a grant from the National Institute of Mental Health Program for Mental Health Services Research on Women and Gender (R24 MH54212-02). Thanks to Joe Flaherty, M.D., and Susan Adams, Ph.D., for their feedback throughout the project. Preparation of this manuscript was supported by a Faculty Scholar Award from the University of Illinois at Chicago Great Cities Institute. Thanks to David Perry, Director, and all of the 1998–1999 scholars for their interest in this work.

The Department of Psychology at the University of Illinois at Chicago has provided a good professional home for my work. Thanks to Roger Weissberg, Robin Miller, Jim Kelly, Ed Trickett, Linda Skitka, and Andy Conway for their encouragement. Special thanks to Stephanie Riger for helping me find a publisher and for providing feedback on early drafts of this manuscript. To Chris Keys I owe a special debt of gratitude for recognizing the right moment when this manuscript was ready to be shared with others—his complete conviction that it was ready helped me feel ready. To my upstairs neighbors in the Department of Sociology and Department of Criminal Justice, thanks to Tony Orum for advice on publishing and multidisciplinary writing; Sarah Ullman for sharing her incredible command of the rape victimology literature; and Lisa Frohmann for sage methodological guidance and her many acts of kindness during the bleaker moments. To my across-two-states neighbors at the Michigan Public Health Institute, thanks for keeping me grounded in the real world.

Throughout the preparation of this manuscript, my writing group—Ann Feldman and Sharon Haar—provided appropriate doses of encouragement and whoop-ass. Being professors of English Composition and Architecture (respectively), they wouldn't buy disciplinary jargon, instead dealing only in the currency of clear prose—for which I am grateful. Many thanks to Tracy Sefl, Courtney Ahrens, and Sharon Wasco for culling the library in search of answers to my vague "Can you find something on . . ." questions and for providing thoughtful feedback on ideas in progress. Thanks to Valerie Lorimer for her assistance with transcription and Cherise Watkins-Jones for her help with coding. Long-distance support from Holly Angelique, Karen Bachar, Charlene Baker, Bill Davidson, Kim Eby, Mary Koss, and Pat Martin kept me believing this was worth writing.

For the intangibles—thanks to Joseph Bauers who taught me to write and love writing; and Shelley Smithson who helped me find the emotional courage to write in my own voice.

For the tangibles—much appreciation to my editor, Ilene Kalish, who never lost faith (or at least never let on that she had lost faith) that there would be good news at the end of the bad news parade. Thanks to all the staff at Routledge who helped transform my manuscript—visually and substantively—into a real book.

To those I hold dear in my heart, I thank them for their simple gifts that are far from simplistic: the members of the Women & Violence research team for their honesty; the rape survivors we interviewed for their trust; my grandmothers for their presence; my parents for their guidance; and my husband Eric for his love.

I finish this project where it began, in the desert of Tucson, Arizona. Witnessing bloom in vast scorched earth inspired me to write this book and gives me peace as I lay it to rest.

Tucson, Arizona
April 2001

Emotion is the chief source of all becoming-consciousness. There can be no transforming of darkness into light and of apathy into movement without emotion.

—Carl Jung in *Four Archetypes*

I didn't realize that it's emotion, not event, that creates a dynamic response in the mind of a reader. The artist's job is to sink a taproot in the reader's brain that will grow downward and find a path into the reader's soul and existence, so that some new emotional inflorescence will grow out of it.

—Barbara Kingsolver in *High Tide in Tucson*

In nine out of ten cases the original wish to write is the wish to make oneself felt.

—Elizabeth Bowen,
quoted in *Elizabeth Bowen* by Victoria Glendinning

The university buries emotions and faculty look for "balanced" opinions.

—Laura Nader in *The Cold War and the University*

I am a researcher who studies rape. That means I think about rape for prolonged periods of time. I read about it, talk about it, write about it, and bear witness to it. That means I might, depending on how I choose to conduct my research, actually sit face to face with a rape survivor and listen to her tell me what happened to her. I might see up close and personal the devastation of rape over and over again. I do, in fact. My job is to listen to women's stories of rape. Colleagues I have worked with for years, who know what I study and have even read my research articles, have never pieced this together. It has never occurred to them what it means to research rape, as a woman. They have not considered what it might feel like to do this research. This book is about how it feels to study rape. This is the story of how listening to and learning from women's stories of rape affects researchers, emotionally and intellectually.[1]

My experiences as a community volunteer and researcher have made me not so much bitter as extremely grim. It's a rare day that I don't think about rape. There are words and images I wish I could forever purge from my memory, but cannot. I carry them with me, and try to make peace with them and learn from them. I don't think I have ever truly believed that "I've seen it all" because I know it can always be worse. But very little surprises me anymore, and very little shocks me anymore. My realm of possibilities knows some sickening bounds. But what happened one day, in painstaking slow motion, completely recalibrated my expectations. I had never heard anything so devastating in my life, and I had never borne witness to such agony and strength. A single interview, the experiences of one rape survivor, forever changed how I understood myself as a researcher.

I was 19 years old when I started volunteering at rape crisis centers. I didn't experience college in a blissful haze of beer bashes and fraternity parties—I cleaned up after them. I spent college in hospital emergency rooms, police departments, and courtrooms working with rape survivors who were victimized occasionally by complete strangers, but more often than not by someone they knew and trusted. I spent college knee-deep in rape. I was deeply affected by what I saw, and became an academic psychologist specializing in violence against women. Interviewing rape survivors for my research projects added to the countless stories I had already collected as a rape victim advocate. After nearly seven years of practice as a researcher, I began my second major research project on rape, funded by the National Institute of Mental Health. It was a study of how community agencies, such as the police, courts, hospitals, and mental health centers, respond (or don't respond) to the needs of rape victims. I assembled a team of bright, passionate women—undergraduate and graduate students—to help me plan and execute this study. We finalized the research design, devised the sampling protocol, constructed the interview protocol, trained the additional interviewing staff, and began to recruit and interview rape survivors.

Our research team had been interviewing victims for about one month with no problems. We wanted to respect survivors' healing process, so we favored noninvasive sampling strategies. We developed posters and fliers about our project and systematically distributed them throughout Chicago. We let women know we wanted to hear from them when they were ready to talk about their experiences of rape. The decision when and if to call our research office was theirs. To reach out to women in our communities, we targeted nail salons, among other places. Women of many different races, ethnicities, and social classes pass through nail salons, so they seemed both strange and obvious recruitment sites. One owner of a nail salon received our recruitment fliers in the mail. She read the materials, and liked what they had to say enough to place them in her salon at the drying table where women sit to wait for their nails to dry. She placed all of the fliers out, except one. She kept that one for herself. She carried the flier in her purse for weeks. She read it over and over again. Months passed, but then she called us.

The woman was clearly nervous on the phone, but after some calming chit-chat, our undergraduate interview coordinator proceeded through the screening questions. Our screening criteria stipulated that women would be eligible for participation if they had been assaulted within the last three years. We needed reliable data, and if survivors' contacts with various social systems were a long time ago, some memory distortion could have occurred. The interview coordinator asked this woman if she had been raped within the last three years. Because she answered no, the coordinator went through the "screen-out" script we had so meticulously constructed. The woman would hear nothing of it. As our coordinator told us later, "she went off," really gave her an earful. She was absolutely furious. She had thought and thought and thought for so long about calling, and then did, only to hear she couldn't be interviewed?! She told our coordinator in no uncertain terms that it takes more than three years to be emotionally ready to talk about something like this.

At our next research team meeting, the interview coordinator brought this call to our attention. She asked us very hard questions: If we were supposed to be studying how the community may revictimize rape survivors, then could we do this to this woman, and to other women? Were we really all that different? This was, I believe, our most intense and stressful meeting ever. Emotions ran very high. I sat quietly and watched the members of the research team debate: yes, the screening criteria should stay; no, they shouldn't. What are the pros of keeping these rules? The cons? Could we change the rules? Would we be sacrificing our methodology by making these changes? Did we care? These discussions were spoken through many voices—the voices of researchers, of rape victim advocates, of survivors. These voices and perspectives led us to very different conclusions about how to proceed. I sat in confusion. I had never felt so trapped by my role as a researcher. My experiences as a rape victim advocate were chastising my project and me. I kept imagining this woman carrying around our flier, and how hard it must have been for her to call. I kept thinking about how our coordinator must have felt to be the one to take that call.

I owed this rape survivor something—I had a responsibility to her, and so did our project. We decided to change the screening criteria. If a woman had been raped as an adult (18 or older), then she was eligible, regardless of how long ago the assault occurred. We would carefully document at what point this change in our protocol occurred and how many women we had screened out prior to the change. We weren't sure if women would be able to accurately remember the specifics of their contact with social systems for rapes long ago, but we also weren't sure that they could not.

But what should we do for this survivor, the one who sparked this whole discussion? We listened to her concerns, and we changed our rules. Would we dare call her back? The interview coordinator was emphatic: we must call her back, tell her about the change, and thank her. If she still wanted to be interviewed, we would gladly do it. We decided to call the other screen-outs as well to offer them the opportunity to participate. Everyone we could reach was pleased with the new criteria, and all signed up for an interview, including the woman who started it all.

This rape survivor's interview was scheduled for a Tuesday morning at 10:00 in our project office on campus. We ask the women we will be interviewing to meet us at the building next door so we can escort them to the project office, because the architecture of our building is very confusing and it's easy to get lost. The interviewer who was assigned to this case had been briefed about its history and was nervous, but ready to go. Ten o'clock came and went. She waited, and waited some more. She decided to run back to the project office to check the phone messages to see if the woman called. No calls. She went back to the meeting location and waited some more. A no-show. She came back to the project office, and logged it in the interview book as a no-show.

At noon, I was preparing for a class I was about to teach when my office phone rang. It was another interviewer who worked on the project, and she was frantic: "There's a woman here looking for the project office for her interview!" "Where is the woman now?" I asked. She was upstairs, and very upset. I told the interviewer to tell the woman to sit tight; I was on my way up. In the elevator, I pieced together who "this woman" must be. My heart sank. She was supposed to have her interview at 10:00, but something was very wrong, because it was now 12:00. Her interview was scheduled with someone else, not the interviewer who had just called me. What was going on?

The woman and the interviewer were sitting outside our project office. As I opened up the office, I introduced myself as the project director and apologized for the confusion. The woman was already trembling and crying. The interviewer ran down to the cafeteria to get her some coffee while I asked what happened. This woman had taken the entire day off from work to come to the campus for her interview. She told me she wanted to do the interview because she had important things to say. She got to the campus late because she was so scared about the interview and got lost on campus. She was not so much mad as upset. And scared.

My guess was that the assigned interviewer and the woman had missed each other when the interviewer ran back to check for phone messages. That's exactly what happened. When the woman couldn't find her interviewer, she panicked and wandered around campus for two hours trying to find our project office or anyone who could help her. At one point in this search, the woman stopped in the German Department to see if they could help. A secretary calmed her, gave her a place to sit, and called the Women's Affairs Office, hoping they might know about the project. Coincidentally, one of the other project interviewers works there, and was at the office that day. She figured that something had gone wrong, and asked her boss if she could step out for a minute to collect the rape survivor and call me. I was devastated. Nothing like this had ever happened before. We were so careful; we had detailed procedures, clear instructions, safeguards on top of safeguards. We had been interviewing for about a month with no snags.

I told this rape survivor that as the project director, I accepted full responsibility for what had happened, and I was sorry. I told her I would be doing everything in my power to make sure nothing like this ever happened again. But, then the most amazing thing happened. She looked me straight in the eyes and said, "I still want my interview." I told her I would personally do the interview if she wanted me to. She did. She said she felt like she could talk to me, that I seemed to care, that I seemed to want to hear from her. And I did. I told her I would need a few moments to get my materials ready and set up the interview room. I found our graduate student interview coordinator, who coincidentally was enrolled in the course I was scheduled to teach in five minutes. When she heard what was going on, she offered to do the interview for me so I could go to class, but I told her that in good conscience I could not pass this victim off to yet another person. I had to do this interview, so I asked her to cancel class for me.

It was now 12:30, two-and-a-half hours after the interview was supposed to start. I sat quietly with this woman for a few minutes—I told her to take her time getting settled. The first questions in the interview ask victims how they heard about the project and why they decided to participate. We also ask what concerns they have about the interview, and what we could do along the way to address those issues. This survivor told me about her nail salon, how she received our fliers in the mail, and how they touched her. She had never viewed her business as a resource, as a place of expertise for something like this. She told me about the phone call with the undergraduate interview coordinator, and her anger and humiliation. I explained how the coordinator brought this problem to our attention and advocated strongly on her behalf, and how we changed our procedures. She was visibly stunned—"Because of me? Really? It was me? It was what I said?" Yes. "You listened?" Yes.

We ask rape survivors near the beginning of the interview to "tell us your story." As an open-ended narrative, it allows survivors to tell us, in as much detail as they want, for as long or as short as they want, what happened to them. We ask about the rape early in the interview because it's like an elephant in the room. We know they've been raped, they know we know; they assume, correctly, that we're going to ask about it. Many of the women we interviewed in this project acknowledged that they were glad to get it over with near the beginning, so they didn't have to keep waiting and wondering: Will it be the next question? Will it be on the next page? When are they going to ask about it? We tell them when we're going to ask it, and why. It seems to help.

The next question in this interview was the "tell me your story" question. This woman's answer took three hours. She was raped and re-raped and re-raped, first by the rapists, then by the police officer, and then by the doctor. Then she was silent for nine years. She never said another word about it to anyone. She never told a single friend, no family, no one. She reported to the police and went to the hospital emergency room, but what happened there was so bad that she never wanted to talk about it ever again. Never. Never—until she received our fliers at her nail salon. She thought maybe she could talk to us because we seemed to "get it." So she called and screened out. But then she heard from us again, came to the campus, and got lost. The abuse never seemed to end. I so wanted to take back everything that had happened that morning and in those prior phone calls. I was surprised she wanted to do the interview.

As I listened to her preface her story with this information, I realized this was something more than just a research interview. I was not just the project director, not just a researcher. I was the first person she was going to tell about the rape in nine years. I was going to be the first person she was going to trust with this information. I was being given something very fragile, and yet very strong. It was a sobering responsibility. We both knew that what was coming was going to be hard for both of us.

She had been new to the city and was walking home one night because she had no money for the train. She passed three men on the sidewalk, who followed her for several blocks. As she passed an alley, they abducted her, and holding a knife to her throat, ripped her clothes off. They orally raped her, vaginally raped her, and anally raped her, each taking his individual turn with each form of violation. Then they decided to work on her in pairs. Then they all worked on her at once. In the midst of this, one of the rapists expressed some reservations to the others. He said he wasn't sure if he could do this. Another pulled a gun on him and told him to finish the job. After they were done, she was practically dead. The rapist with the gun said he wanted to finish her off—kill her, shoot her, dump her in the street like the rest of the trash, or into someone's lawn like the rest of the dog shit. He pulled the gun out. The reluctant rapist stepped in, and told him no, and then they fled. She said she never really knew how to feel about the reluctant rapist: Grateful to him because he spared her life? Or hatred because he let her live, and live with this?

She somehow managed to pull herself to standing, tied the scraps of her clothes around her, and staggered home. She immediately took a bath. After a couple of hours, she called the police, who brought her to the hospital emergency room. While she waited for a doctor, the police officer took her statement. He listened. He smiled. He smirked. And he continually reached down to adjust his erection. He was aroused by her story, and let her know it. When the doctor came in, the first thing he asked was whether she showered or bathed since "the incident." Yes. He looked at her in total disgust, and said, "Next time, don't bathe—we can't do the exam now," and he walked out of the room. Neither the hospital nor the police had called a rape victim advocate to come be with this woman; no one was there to tell the doctor that exams can be done after showering and bathing; no one was there to take the officer to task. When the doctor left, the police officer said to her, "Well, he says there was no rape, so I guess there was no rape. Case closed," and he left. The woman left the exam room and walked home. And she never said another word about this to anyone. Until now.

It took her three hours to tell this story. She had flashbacks trying to tell me, reliving all the details of that night. She wept throughout the entire story. She trembled. She shook. She rocked back and forth. She buried her face in her hands. She shredded tissues. She dug her nails into her skin. I held her hand, wiped her eyes, and passed her tissues. I talked her through the flashbacks, returning her to the safety of our interview room. I knelt with her when she asked me to join her in prayer for the strength to tell this story. My emotions ran the gamut from shock to anger to pain to fear, but I didn't have time to process them. What attention I could afford to my own reactions had to keep the waves of nausea in check. My only job was to bear witness to her story with support and comfort. It was more job than I had ever attempted before.

After she had told her story and we had both lived through it, I had in my lap an interview packet that was less than one-third complete. We had more questions to go, about how the assault impacted other aspects of her life. I asked this woman if she wanted to go on and she said she did; I wasn't entirely sure I wanted to. But when she was ready, we moved through the rest of the interview.

After two more hours, the interview was over. At the end, she said very quietly, "I should have walked home a different way. I should have known better." "It's not your fault," I said, "There's no way you could have known. You did nothing wrong." "It's not my fault?" she asked very quietly. "It's not your fault," I repeated. Over and over again, she would ask, and I would affirm. It's not my fault? It's not your fault. After several minutes of repeating this exchange, she started crying again, "It's not my fault. I've thought for so long it was. I can't tell you what it means to me that you told me it wasn't." She hugged me, and we both cried. I offered to walk her to her car.

On the way, she told me about a cruise to the Caribbean she was planning. She had the trip booked, but was scared. She said she felt so heavy, so weighted down that she was afraid she might sink the cruise ship. Of course, she knew she wouldn't literally sink the ship, but she felt so burdened by the assault that she didn't think she could enjoy the trip. After talking with me, she said she felt like she could get on the ship now without risk of sinking. She hugged me again, and we said good-bye. I watched her car leave, oblivious to the world around me. I could not speak, I could not think, I just wanted to be anywhere else. I felt strong and weak—proud about what we had accomplished together, drained because of what it took from both of us. The nausea that I had held at bay throughout the interview was returning. I walked back to my building, found a deserted bathroom in a corner on the upper floor, and vomited, expunging everything that I had taken in that day. This was only the second time I had gotten sick from my work, once after my first case as a rape victim advocate in a hospital ER, and now this day. Both were initiations, rites of passage from which there was no return. As I splashed cold water on my face, I decided to go home for the day. I could not bear the thought of running into any of my colleagues and being asked how my research was coming along, or anything else for that matter. I was quite sure that any detail of academic life—a reminder memo about a faculty meeting, a grant budget—would prompt me to snap. The contrast would be too great.

• • •

After that day, after that interview, I was never able to think about rape the same way again; I felt rape as I never had before. The woman's story was gruesome—one of the worst I had ever heard. The treatment she received by the legal and medical communities was abominable, but also was not entirely surprising. I had shed tears of anger, fear, and pain before, and I had certainly experienced days as both a community volunteer and researcher that were emotionally draining. That was not new.

What was different was that my emotions during the research process were impossible to ignore and impossible to separate. All of the feelings unfolded before, during, and after the interview, in the midst of supposedly objective phases of research. I was thinking about this topic from an emotional standpoint. Intellect and emotion had fused, and thinking and feeling had become one. This is something of a touchy subject in academic psychology, as our field has a long-standing tradition of wanting to appear unbiased and unaffected. The emotional detachment afforded by research has been helpful to me if for no other reason than personal comfort. But maintaining this agenda is not a primary goal of my work: I have long considered emotions as a useful and honest part of the research process. Before this interview, my careful divide between thinking about rape and feeling rape had been clear and essentially unchallenged. After that day, the role of emotions took on a new meaning in my research.

At the end of the interview, as we walked to her car, this woman asked me a question that has stuck with me ever since: "So, this is what you do for a living? Listen to women talk about rape? Talk about all the bad things done to us, you know, by the rapist, the police, the doctors? Talk about how much this hurts, how rape feels?" "Yes," I replied slowly, feeling every story over the past nine years sink into me, "this is what I do for a living." "How can you think straight in all that pain?" she asked.

• • •

This is an important question for researchers to consider, because the emotional nature of studying violence has received little attention in academic discourse. The process of managing difficult emotions has drawn interest in many other fields, spawning an entire literature—termed "emotion work" (Hochschild, 1983)—on the sociology of emotions. Researchers have discovered how people in a variety of jobs—airline staff, nurses, social workers, doctors—understand and cope with stressful feelings. But what if the research focus turned inward? What if the difficult job was being a researcher who studied an emotionally charged topic? Do researchers engage in emotion work too? Do they become emotionally involved in their research? Researching social issues can be arduous and painful. I term this focus on emotional experiences of researchers "researching the researcher," and it is a much-needed new area of investigation.

The emotional nature of researching violence against women presents a prime example for exploring the affective component of science. The rape researcher can bear witness to the pain of sexual assault over and over again, hearing story after story of victimization. What is the impact of conducting such emotionally charged research? How do scientists' feelings influence the research process? Only a handful of researchers have stepped forward to "admit" that it can be emotionally draining to investigate these topics (e.g., Alexander, et al., 1989; Dunn, 1991; Gordon & Riger, 1989; Hippensteele, 1997; Huff, 1997; Kelly, 1988; Mattley, 1997; Moran-Ellis, 1996; Naples, 1996; Schwartz, 1997; Stanko, 1997). The victimology field, therefore, is ripe for an in-depth study of researchers' emotional experiences.

This book is one answer to that rape survivor's question: How can we, how do we think straight in all of that pain? How does studying rape affect the researcher? This book presents a systematic study of researchers' emotions—my emotions and the emotions of my research team as we conducted this study on the community response to rape. Over the course of two years, we—the Women and Violence Project—conducted interviews with over one hundred rape survivors. During that study, I also kept detailed field notes on how we were emotionally affected by what we were learning. In addition, I conducted in-depth, qualitative interviews with all staff at the completion of the project. These interviews covered four domains: 1) our most emotionally difficult interview; 2) the emotions we experienced throughout the project; 3) how we coped with these feelings; and 4) how these emotions affected our understanding of rape. The Women and Violence Project unfolded as two parallel research studies: one interviewing rape survivors about their experiences postrape, the other examining how we as researchers were affected by doing this kind of emotionally charged work. In this book, the researching-the-researcher component of our project is explored. This is not a memoir, but rather a qualitative multiple case study steeped in the theoretical traditions of the sociology of emotions and the psychology of trauma literatures. Using my field notes and the staff interview transcripts as data sources, I describe how and why we were emotionally affected by studying rape.

The central theme in these data, which guides the organization of this book, highlights the difference between thinking about rape and feeling rape. Many of us on the research team began this work thinking about rape: rape was a concept to be operationally defined and debated. But, as the project continued, and the idea of rape was paired with the reality of names, faces, and tears, abstractness gave way to emotions. Feeling rape took over: an understanding based upon shared emotions—shock, betrayal, guilt, anger, hurt, and hope—with the rape victim. Rape was no longer something we thought about at work, but something we felt throughout the entire day. The strict dichotomy between thinking and feeling softened. Although we had to cope with these emotions to continue the project, feeling rape brought a sharper understanding of sexual assault. The emotional experience of feeling rape became a resource for thinking about rape. Using the techniques of ethnography and qualitative interviewing, this book examines the struggles of becoming what I term an "emotionally engaged researcher." By drawing upon the experiences of a diverse group of researchers, we move beyond simply declaring that investigating rape can be emotionally difficult. This project sheds light on the specific emotions, the situations that gave rise to them, the strategies for coping with painful feelings, and the intellectual gains that can come from this emotional reflection.

• • •

This book is organized into five sections.[1] The first chapter, "Creating Difference—Thinking versus Feeling: The Role of Emotions in Research," explores how the social sciences create and maintain a hierarchical separation between thinking and feeling. Often viewed as a source of bias, emotions are traditionally excised from science, and researchers are socialized to emotionally disengage. Yet, for as much as we might not want to believe that our values and feelings influence our work, we cannot rid ourselves of these factors by pretending they're not there or valuing their exclusion. The researcher is a key actor in the scientific process, whose personal experiences are worthy of reflection and examination. To date, analyses have focused primarily on *cognitive* influences: the effects of researchers' attitudes, beliefs, and values on research outcomes. What seems to be missing from these discussions is an understanding of the *affective* influences. A fundamental aspect of our humanness is our capacity to feel. It is normal to have feelings; therefore we are entitled to our feelings, even during research. I examine what role emotions could have in the research process. Drawing from philosophy and the sociology of emotions literature, I argue that emotions can provide intellectual, substantive insight and therefore can be a valuable tool for social research. To set the stage for this exploration regarding the interdependence of thinking and feeling, I also describe the background and methods for this researching-the-researcher project.

The second chapter, "From Thinking to Feeling: The Stories That Bring Feeling to Researching Rape," describes the research team's journey into the world of emotion. We began this project *thinking* about rape. Whatever prior experiences we had with rape—as a rape victim advocate, as a counselor, as a survivor—certainly informed our choices and decisions, but our key focus was to *study*—not feel, not fight—rape. We knew intellectually that this work would be emotionally challenging, yet that didn't necessarily register emotionally. But slowly, week by week, that changed. Shocked and surprised by what we were hearing from survivors, each one of us on the research team was jolted from the safety of thinking about rape. A case, then cases, got under our skin. It became personal, and no amount of abstract thinking could quell the emotional violation. This chapter describes specific interviews that moved us, forever changing how we understood rape. Many of the most painful cases hit close to home, reminding us that all women are at risk for sexual assault. As a society, we want to believe that our social systems will help people in need, but we were often faced with stories to the contrary. We also wanted to believe that all survivors could recover from rape; however, some cases were so severe that they shook this belief to its core.

The third chapter, "Feeling: The Emotions of Researching Rape," describes the emotions we felt throughout this research in our near-constant exposure to rape. This is what it felt like to study rape, up close and personal. It hurt—a lot—a great deal of the time for most of the project staff. Yet interspersed with the overwhelming anger, fear, loss, and pain was undeniable hope. The rape survivors we interviewed entrusted us with their stories, which were indeed devastating to hear over and over again. But in witnessing the telling of these stories, we also felt the incredible strength and resiliency it takes to survive rape. More often than not, we could walk away from an interview feeling good about our work and having something uplifting to remember about each woman and each story. This chapter examines the five primary emotions experienced by members of the research team: loss, pain, fear, anger, and hope. We mourned for the victims and ourselves: our loss of innocence, safety, and well-being. Bearing witness to these stories of trauma was painful, and we became saturated with hurt. This constant contact with rape reminded us that we too could be victimized, instilling us with fear. The fact that rape had taken so much from these women, and was taking so much from us, made us angry at the injustice of violence against women. Yet this pain was interrupted with happier feelings: joy, warmth, compassion, connection, support, and hope. How we coped with the negative emotions and attuned to the positive aspects of this work is also explored in this chapter.

In the fourth chapter, "From Feeling to Thinking: The Insights Feeling Rape Bring to Researching Rape," I describe how feeling rape can enhance our conceptual understanding of violence against women. Feeling rape reveals the varied effects that sexual assault has on women's lives. Based on my analysis of how researching rape has affected me and my research team members over the years, I argue that harm of rape has been too narrowly defined. Research on the cognitive and affective consequences for victims has been and will continue to be an important area of investigation, but the effects of sexual assault extend far beyond individual-level symptomatology. Who is affected by rape, how they are impacted, and what effects rape has on all of its victims are critical questions that have gone largely unexplored. The secondary victims of rape—those caught in its wake—are also deeply affected by this crime. Furthermore, the intensity of the devastation caused by rape is rarely reflected in academic discourse, which inadvertently presents a cleaner, less disturbing vision of rape that may not be wholly accurate with the experiences of survivors. It is not the scientific accuracy of the rape victimology literature that concerns me; it is its emotional accuracy. The degree to which the academic language of rape conveys the inherent emotionality of this crime, the gap between the lived experiences of the victim and social science research is narrowed. Drawing on compassion fatigue theory and emotion work theory, I examine how future research can tap into the multitude of ways rape affects its victims from an emotionally engaged vantage point.

Finally, the fifth chapter of the book, "Creating Balance—Thinking and Feeling: The Possibilities for Emotionally Engaged Research," explores how social science research can be reconceptualized to balance the unique contributions of intellectual thought and human emotion. Drawing from the feminist methodology literature, I propose a framework for what I term "emotionally engaged research." Such an approach emphasizes attuning to the emotional needs of both the research participants and the social scientists themselves throughout the research process. In all phases of a project—from design and sampling, to data collection and analysis, to dissemination—I outline the emotional choice points we face and suggest ways to balance methodological rigor with human caring. In addition, I describe specific self-care strategies for researchers and discuss useful organizational and institutional supports needed for emotionally engaged research.

Throughout this book, I have deliberately chosen words like "we," "our," and "us" to refer to the community of applied researchers (in general) and/or violence against women researchers (in particular). I use these words in an attempt to build a common interest in these issues, not to suggest presumptively that others in these disciplines may agree with my perspectives. Furthermore, I am interested in getting the researcher out of the silent margins—the never-seen, rarely-heard-from creators of the scientific work—and into the central picture that defines how social science is really conducted. As a result, more often than not, I have to use a subject in my sentences; passive voice obscures the actor, which is precisely what I do not want to do. It may feel odd to read "we," especially in instances where a reader may not necessarily agree with such inclusion or want to be included in that "we," and it certainly felt strange writing it over and over again. Nevertheless, I believe it may be a useful experience to try owning it a bit more. My goal throughout this book is to challenge myself and other researchers in social sciences to look at our work from a different point of view. I speak in the general "we" and "us" because it is precisely these general issues that concern me.

This book makes public a very private side of researching difficult social issues. The emotional impact of studying emotionally charged topics has come up before, but often peripherally in brief references in our writings, hushed conversations outside lecture halls at conferences, cloistered talks in our homes and offices. It is there, but it is not something that has been explored in depth. As one of my interviewers told me when learning about my plans to do this book, "Good, it will help all of us and all the students of the future to know we're not crazy." My aim is not just to normalize these emotional experiences, but to transform them into useful components of our scholarship.

Creating Difference—
Thinking versus Feeling

The Role of Emotions in Research

Historically, social scientists have been silent, absent researchers. We are ghostwriters for our own work. The work "was done," the experiment "was conducted," the setting "was observed," the results "were obtained." This affinity for the passive voice reflected not only stylistic preferences but also ideological norms regarding the researchers' role in the scientific process. There is no subject in passive constructions: things happen, things occur. Who did those things and what those individuals think, value, and feel is difficult to discern. It's as if it doesn't matter who conducted the study because what really matters is the method by which the knowledge "was acquired" and the actual knowledge itself. The "I" is not in our sentences because who we are as social scientists—what we value and feel—is of less scientific interest. In some respects, this makes sense. More often than not, we are studying those other than ourselves. Who we are really isn't the focus. Yet who we are undoubtedly affects how we understand the world and hence how we understand our research. We may try to erase ourselves in written discourse, but we cannot erase our effect on our research.

Although notable philosophers of science (e.g., Jürgen Habermas, Thomas Kuhn) and empirical social scientists (e.g., Donald Campbell, Lee Cronbach) have generally agreed that researchers do indeed exert their humanness on research, this is not necessarily viewed as a good thing. The perspective of scientist-as-contaminant is a strong and enduring norm. Psychology instructors specifically teach students how to avoid contaminating their own studies (e.g., don't let your subjects know what you hypothesized). Students in other social science disciplines receive equivalent warnings (e.g., the don't-go-native advice still applies for many sociologists and anthropologists). Yet, for as much as we might not want to believe that our values and feelings influence our work, we cannot rid ourselves of these factors by pretending they're not there or by valuing their exclusion. The researcher is a key figure in the scientific process whose personal experiences are worthy of reflection and examination.

To date, such analyses have focused primarily on *cognitive* influences: the effects of researchers' attitudes, beliefs, and values on research outcomes. What seems to be largely missing from these discussion is an understanding of the *affective* influences.[1] In this chapter, I examine what role emotions could have in the research process. Understanding how emotions enter into research is inextricably linked to ontological and epistemological views on the nature of knowledge. For instance, researchers' emotions have limited utility within a positivist framework, which postulates an objective reality that can be objectively verified. Feelings, like other potential "biases" (values, beliefs, expectations) may hinder researchers' abilities to capture reality. Although most positivists acknowledge that such an idealized process cannot be achieved (e.g., Campbell & Stanley, 1963; Cronbach, 1975), researchers should at least try to minimize the effects of emotions. By contrast, post positivist theorists (e.g., Habermas) question the existence of objective reality and instead stipulate that "reality" is socially constructed. Embracing the subjectivity of science provides some place for humanness in research. My goal here is not to continue the positivist/postpositivist, objectivity/subjectivity debates, but rather to examine how different disciplines in the social sciences, with their associated epistemological allegiances, construct a role for emotions in research. My analysis suggests that feelings, like our beliefs and values, do indeed shape our research and are a natural part of inquiry. Furthermore, I argue that this is a reflexive process: our emotions influence our research, and our research can affect us emotionally. This emotional dialogue between our inner feelings and our research can be an important intellectual resource. Examining our feelings and the emotional impact that research has on us can bring a deeper intellectual understanding of social phenomenon.

In this chapter, I first examine how this difference between thinking and feeling is created and maintained. Drawing on the works of sociologists Susan Krieger and Shulamit Reinharz, I argue that the socialization of a researcher involves learning not to feel. Examples from "classic" texts in psychology and sociology, as well as contemporary training texts, demonstrate the specific ways in which social scientists are taught to devalue emotions as a source of knowledge. Second, because emotions are indeed an integral part of our lives and influence our thinking, we can challenge these enduring disciplinary norms and consider the possibilities for emotion in research. Philosophers Chesire Calhoun and Alison Jaggar have provided an epistemological foundation for emotions as a legitimate source of knowledge. Building upon the arguments of sociologists Carolyn Ellis and Ruth Wilkins, I consider what can be gained intellectually through the systematic investigation of researchers' emotions. Some research topics by their very nature are highly emotional and can provide a useful context for understanding the role of emotions in social science. In the final section of this chapter, I turn to the violence against women literature to explore how studying rape, domestic violence, and incest affects researchers emotionally. But the question remains: How can these emotions inform science? To provide one answer to this question, I then outline the specific research project that is the focus of this book. Over the course of a year, my research team members and I interviewed over a hundred rape survivors, listening to and bearing witness to their stories of trauma and recovery. At the conclusion of this phase of data collection, I then interviewed the project interviewers to learn more about how this work affected them emotionally, and if and how these emotions developed their substantive understanding of sexual violence. This researching-the-researcher project provides one model of reflexive learning where emotion and intellect are not forced separate, but allowed to mingle and inform each other.

The Socialization of the Researcher: Learning Not to Feel

It's a strange thing: feeling, sentient beings try very hard to be, for a specific role in their lives, only rational, not emotional. Whereas I doubt any scientist has ever truly been able to achieve that feat, we nonetheless learn not to admit feeling. As sociologist Susan Krieger argued in her book *Social Science and the Self* (1991), we learn that the self, and all of its associated emotions, has no place in science:

> The social science disciplines tend to view the self of the social scientific observer as a contaminant. The self—the unique inner life of the observer—is treated as something to be separated out, neutralized, minimized, standardized, and controlled. At the same time the observer is expected to use the self to the end of understanding the world. . . . We are taught to avoid attention to the authorial first person, whose view, and whose choices, a study represents. We learn to become invisible authors. If we cannot be objective, at least we should not call too much attention to the fact of our subjectivity. (p. 1)

> The expression of an individual perspective in social science is a difficult accomplishment in part because individuality is theoretically unpopular. The social sciences tend not only to view the self of a researcher as a contaminant, but they also view the selves of people studied as invisible. (p. 43)

Drawing from her own personal experiences, Krieger reasoned that this norm of emotional distance is created within us over years of socialization.

We are taught to speak and write in a standardized way that reflects the standardized way in which we are supposed to think about and understand the world. The key to this socialization process is its emphasis on *thinking* and developing normative practices for conceptualizing research. What we learn about feeling and emotion is that we're not supposed to feel. For example, Krieger writes,

> These are ideas I have internalized at least since graduate school. They reflect the fact that social science ideology is full of prohibitions against conspicuous use of the self. It is full of guidelines that suggest that the standard forms of expression are the only correct forms. (p. 2)

Krieger contends that by detaching ourselves from the research process, social scientists distance ourselves from our research subjects, thereby rendering what we study more difficult to see and understand. She encourages us to acknowledge more honestly than we do the extent to which our studies are reflections of our inner lives:

> I wish to suggest that the self is not a contaminant, but rather that it is the key to what we know, and that methodological discussions might fruitfully be revised to acknowledge the involvement of the self in a positive manner. The self is not something that can be disengaged from knowledge or from research processes. Rather, we need to understand the nature of our participation in what we know. The problem we need to worry about is not the effect of an observer's inner self on evidence from the outside world, but the ways that the traditional dismissal of the self may hinder the development of each individual's unique perspective. (pp. 29–30)

A similar concern about this socialization not to feel was raised by sociologist Shulamit Reinharz. In her book, *On Becoming a Social Scientist* (1979), Reinharz explores the contradictions in sociological method and describes how students of sociology are socialized not to question dominant ideologies:

> During the socialization process students confront conflicts but are unsure of the extent to which they can explore them since strong pressures to specialize compel students to choose a substantive camp early and develop a firm commitment expressed in competence. In addition, the student does not know to what extent the values inherent in the discipline can be challenged. Are there certain questions that may not be asked at all without violating the definition of the profession itself? (pp. 12–13)

This socialization can stall individual expression and creativity. Before students can learn otherwise, they are taught that sociology must be impersonal and objective, and be oriented to the prediction and control of events. But, as Reinharz argues, the sociologist must use one's self in the research process—the entire process is touched by the researcher's humanness. In highlighting this contradiction, Reinharz calls for a sociological method that acknowledges the personal elements of research and seeks to understand how researchers' values, beliefs, and emotions contribute to knowledge: "The sociology I would do, therefore, would stem from my personal values as much as from my understanding of methods" (p. 9).

Krieger and Reinharz suggest that there is a hierarchical relationship between thinking and feeling in the social sciences. This difference is created and maintained by teaching students to reject the role of the self, which includes rejecting emotionality. Certainly my own experiences of being trained as a psychologist and my current encounters training doctoral students resonate with Krieger's and Reinharz's socialization theory. But how does this happen? How are students trained not to feel in research? Both Krieger and Reinharz describe how, as students, their classroom climates did not encourage questioning these norms. Certainly the attitudes and behaviors of instructors communicate expectations, but there is also more concrete and enduring evidence of this socialization process. Analysis of the "classic" texts in psychology and sociology, as well as their contemporary counterparts, reveals one way in which students are taught to devalue emotionality in social science. These training texts specifically state that emotions have minimal use in research.

The classic texts of psychology and sociology set the stage for the exclusion of emotions in research by reminding researchers how they can unduly and inappropriately influence the scientific process. Often assigned by instructors for historical orientation, these texts indoctrinate students into standard ideologies. The readings we were assigned as students, and those we assign to our students, begin that socialization process through their emphasis on rationality, not emotionality. By labeling these works as "classics," they become the referent norm. In psychology, classic texts emphasize objectivity as a fundamental goal. As a student of psychology, I was raised on a steady diet of logical positivism and experimental studies through the writings of Donald Campbell, Lee Cronbach, Julian Stanley, and Robert Rosenthal. These writings taught me that there is truth and order to the social world. My job, as I came to understand it from these texts, was to find that truth, verify it, and replicate the process by which I found it. The dispassionate language of these writings reinforced the value of neutrality and objectivity. It is important to note, however, that these classical texts readily acknowledge that bias is impossible to avoid because our humanness will always come through. In fact, Campbell and Stanley (1963) once referred to social sciences as an "impure art." My reading of these texts and my experiences of being taught them suggest a longing for "pure" science. That we cannot mimic the physical sciences is disappointing but perhaps unavoidable. At the very least, we should strive to remove as many extraneous influences as possible.

Underscoring this need for attention to our biases, decades of research in social psychology has demonstrated that people are indeed influenced by their attitudes, beliefs, and emotions. Researchers are no exception. For example, classic texts by Robert Rosenthal, such as *Experimenter Effects in Behavioral Research* (1966) and *Artifact in Behavioral Research* (with Ralph Rosnow) (1969), enumerate the varied ways in which experimenters' personological factors can bias a study's findings. Rosenthal's laboratory studies demonstrated that researchers can systematically attune to or ignore key behaviors in observational research. We can also communicate, subtly or overtly, to our research participants the nature of our experimental hypotheses, thereby creating a demand for the very effect we hoped to objectively verify. Quite simply, Rosenthal's work demonstrates that if researchers are not careful, we could find exactly what we're looking for, but for all the wrong reasons and by all the wrong methods. Rosenthal's experimental laboratory studies beg the question about bias in the real world: If we can be so "flawed" in lab work, dare we ask what happens in the real world? The same effect. As Charles Lord and his colleagues found:

> People who hold strong opinions on complex social issues are likely to examine relevant empirical evidence in a biased manner. They are apt to accept "confirming" evidence at face value while subjecting "disconfirming" evidence to critical evaluation, and as a result to draw undue support for their initial positions from mixed or random empirical findings. (Lord, Ross, & Lepper, 1979, p. 2098)

Because "strong opinions" are often emotion-laden, Lord's research suggests that emotions can adversely affect the quality of research. This seemingly detrimental effect continues to be documented in more recent work. Timothy Wilson and his colleagues found that scientists—faculty in major medical schools and research psychologists—were significantly more likely to overlook methodological flaws on research that they deemed more important (Wilson, DePaulo, Mook, & Klaaren, 1993). When considering research about an "important" topic, one with social and personal meaning (manipulated in their experiment as heartburn versus heart disease), scientists were more forgiving of methodological transgressions (demonstrated by more lenient ratings regarding publication). "Bad" work can, and does, get published. The more we "care" about a topic, the less likely we are to critically evaluate its research. Although Wilson's and his colleagues' work does not specifically address the role of emotions, the "importance" dimension is probably emotionally charged. These results indicate that our emotions may cloud our scientific judgments. What, then, is the role of emotions in research? What is the take-home message to students who read these Rosenthalesque studies? Emotions appear to hinder good work, and therefore, like all other forms of bias, they should be excluded.

It is interesting to contrast psychology's rhetoric on the role of emotions in research with the struggles sociology has undertaken on these matters. In psychology, a researcher's values, beliefs, and emotions are essentially viewed as sources of bias, and because we should strive to avoid bias, we must try to avoid emotionality in our work.[2] The classic texts of sociology lead researchers along a different path of thinking about objectivity in science. In many classic texts of sociology, the following is at issue: Can social scientists view the data of their research in some objective manner or not? If not, what influences and biases these views? The classic writings of Max Weber, such as *The Theory of Social and Economic Organization* (1947) and *Methodology of the Social Sciences* (1949), maintain that the social sciences could be value-free. Yet sociological philosophers such as Habermas strongly questioned Weber's thesis. In such texts as *On the Logic of the Social Sciences* (1967) and *Knowledge and Human Interests* (1971), Habermas challenged the objectivist illusion. The social world does not operate in law like universal order. His postpositivist critical theories stipulate that the search for one truth is futile because there is no such thing. We should not be so worried about the potential "damage" our humanness may inflict upon our investigations because there is no one single truth to be tainted. Knowledge is socially constructed, so Habermas advocates for a paradigm of mutual understanding in which the researcher and the research participants engage each other in the identification and creation of knowledge. Similarly, Anthony Giddens concluded in his book *New Rules of Sociological Method* (1993) that researchers always influence what they research. "Bias" is a natural part of inquiry because it cannot be removed and therefore must be studied in its own right. These sociological theorists make more provision for emotions in research as part of their general interest in understanding subjective influences.

In many respects, classic texts of both psychology and sociology came to the same conclusion: researchers can't be truly objective because there is always some form of "bias"—values, beliefs, emotions—influencing our research. Yet the rhetoric of these two fields has different implications for practice. By and large, psychology remains deeply committed to a positivist epistemology: objective truth can be obtained through rigorous method. The goal must be to identify and remove, or otherwise nullify, those biases in order to get closer to the truth. Emotions can thwart our quest for truth and must be avoided. In sociology, the general conclusion is similar. We are hopelessly "biased," but because reality is socially constructed, the job of a social scientist is to understand how individuals, or groups of individuals, come to construct and understand those realities. In doing so, researchers must also attune to how their own values and beliefs shape this construction.

Whereas authors of these classic texts rarely address the specific role of emotions in research separate from other sources of bias or humanness, their contemporary counterparts take on this issue directly. In fact, many of these recent texts hold an even stricter position than the classics that emotions should not influence science. Contemporary training texts provide specific instruction regarding the exclusion of emotions in research. For example, John Cone's and Sharon Foster's book, *Dissertations and Theses from Start to Finish: Psychology and Related Fields* (1993), is a key resource for how to create a first research project in psychology and is an assigned text in numerous psychology programs. As a socialization tool, it defines standards and norms for beginning researchers about acceptable practice. Upon learning that I was writing this book, my colleague, who uses this book in his courses, called this passage to my attention:

> In fact, many of us in the behavioral sciences, especially psychology, [are interested] in some aspect of our own experience. Don't get us wrong. This is not a bad reason for being in psychology in the first place. But, it is probably not a good idea to plan thesis or dissertation research around something with a high degree of personal emotional relevance. Save these issues for therapy. Research is difficult enough without having it serve as the stimulus for a lot of personal soul searching every time you pick up the pen or run a subject. Besides interfering with your progress, personally loaded issues are unlikely to be approached from the detached, objective, analytic perspective necessary in science. You are likely to have a "position" on the subject that will interfere with your completing the research satisfactorily on a number of levels. . . .
>
> Choosing a research topic that evokes strong emotional reactions can interfere with your objectivity in other ways. For example, otherwise helpful suggestions from committee members might be hard to accept if they "don't fit" your personal understanding of the problem. This can result in your appearing rigid, defensive, and inflexible, characteristics faculty do not view positively. In fairness, however, we should note that issues of personal relevance can be a good source of research ideas under some circumstances. Your motivation is likely to be higher for such topics, and you might know the area in unique ways that might challenge the conclusions of current investigators.
>
> The bottom line is that issues of personal relevance should be considered as a source of research ideas only if you can approach them objectively. If you have resolved the emotional aspects of the issue and can approach it in a detached, relatively disinterested, and unbiased manner, go ahead. You might make a truly useful contribution. (p. 32)

The message of this passage is straightforward: personal topics with emotional meaning probably have no place in psychological science. Just therapy. But, interestingly, Cone and Foster suggest that this personalness may be an important resource and could provide useful insights. But they caution students not to attempt such projects unless they can approach the topic objectively.

Coincidentally, a student who was assigned this book by my colleague for her methods course brought this very same passage to me. She wanted to do a project that was deeply personal. Did this book mean she couldn't do research on this topic? I found it interesting that she came to me to talk about these issues. I even had some momentary panic about how I might be regarded more generally in my department. Was there a big sign, "Biased," on my office door? So I asked the student why she decided to come talk to me about these issues. After all, I am not her instructor nor her advisor, nor am I even a member of her division of psychology. She said it was because she knew what kind of research I did, and although she didn't know or need to know whether I was a survivor of violence, I was studying violence against women as a woman. Therefore I was studying something that is personal. Violence against women is personal to women. So she assumed (correctly) that I had given some thought to if and how one could study something personal and potentially emotional. The fact that I was doing such work meant that she had at least one example, so far, that contradicted her text.

The essence of my reply to this student was that yes, I didn't completely agree with Cone's and Foster's message. Nevertheless, I found some aspects of that passage to be instructive. I also believe it is important to find some (initial) emotional peace with a topic before studying it. I don't think this peace affords objectivity, but it is useful to know how to identify your own emotions, feel them, work with them, find ways to cope with them, and learn from them. If a topic is still quite raw and emotional for someone, I also express some concerns about planning research around it because it will hurt a lot—to study something so painful. For beginning scholars, that may be too much to take on—learning and hurting. In general, I don't steer students away from the topics that have emotional meaning to them, but I do encourage them to locate their first studies in a less emotional vein. I do not know how normative this advice is within psychology. At the very least, it is different from some dominant recommendations.

Some contemporary training texts in sociology also admonish emotional involvement in research. Despite broad disciplinary interest in postpositivist ideologies and an exploration of subjective influences in research, one often-used text recommends against examining researchers' emotions. In their book, *Analyzing Social Settings: A Guide to Qualitative Observation and Analysis* (1995), Jon Lofland and Lyn Lofland write:

It is often said among sociologists that, as sociologists, we "make problematic" in our research matters that are problematic in our lives. With the proviso that the connection between self and study may be a subtle and sophisticated one, not at all apparent to an outside observer, we would argue that there is considerable truth to this assertion. . . . That such linkages are not always, and perhaps not even usually, publicly acknowledged is understandable: the norms of scholarship do not require that researchers bare their souls, only their procedure. . . .

Some researchers have argued that there is much to be learned by making oneself the (mostly) exclusive focus of one's study; that is, by doing what Norman L. Friedman (1990b) calls "autobiographical sociology" and Carolyn Ellis (forthcoming) refers to as "telling personal stories." We would grant that for some kinds of research concerns (the phenomenology of ongoing emotional experience for example), one's self may be the only available data site. And we would grant that in the hands of a skilled analyst and wordsmith, staying where you are [studying topics of personal relevance] may result in meaningful and insightful works of social science. Nonetheless, we strongly advise most researchers, especially beginners, to avoid it. Even when exceptionally well executed, reports analyzing autobiographical data are often viewed by readers as borderline self-indulgence, when only competently executed, they are likely to be labeled "narcissistic" or "exhibitionist" and simply dismissed as uninteresting. (pp. 13–14)

Lofland and Lofland do not critique emotionality as strongly as do Cone and Foster. The Loflands acknowledge that some sociologists are indeed quite interested in studying researchers' emotions. Because the fields of psychology and sociology have different perspectives on the issue of objectivity and bias, the caution in this text isn't so much about being biased but about being boring. This kind of work is not for beginners. It may not even be for nonbeginners.

Step back and think about this message. If not now, then when, if ever? When is it acceptable to analyze our own emotions as part of the research process? I concur with Cone and Foster, and Lofland and Lofland, that this kind of work could be quite risky for beginning researchers. Doing emotionally charged research is a difficult place to begin your career—in pain and under suspicion by your colleagues. But when can we research an emotional topic? Can we research an emotional topic emotionally? If the socialization of a researcher involves reading classic and contemporary texts that devalue emotionally derived knowledge, then why would we believe it is acceptable to do otherwise? Because socialization goes only so far in creating the identity of a researcher, and because there are other traditions in the social sciences that do not call for the exclusion of our personal values and feelings. The difference between thinking and feeling does not have to be so painstakingly created, maintained, and reinforced. Contemporary philosophers of science have challenged these norms of difference, providing an epistemological grounding for emotions in social science. From this conceptual starting point, an emerging literature articulates how and why emotions can be a resource, not a hindrance, in the process of science.

The Possibilities for Emotion in Social Science Research

In her essay "Love and Knowledge: Emotion in Feminist Epistemology" (1989), philosopher Alison Jaggar noted that " . . . western epistemology has tended to view emotion with suspicion and even hostility" (p. 154). Jaggar deconstructs this false dichotomy between thinking and feeling, which she terms "the myth of dispassionate investigation," reminding us that even Plato himself came to accept that knowledge requires love. Jaggar's work begins building an epistemological foundation for emotions in the creation of knowledge. For example, she writes:

> Time spent in analyzing emotions and uncovering their sources should be viewed, therefore, neither as irrelevant to theoretical investigation nor even as a prerequisite for it; it is not a kind of clearing the emotional decks, "dealing with" our emotions so that they not influence our thinking. Instead, we must recognize that our efforts to reinterpret and refine our emotions are necessary to our theoretical investigation, just as our efforts to reeducate our emotions are necessary to our political activity. Critical reflection on emotion is not a self-indulgent substitute for political analysis and political action. It is itself a kind of political theory and political practice, indispensable for an adequate social theory and transformation. (p. 164)

> Emotions are neither more basic than observation, reason, or action in building theory, nor are they secondary to them. Each of these human faculties reflects an aspect of human knowing inseparable form the other aspects. (p. 165)

Jaggar contends that our experiences are legitimate sources of knowledge. In the context of feminist philosophy, Jaggar argues that ordinary and extraordinary events of women's lives are worthy of critical reflection, as they can inform our understanding of the social world. No different from reason, feeling is also part of our everyday experiences, and as such, emotions contribute to knowledge.

In "Subjectivity and Emotion" (1989), philosopher of science Cheshire Calhoun similarly argues that emotions, like cognitions and sensory perceptions, are one of many vehicles through which we view the world, thus they are also capable of providing information and knowledge. Calhoun's work delves more deeply into why emotions are excluded in science and, in doing so, articulates a foundation for their inclusion. Calhoun reasons that it is the inherent subjectivity of emotions that gives some scholars pause:

> The most common uses of "subjective" and "objective" are both epistemic and evaluative. "Subjective," always used pejoratively, indicates a lack of adequate justification or of representativeness. Saying that a belief is subjective is a way of critically implying a lack of good, justifying reasons. When applied to emotions, this pejorative label implies that emotions are based on false or unjustified beliefs, or that viewing the world emotionally is a biased or myopic way of seeing things, or that emotions have no cognitive content at all. Thus we should take emotional peoples' judgements with a grain of salt; and in pursuing objective knowledge, we should purge ourselves of the biasing influence of emotion. (pp. 196–197)

> Yet, emotions do not always rest on false beliefs, nor do they always imbue objects with unreal qualities . . . nor do all emotions myopically bias our perceptions . . . rigidly adhering to any point of view, emotional or nonemotional, may incur judgement errors; but simply adopting a point of view and being selectively attentive does not entail epistemic subjectivity. (p. 197)

> If emotions mirror the world as reliably as other faculties, then we should begin trusting our emotions to deliver truth in the same way we trust our perceptions or our chains of reasoning or the voice of experts . . . but there is a lingering sense that emotions are not trustworthy, are not deliverers of the kind of truth pursued in academia and science. (pp. 198–199)

Then how can emotions be both personal and sources of knowledge?

> The pursuit of knowledge is always to some extent personal . . . if it makes sense to continue talking about knowledge under these circumstances, we will need a revised notion of epistemic objectivity in which truth might reliably be delivered from a, at least partially, personal point of view. That means emotions could plausibly be used as a resource for knowledge. . . . If . . . our ideal of knowledge is that it be relevant to living some kind of life, then getting the truth will be comparable with taking a biographically subjective point of view. And we might reasonably expect emotions to come into play in the pursuit of knowledge. (p. 200)

Calhoun uncovers the deep irony that pervades the epistemological foundation of much research. If it is observation and reason upon which we should build knowledge, then because emotions actually involve both, feelings would thereby qualify as legitimate ingredients for theory. But rather, the collective devaluing of emotions is really the issue. Emotions are central to knowledge, and rather than continuing to value their exclusion, perhaps the sciences would be better served through systematic investigation of how such subjective points of view inform the construction of knowledge. It is not, then, the case that only "accurate" feelings could contribute to knowledge. Rather, Calhoun and Jaggar argue that our individual experience of those emotions contributes to our unique understandings of the world, and it is these understandings that create knowledge.

That emotions could be a resource for knowledge opens up a world of possibilities for social scientists. Emotions are not a new topic of investigation by any means. Research *about* emotions in *other* people (i.e., not researchers) has been one of the most enduring literatures in both psychology (e.g., Ekman & Davidson, 1994; Ortony, Clore, & Collins, 1988; Schachter & Singer, 1962; Singer, 1995) and sociology (e.g., Denzin, 1990; Kemper, 1978, 1981, 1990; Shott, 1979). Jaggar's and Calhoun's work contributes a theoretical grounding for what I term "researching-the-researcher": the study of how researchers' emotions affect science, how research can in turn stir the emotions of its investigators, and how these emotional exchanges contribute to knowledge. Within some literatures in the social sciences, there is growing interest in examining the researcher's self and how our personal experiences shape our research. For example, sociologist Carolyn Ellis (1991a) writes:

> We can [also] view our own emotional experience as a legitimate sociological object of study and focus on how we feel as researchers as a way of understanding and coping with what is going on emotionally in our research. . . . Emotions affect how mainstream sociologists formulate questions, conceptualize, gather data, and draw conclusions. Many interviewers respond emotionally to their subjects. And, most participant observers become emotionally connected to the people they study. (pp. 125, 127)

Researching researchers' emotions serves two purposes. First, it can more accurately reflect the nature of the research process. If we have emotional experiences as researchers, but don't write about them, then we have not truly reflected the process of inquiry. I suspect this argument may have appeal for the positivist-minded, tapping into a general interest in assessing the accuracy of science. I raise this issue not to invoke more investigation into the "biases" that affect science, but rather as part of broader call to capture the actual lived experiences of researching human behavior. What is it that we do in the social sciences? How do we construct knowledge regarding the social world? How does our particular standpoint as a scientist and member of society shape that construction?[3] Feeling is a natural part of research. Feeling and thinking, therefore, are simultaneous and reflexive activities; they are inseparable and should be described accordingly. For instance, Krieger (1991) states:

> For me, the strongest statement is always the direct personal one. That type of statement brings me closer to an experience and helps me feel grounded and honest. It gives me more confidence concerning what I say than a general statement does. (p. 4)

Sociologists Sherryl Kleinman and Martha Copp (1993) make a similar point about field research:

> By censoring their notes, fieldworkers may believe that they can prevent their views from contaminating the research: They did not just see what they wanted to see. . . . But, if we avoid writing about our reactions, we cannot examine them. (p. 19)

Psychologist Kathleen Gilbert (2001) also argues:

> It is not the avoidance of emotions that necessarily provides for high quality research. Rather, it is an awareness and intelligent use of our emotions that benefits the research process. (p. 11)

In other words, not examining our own emotional reactions to our work can actually be a disservice to the quality of our research. Whether the concern is compromised "accuracy" or a missed opportunity to illuminate the process of science, censoring ourselves doesn't seem to provide any benefit. We create difference between thinking and feeling when we exclude emotionality from our work, and we create difference where it isn't there.

A second argument for focusing on researchers' emotional experiences is that by distancing ourselves from our research, what we study can become more difficult to see and understand. By emotionally engaging our work, we can gain a closer and potentially more insightful perspective. In other words, this kind of emotional inquiry could be an intellectual resource. As Krieger (1991) argues: "I believe that increased personal understanding can help us think more intelligently and fully about social life" (p. 2). Expanding on this concept, sociologist Ruth Wilkins (1993) encourages researchers to "take [our] research personally":

> "Taking it personally" requires us to become articulate about our social and emotional resources and their utility or otherwise in the context of research. . . . The researcher needs to consider emotional resources from

an *existential perspective*, for our emotional responses constitute key *cognitive* and *analytic* resources in the "here and now" of the research setting and are capable of yielding important sociological insights. . . . In my research, I found my emotional resources gave me insight into the *substantive* aspects of the research. Far from being an encumbrance, my positive feelings were the most essential resources in research dealing with the deep emotions engaged during pregnancy and childbirth. My own experiences, whether as a mother or researcher, do not guarantee understanding, for understanding transcends experience. But it remains important to appreciate how our personal biography creates and situates us vis-à-vis the research; and I for one would not have attempted my particular piece of research without such feelings and experiences to draw upon. (p. 97, emphases in original)

We could learn more about our phenomenon of interest by examining how we emotionally respond to our research. How we feel about what we witness and what we do in the process of research could tell us something about that which we have studied. Why do we feel anger? Fear? Sadness? Joy? What do we feel conflicted about, and why? Emotionality can provide some common ground between social scientists and their research participants. We may not be feeling the same things, or feeling with the same intensity, but emotionality can create a connection that doesn't require disciplinary jargon or specialized language. However, it is not simply enough to feel our research. Emotions can provide substantive perspective, but this insight must be developed through analysis and critique. Feeling science creates the potential for critical social analysis, but such a standpoint emerges only through consciousness-raising experiences and reflection (see Hartsock, 1998). If indeed emotions are treated as data and analyzed as such, then it is quite possible that feeling can become a resource for thinking. How and what we feel could shape—in a positive way—what we know.

Researching the Researcher: Methods of Capturing Emotionality

If researchers' emotions are indeed a worthy subject of investigation, what would such an approach to inquiry look like? If emotions provide another form of data for researchers, then how could such information be collected and analyzed? Because this is an emerging interest in the social sciences, there are few published examples to draw upon. Most typically, the study of the researchers' emotions is a secondary project, an offshoot from a "main" research project. Not surprisingly, the topic of the "main" research study is often emotionally charged: violence, illness, trauma, death. The process of conducting the "main" study touched emotional nerves within the researcher, prompting a critical analysis of those feelings. In these projects, investigators have combined narrative techniques with traditional methods of social science to reflect upon the emotional impact of researching such emotionally difficult topics.

One such approach for exploring researchers' emotions is what sociologist Marjorie DeVault (1997) terms "personal writing." Confessional in tone, memoir-like in style, these writings are "behind-the-scenes" accounts of what happened in a research study. These writings are often done after the fact, after the "main" study has been published, and are published separately from the main study. The primary goal is stating what one experienced:

> Personal writing is autobiographical or introspective material in the service of a sociological analysis. . . . Rather than simply criticize or defend personal writing (the most common sociological responses to date), I propose that we consider in a more thoughtful way what is involved in the production and interpretation of research texts that include personal accounts . . . personal writing can be more or less self-conscious, but it is most often designed to appear immediate and confessional. It speaks to readers with an individual voice, and that voice often claims something like "Here is my truth, complete and unvarnished." A personal account works well when it reads easily and gives the impression of direct access to an individual reality. The author disarms (and thus wins the reader) by telling it "like it is." (pp. 217, 221)

Personal writing names, identifies, and describes researchers' emotional experiences so that the readers may feel as well. The purposes served by such writing are complex. For the researcher, personal writing can provide catharsis, reflection, a vehicle for processing the experience, and an opportunity to build community with other researchers. For the reader, the vicarious emotions could deepen understanding of an issue. One topic that has initiated this kind of personal writing is researching trauma and abuse. For example, in her essay "Close to Home: The Experience of Researching Child Sexual Abuse" (1996), sociologist Jo Moran-Ellis (1996) brought to light the hidden aspects of this work—what she has heard from child survivors, what she has witnessed, how others react to her work. One particularly difficult experience at a conference on child abuse, an infuriating conversation with a probation officer, epitomized her struggles:

> [His] suggestion was that a significant proportion of mothers were satisfying their own sexual needs on the bodies of their sons. My initial reaction was a desire to say "Show me how that compares with men who anally fuck their sons, orally rape them, make them take part in pornography; who do the same to their daughters, tear and bruise and split their children's mouths, anuses, and vaginas; who blame the children for being seductive, or their 'wives' for being unavailable." I felt anger and frustra-

tion in the face of what seemed like a diversion away from recognizing male violence. (p. 180)

At this point I felt lonely and in need of support. Conferences can be a lonely place, and this was not a feminist event. I looked at all men with suspicion: Were they perpetrators? Were they apologists for perpetrators? The effect of these encounters on me was such that after the conference I avoided male company at work and in my social life. (p. 180)

I have resisted the impulse to deny or apologize for some of the emotional experiences I had during the research since I feel this would constitute "coming to terms" with sexual abuse. Violence against women and children must never be accepted. Instead reflecting on and reviewing our reactions to what we encounter through our research as well as our everyday lives can be incorporated into working to end these oppressions. Ignoring something that is painful is an effective strategy but it does not lead to the situation being changed. (p. 186)

As a method for examining researchers' emotions, personal writings can be quite effective in demonstrating how feelings enter into the research process and thereby provide a more complete picture of the process of science. The very nature of Moran-Ellis's work requires her to engage emotionally painful material throughout all phases of the research—even at the supposed end, when one is presenting work at a professional conference. What personal writings, like Moran-Ellis's essay, do is fill in the details of what it means—emotionally—to do some kinds of work. Moran-Ellis's essay reminds us that asking victims of child sexual abuse about their experiences means someone will hear those voices. Someone's job is to hear and bear witness to these stories. Not just anyone, but the researcher. The researcher must then find some way to cope with what has just been heard. This kind of personal writing shows that thinking and feeling are not separate entities. For many researchers, they are simultaneous activities, and the challenge becomes how to think in the midst of some very difficult emotions.

Personal writings are often published separate from the "main study," yet they often provide as much information about the phenomenon of interest as the "official" story. For example, Barbara Katz Rothman's essay "Reflections: On Hard Work" (1986a) describes how it felt to research women's experiences of tentative pregnancies. She examined how reproductive technologies, such as amniocentesis, affect women's decision-making regarding mothering. What happens when women learn that they are carrying fetuses with birth defects? How do women decide to abort such fetuses? In this essay, which is separate from her primary book (*The Tentative Pregnancy* [1986b]) on this research, Rothman reveals what it felt like to study such painful issues:

It was like lifting the proverbial rock and having it all crawl out—ugliness, pain, grief, horror, anger, anguish, fear, sadness. Women in their fifth month of pregnancy afraid to feel their babies move—because they may not be babies at all, but genetic mistakes, eventual abortuses. Women having abortions but using the language of infanticide, because these were not "accidental" pregnancies, but wanted babies. It was a nightmare. . . . I had *no* idea how much pain was there, or how much pain I would suffer. (p. 48)

I kept everything to do with these bad diagnoses in one drawer, in my office at school, in a building locked nights and weekends, at best nearly an hour away from home. Inaccessible. No way I could work all night, not even put in the odd hour after dinner, run in while the baby slept. A locked drawer in a locked office in another borough. Almost far enough. (p. 50)

I needed it far away because it was making me crazy. I could not stop looking at it, and I could not bear looking at it. Why was it so painful for me? For one thing, the women became so real to me; I came to know them, to care, to identify. Especially to identify. I had a baby at home. My second, born when I was 33—too young in 1981, if not now, for an amniocentesis. I was so close, emotionally, and physically, to the pregnancy experience, to the terrible, urgent intimacy of that relationship. (p. 50)

I read Rothman's book, *The Tentative Pregnancy*, which does not gloss over the emotional turmoil of difficult pregnancies, and I felt like I "got it" after reading this text. Yet this separate essay of personal writing, "Reflections: On Hard Work," taught me that the "it" to get was a lot more complicated. To study risky pregnancies, as a woman, as a mother, is to be reminded of one's own risks. If this is what it does to the researcher, what does it do to the participants? If studying the problems associated with amniocentesis was that emotionally draining for Rothman, what is it like for the women? Rothman's emotional experiences of this work provided another source of data, and through that contrast, I believe both authors and readers can walk away with a deeper understanding. Doing this research is emotional, and it requires both thinking and feeling. They are inseparable.

The personal writings method of capturing researchers' emotional experiences raises interesting questions: Is this science or is this good nonfiction writing? Should we read these personal writings as sociological record, as research "findings," or should we read them as research memoirs? They indeed document that researchers do have emotions, that emotions do enter into the research process, and that emotions can provide intellectual insights. It's as if these personal writings can attain the goals of science—discovery, insight, explanation, education—without actually going through

all of the methods of science. Is that possible? Perhaps. DeVault (1997) provides a useful explanation of the relationship between personal writing and
sociology as a science:

> Both projects [two examples of personal writing] represented work that I
> thought of as "not quite sociology," but I have also felt, at times, a desire
> to present and defend them as sociology because they express many of the
> same analytic themes as my more conventional scholarly work. (p. 217)

To create personal writings, the author must engage in a critical thought
process that is not unlike how other more "research-y" pieces are constructed. Thus, their methods of generation may reflect similar critical-
thinking skills, if not similar methodologies.

In addition to these examples of personal writings, the literature on
researchers' emotions has expanded in recent years to include now a handful
of studies that formally investigate the emotionality of social research. In
these projects, the study of the "main topic" and a formal study of the
researchers' emotions proceed concurrently, with a defined methodology to
capture the role of emotions in research. Typically, investigators keep detailed
field notes or other written documentation that is then content-analyzed as
would be done with any textual data. For example, psychologist Frances
Grossman and her colleagues collected and analyzed their emotional struggles
in researching childhood sexual abuse (Grossman, Kruger, & Moore, 1999).
Throughout all phases of the research project, they kept detailed notes and
memos regarding their individual feelings and group conflicts. The content
analysis of these notes revealed as much about the painful emotions of studying child abuse as it did about the real day-to-day process of conducting feminist research. This work provides unique insight into just how difficult it can
be to try to negotiate power differentials in a setting that strives for equality.

Similarly, Carolyn Ellis and her colleagues have used these techniques
across a variety of projects (see Ellis, 1991a; Ellis, Kiesinger, & Tillmann-
Healy, 1997; Ronai & Ellis, 1989). At the conceptual heart of this methodology is what Ellis (1991b) calls "self-introspection":

> Introspection as a social process is active thinking about one's thoughts
> and feelings. . . . It emerges from social interaction, and occurs in
> response to bodily sensations, mental processes, and external stimuli as
> well as affecting these same processes. It is not just listening to a lone
> voice arising in one's head; usually, it consists of interacting voices, which
> are products of social forces and roles. As such, it is a valuable process for
> sociological research. In self-introspection, the researcher makes a con-
> scious effort to be aware of awareness (meta-awareness), to examine self
> and feelings, and to record systematically self-reflections and their appar-
> ent links to social situations and structural constraints. (p. 129)

For example, in caring for her chronically ill spouse, she kept daily field notes about that experience and analyzed her own feelings for writing her book *Final Negotiations* (1995). Ellis has expanded this methodology in other projects to include group introspection, in which members of a research team systematically record and then analyze field notes regarding their own emotional experiences (Ellis, Kiesinger, & Tillmann-Healy, 1997). On the one hand, these field notes (either individual or group) are not remarkably different from those taken by other sociologists using ethnographic methodologies, except that the thick, narrative descriptions are written by the researcher about herself/himself. Yet on the other hand, they are profoundly different, because what is being chronicled in those field notes is an emotional account of what the researcher is actually experiencing. It is tempting, then, to question whether the creator of such notes could analyze them "effectively" or "accurately," but that is missing the point of doing this work in the first place. It is this very closeness between the researcher and these data that defines this kind of research, and it is this closeness that benefits the analysis. Researching the researcher is by definition a subjective enterprise. The act of telling the story behind the research, with or without formal documenting data, creates a novel vantage point through which we can understand the social world.

Researching the Researcher: Studying Violence against Women

As noted previously, it is often the "difficult" topics—trauma, abuse, death, illness, health problems, violence, crime—that spawn reflection on the role of emotions in research. Although I believe it is important to examine the affective component of research in general, irrespective of the particular substantive focus, it is telling that many examples of personal writing in the literature come from research on violence against women and girls. And most of these reflections are written by women about the experience of researching something that they may have experienced or are at continued risk for experiencing. It is jarring as a researcher to hear a rape survivor's story and realize that, given different circumstances, you could be on the other side of the interview. Consequently, this area of research can provide a rich, albeit grim, context for exploring the interconnections between emotionality and science. It's worth taking a closer look at what it means to research violence against women, because such work provides more than enough data for analysis. Through its expansive set of conflicts and challenges, studying violence against women can evoke a staggering array of emotions. Careful documentation and reflection upon those feelings could help inform our theories of violence but, more generally, could also provide an exemplar for the social sciences regarding the reciprocal nature of knowledge and emotion.

But for many years, the notion that studying this kind of violence can at times be emotionally draining was a fairly private issue. For example, in the rape victimology literature, psychologists Margaret Gordon and Stephanie Riger (1989) were among the first researchers to make any mention of this phenomenon:

> [We] found it difficult at times to separate ourselves from the topic. Constantly reading about and discussing rape and other forms of violence against women often left us anxious and depressed. Staff working with us also found themselves disturbed. (p. xiii)

This is a side comment in their book on women's fear of rape, standing alone as a brief confession to the realities of this kind of research. In addition to Gordon's and Riger's remarks, there have been more detailed personal writings about the nature of researching violence against women. Liz Kelly (1988) described how studying rape caused her to experience flashbacks and acute feelings of fear about personal safety, anger, and sorrow:

> I became increasingly concerned about my own safety. For the first time in years I felt scared walking alone at night. I resisted this fear, told myself that it was irrational, and that I was no more at risk that six months previously, that everything I knew about male violence told me that women had more to fear from men they knew in their own homes than from strangers. As I began interviewing [rape survivors] I was more directly reminded of the threat and reality of sexual violence. (p. 15)

Similarly, Janet Alexander and her colleagues characterized their experience of researching rape as a "parallel reaction"—parallel to that of the victim, including similar feelings of distress (Alexander et al., 1989). Interestingly, their methodology—case record reviews from rape crisis center files—was relatively "impersonal," but even that exposure was enough to be upsetting: "[It] became clear that some of the feelings identified as rape trauma syndrome were being reported by members of the research team" (p. 58). As one member of their research group recalled:

> After collecting data for several weeks, I had a horrible nightmare that someone entered my bedroom while I was sleeping and both physically and sexually abused me. I woke up with my face wet with tears and felt a fear that I will never forget. I began to feel that rape is the ultimate invasion of human life, and yes it can happen to me, but it should never happen to anyone. (p. 59)

The emotionality of researching sexual violence against women gained more public exposure when Martin Schwartz's edited book, *Researching Sex-*

ual Violence against Women: Methodological and Personal Perspectives (1997), included an entire section on researchers' emotions. In four brief vignettes, authors Stanko, Hippensteele, Mattley, and Huff reflected upon the emotional impact of their work. For example, Elizabeth Stanko wrote:

> Emotion and pain are never far from teaching and research on violence. I have wept with my students and my interviewees; I have been so overwhelmed with anger at the treatment of (mostly) women by abusers that I have not known quite how to handle it. After 20 years of academic work as one who has identified (and been identified by others) as a *radical* feminist, I am tired and wonder how all my colleagues have coped with what I now see as inevitable angst accompanying the act of researching sexual violence. The purpose of this chapter is to break my own silence about my experiences of harboring anger, frustration, fear, and pain during my own research experiences. (p. 75)

The personal writings of Kelly, Alexander, and Stanko further demonstrate that researching sexual violence against women provides a rich context for understanding the role of emotions in research. It is common, perhaps even normative, to be emotionally upset by constant exposure to such violence. By breaking their silence, these authors present a more complete picture of what it means to do this kind of work. The behind-the-scenes details are not censored; the empirical research findings that these authors have described in other articles and other books were generated in this setting of emotionality. The context of the work is now known. And after learning these details, it is reasonable then to ask what impact that emotional context had on the research itself. Kelly noted that "moving between the interviews and my own experiences and reactions was an integral part of the research methodology" (p. 19), and Stanko stated: "Such emotion may be tapped as a resource for expanding our insight into the day-to-day realities of sexual violence" (p. 79). Something about these emotional connections was seen as useful. What that "something" is is worthy of more detailed reflection. In what ways were these emotions a resource to Stanko and part of Kelly's methodology?

It is this "impact" question that I am most interested in exploring. Building upon these descriptive personal writings in the field, my goal in the remainder of this book is to develop this link between experiencing emotions in research and the intellectual benefit these feelings could bring to the substantive findings. Researching the researcher provides insight into the actual lived process of conducting research, but also shows us how our feelings are integral to the construction of knowledge. Studying sexual violence, as a woman is, almost by definition, an emotional experience. By systematically attuning to those feelings, what can we learn about rape and violence against women? I examine this question within the context of a project I developed with graduate and undergraduate students at my university. The Women and Violence Project interviewed rape survivors throughout the metropolitan Chicago area regarding their postassault experiences. A particular focus in this work was how victims' contacts with their communities, such as the legal system, medical care facilities, mental health services, rape crisis centers, and religious organizations, affected (positively or negatively) their psychological and physical health recoveries. To recruit participants, we distributed information about our study and our research team throughout the varied places women might pass through in their daily lives, such as nail salons, beauty parlors, grocery stores, churches, laundromats, currency exchanges, libraries, bookstores, gyms, public transportation, and child care centers.[4] We sat down with over a hundred women and listened to their stories of abuse and survival. And then we had to find ways to live with what we had learned and witnessed.

Throughout this project, I kept ethnographic field notes documenting the process—both scientifically and emotionally—of conducting this work. In addition, at the conclusion of the project, I interviewed the members of the research team to learn more about how conducting this research affected them emotionally and how it shaped their understanding of violence against women. I developed an interview that would allow for exploration, examination, reflection, sharing, and closure. As a semistructured interview, I outlined four topics for discussion: 1) our most emotionally difficult interview; 2) the emotions we experienced throughout the project; 3) how we coped with these feelings; and 4) how these emotions affected our understanding of rape. Using a grounded theory approach to analysis, I coded my field notes and these interview transcripts to discover how emotions influenced our work. What follows in the remainder of this book are the findings of this researching-the-researcher project and my reflections upon those results. Over the course of the project, what happened to stir our emotions, what were those emotions we felt, and what did they teach us?

In Appendix A of this book, I tell the story within this story of how and why this researching-the-researcher project unfolded and how I worked with these introspective data. The Women and Violence Project was not my first contact with rape. I have been a volunteer rape victim advocate for several rape crisis centers, and I had conducted other studies before this one. This prior work taught me that attuning to emotions is a critical aspect of survival, and in trying to attend to my own emotional needs and the needs of my research team, I slowly realized that these feelings were helping us understand rape. But it is not easy to study this process. My research team was generally supportive of my effort to capture our diverse emotional experiences, but this was not without conflict. I can present only my understanding and my interpretation of these events. They are informed by my own experiences and values, and as such, this story would be different if told by other members of the team. It is also important to remember that team members are researchers in their own right, used to working with data and shaping it within their own perspectives and values. How I conducted this project may or may not be how they would. How I saw things may or may not be how they saw them. My goal was to find what was similar and common across people and events while acknowledging the diversity of perspectives. The stakes are very high when researching an emotional topic while simultaneously researching the emotions of the very people with whom you're working in that endeavor. Yet it is my position that going into that unknown space can be personally and professionally insightful. Researching the researcher raises complicated issues regarding subjectivity and interpretation, and in doing so, can also reveal new substantive perspectives and hidden information about the process of conducting social science research.

From Thinking
to Feeling

The Stories That Bring Feeling to Researching Rape

I t seemed relatively straightforward. As a research team, we, the Women
& Violence Project, would interview rape survivors throughout the
Chicago metropolitan area about their postassault experiences. Sitting
down to talk face-to-face with victims requires enormous preparation—
conceptual, emotional, and practical. Our core planning group spent over
six months developing the interview protocol and a training program for
the interviewers. The graduate student team members and I had been volunteers at rape crisis centers and other women's organizations, so we began
with extensive knowledge regarding the challenges of working with rape
victims. Having already heard numerous survivors' accounts, we generally
knew what to expect and we knew how to prepare other team members
who had less practice coming into this project. We had the benefit of both
direct service work with rape survivors and our familiarity with the academic rape victimology literature to guide our efforts. Yet, for all our prior
involvement and planning, we were still, at times, shocked and surprised.
All of the preparation and training couldn't completely protect us from
what it felt like to listen to story after story after story.

We knew intellectually that this work would be emotionally challenging, so we created structures within the project to address these feelings.
We scheduled weekly staff meetings to vent our emotions, and many of
the senior graduate students took key leadership roles in providing mentorship and social support to the less-experienced interviewers. Indeed, it
would be hard to argue that we weren't well prepared. But that was what
was so striking—even we weren't immune. Even though we were a
research team, even though many of us had prior volunteer experience,
there was still room for the pain of rape to seep into our lives. We began
this project thinking about rape, intellectualizing it as a topic of scientific

inquiry, but we were hardly naïve about the possible emotional toll it could take on all of us. We *knew* it would be emotionally difficult to conduct this study, but in retrospect, I don't think that registered emotionally. But slowly, week by week, that changed. Shocked and surprised by what we were hearing from survivors, each one of us on the research team was jolted from the safety of thinking about rape. A case, then cases, got under our skin. It became personal, and no amount of abstract thinking could soothe the emotional violation.

In the first chapter of this book, "Creating Difference—Thinking versus Feeling: The Role of Emotions in Research," I explained why we could approach this project as a predominately thinking enterprise. The socialization of the scientist begins very early, and no matter how hard I worked as the project leader to make it okay for all of us to step away from that detached stance to allow for more emotional exchange in research, the baggage was still there. Yet our need to create this difference between thinking and feeling tapped into something much more powerful than socialization norms. There are other reasons why we preferred to think about rape rather than feel rape, and they had far less to do with our roles as researchers and everything to do with the fact that we are women. The horror of rape makes us—women in this society—want to separate ourselves from it. We did not want to feel rape because we did not want to come that close to our own vulnerability. We even knew that at the start—we knew that there are things women need to believe in order to feel safe in the world. It turns out that the role of researcher doesn't void that need.

We were studying something from which we have no immunity. There is no line that separates us, the researchers, from them, the survivors. We knew we could be or could have been on the other side of the interview— telling a story of surviving rape, not listening to one. It became more and more difficult to *think* about rape when the very things we were hearing and learning in our research project reminded of our own vulnerabilities. Although the primary focus of this book is the emotional experiences of the research team, in this chapter I must reach back into our "main" research project. What we heard in our interviews with rape survivors startled us out of thinking and propelled us into feeling rape. I focus on eight specific interviews of over a hundred our research team conducted with rape survivors. These eight are significant in that they marked our turning points—these eight stories shattered our beliefs and assumptions about sexual assault. These stories are not the "worst" we heard. Substantively, they are not all that different from the other 90-plus interviews our research team conducted. What is different about them is that they made us *feel* rape. They were identifiable moments in the research project where the cool intellectual boundaries of knowledge melted into an undifferentiated puddle of anger, hurt, fear, and pain. These stories forced us to cognitively recognize and emotionally absorb that we too are very much at risk for being raped.

There are things women need to believe to feel safe in this world, and over time, these beliefs proved themselves flimsy defenses against the realities of rape. As women, we need to believe that rape can't happen to us. Yet two stories in particular reminded us that it's hard to maintain that belief when you're sitting across from someone who looks like you, lives near you, or shares your interests and passions. We want to feel that we can escape rape by playing it safe: not walking alone at night, not living alone, locking our doors, not opening our windows on ground levels. Two other stories challenged the efficacy of those "safety rules." When you hear about a rapist using a ladder to climb through a fourth-story window to get to his victim, or when you hear about a "friend" deliberately trapping someone for a gang rape, it becomes painfully obvious that these "safety rules" do not provide safety and rapists do not play by any consistent rules. We also want to know that even if we were assaulted, there would be people in society who would help us and care for us. We want to have faith in the legal, medical, and mental health systems. Two stories in particular were no less than sacrilege: it's hard to believe in the concept of "help'" when you hear that the rape was committed by a police officer, or when you hear about women turned away from community agencies where they were offered no services. Above all else, we need to believe that if we were raped, we would survive. Even that belief can be shaken. In two other interviews, we saw women suicidally depressed and permanently disabled from the assault. We hoped for their survival but realized it's not guaranteed.

Over and over again, we heard stories in our research interviews with rape survivors that decimated every defense we constructed to protect ourselves from rape. Being rape researchers brought us more awareness than the "average" woman, but even so, all of our preparation and training didn't insulate us. We were surprised and shocked at times, and we were surprised that we were surprised. Think it can't happen to people like you? Yes it can. Think social systems will help you? Not necessarily. It is precisely because women are so vulnerable that we have had to find ways to believe in our safety or, at the very least, ways to selectively attune to possible risks. Those tricks stopped working. We felt rape when our safety zones were violated. In the face of overwhelming evidence to the contrary, we wanted to believe we were safe. We felt otherwise. This chapter describes what we heard in our interviews with survivors that got under our collective skins, the specific cases that shocked, upset, challenged, and forced us to feel rape.

It Can't Happen to Me

We need to believe we will not be raped. Yet such thinking creates a paradox for women: if it won't happen to me, then, because rape does indeed happen, and frequently at that, it must be happening to others. There must be something different about me—the one who won't be harmed—and them—those who will. We must believe, at some level, that others do something or don't do something to prevent their own victimization. But rape is never the victim's fault. By definition, rape is an act of unwanted, forced (or coerced), sexual contact. The rapist, not the victim, deserves the blame. To feel safe, however, we must believe in our own capacity to control our lives and protect ourselves. But there is no control in rape; it is outside the control of the victim. Therein lies the problem: How can we feel safe in this world when we are at risk for something so terrible over which we have no control?

Ronnie Janoff-Bulman (1989, 1992; Janoff-Bulman & Frieze, 1983) and other researchers have found that victims' postrape distress is due, in part, to their realization that they are not safe because the world is not a just, kind, predictable place (McCann & Pearlman, 1990a; Perloff, 1983; Ullman, 1997). The feelings of distrust and alienation victims endure after the assault may be the result of their shattered beliefs in a safe world. These empirical findings generated Janoff-Bulman's just-world theory, which suggests that people need to believe their world is fair, orderly, and stable in order to maintain a sense of personal control and purpose. To hold this belief, observers must attribute the unjust suffering of others to flaws in that person's behavior or character. In other words, observers believe that the world is just (i.e., people get what they deserve) and the victim's "bad" behavior, or personal character, must have caused the event (Lerner & Miller, 1978; Montada & Lerner, 1998; Williams, 1984). Such schemas about the world as an inherently safe and predictable place are not easily modified. People may resolve the cognitive dissonance that is generated by blaming victims rather than changing their worldviews. Furthermore, by convincing themselves that they are different from victims or would behave differently, people can believe in their own safety from victimization (Drout & Gaertner, 1994; Janoff-Bulman, 1982; Montada & Lerner, 1998).

[margin note: explanation of why people blame the victim]

Other work, however, suggests that empathy with victims reduces victim-blaming (Barnett, Tetreault, Esper, & Bristow, 1986; Barnett, Tetreault, & Masbad, 1987). Perceived similarity with the victim can override this just-world ideology. This association between empathy and nonblaming attributions has been referred to as the defensive attribution model (Shaver, 1970, 1975). In this situation, observers are less likely to blame victims with whom they can identify in order to symbolically protect themselves from blame. They imagine themselves in a similar situation. They cannot blame the victim because they cannot blame themselves. When observers perceive a shared fate with the victim, they are less likely to engage in victim-blaming. Our experiences in this project were in many ways consistent with the defensive attribution model. Empathy was a critical component of our interviewing methods. Furthermore, the cases that shocked us, moved us, and dug deep into our feelings were the ones where we could all too clearly imagine ourselves in the victims' situations. Although we also wanted to believe in a safe world where rape wouldn't happen to us, we were forced to reexamine that belief. Each interviewer had her own story about what hit close to home and why, but there were two stories that captured the group's collective attention. These cases rattled us because they reminded us realize that rape can happen to anyone. The us-them, me-other distinction is arbitrary and false.

For one of the interviewers, the belief in a safe world did not last long. One of the first interviews she conducted shattered her illusion of safety, and when she told the research team in our staff meeting what happened in this interview, it disturbed all of us. In the staff exit interviews at the end of this project, she explained what happened in this case and how it affected her:

> She [the rape survivor] was my age. She was 19 or 20. I had turned 20 that day. I think she was 20. That struck me, too. This is her life up to this point, and this is my life up to this point. It was hard to think about how lucky I am. I'm conducting the interview, I'm not being interviewed.

> She had been raped by her sister's boyfriend. Other people were in the house, but she couldn't do anything to get away. She told her sister a few days later that she was raped, but didn't tell her who did it. She later found out she was pregnant from the rape, and she decided to have the baby and everyone [in her family] supported her. They knew it was from a rape, but didn't know anything more. She never told her sister what really happened.

> You know, we're [the interviewer and the survivor] the same age, and that's what she's been through. But what also got to me about this interview was that she brought her baby with her. And it was the baby she had from the rape. I will always remember it because I held the baby. She left to go to the bathroom during the interview—it took a long time. It seemed to take forever. But I held the baby while she was in there for a long time, and it seemed so real. The baby was so beautiful. You wonder what's going to happen. How the baby's going to grow up? How can you love this baby? You know, it'd be so half and half. You'd be so torn in your mind all of the time.

> It was such a moving experience. Sitting there holding this life that came about because of something so horrible. It was a little girl. It was really hard for me holding this little girl because we know the odds are really high. When she grows up, she might be assaulted. And she was born from an assault.

> It was hard to think of how lucky I am. I talked to so many women and I think, how have I been so lucky? You know? I worry about my friends and them being hurt all the time. . . . I know full well when I walk around, I could get jumped and hurt and beat up like anyone else.

> [Doing this interview so early in the project] made me realize that after all my interviews, I was going to have to take some time and sit down and be sad for a while. The first one was a little upsetting. Then I breezed through the second one. Oh, this is no big thing. Then this one hit. It stopped me dead in my tracks. This is what rape is all about. This girl's now a mom because of it—a new life is here in the world because of it. And it could have been me or any of my friends in that same situation.

As this interviewer relayed this story to us in a staff meeting, her voice was very quiet and she made no eye contact with any of us. That's how she spent her birthday that year: doing an interview for her research practicum that forever changed how she understood her safety in the world. When she finished the story, I glanced around the room—heads were bent, and on those faces I could see watering eyes. I opened my mouth to say something, but the words got caught in my chest and I couldn't get anything out. I was trying to say something that would contextualize this experience, normalize it—anything to make the sting go away. But my voice failed me. There was nothing I could say to make it hurt less because I knew we were picturing this interviewer holding that baby, completely dumbfounded. That image cannot be undone by any words. Later that night, I wrote in my field notes:

> I was ineffective helping the group with this interview. I couldn't think of a damn thing to say; we just sat there. I finally managed the standard empathy line of something to the effect of, "That must have been very difficult for you." So empty. She had to hold the baby that resulted from the rape. Hold her, feel her warmth, feel her breathing. I can't imagine what this was really like for her. She held the baby. I'm not surprised it was uncomfortable for her to hold that child. It's this completely unknowing, unwitting reminder. She's a little baby who never asked to be born from a rape. But she's here now and she's wonderful.

> It's interesting that people mentioned the option of abortion as we talked about this case. Even though some would have made a different choice than this woman made with regards to the pregnancy, we still talked about how it could have been any of us in that situa-

tion. But [this interviewer] got to feel that in a different way because
she actually held that child.

After a few days, I stopped beating myself up about not having the perfect
magic words for the situation. Maybe the best thing to do was to stop talking and stop thinking, and just feel what we were feeling. That case
knocked the words right out of me. I later learned that many of the other
interviewers were shocked that I was shocked by this case. Another interviewer told me in her exit interview:

> Another thing that has always stood out in my mind was the reac-
> tion on your face when [this interviewer] told us about the case with
> the baby born from the rape—the one she did on her birthday,
> interviewing a woman the same age as her. It was quick, but I saw
> you catch your breath, like you were also caught off guard by it.
> That made me feel better. Damn, if this got to Becki, then I guess I
> won't feel bad about feeling terrible about this case. . . Even though
> I didn't do this interview, it's been one of the ones that really stuck
> with me. I couldn't shake the image of holding that baby. That must
> have been so hard for her [the interviewer]. I feel for her having to
> go through that. To think about how you're so similar to someone,
> and yet, we're here in college doing a research project, and she's
> raising a baby because of being raped. . . . It reminds you of two
> things: It really can happen to anyone—anyone just like us, and
> anyone different than us. And also, that the effects of rape last a
> long time. My god, in this case, they last the entire lifetime of
> another person. She's the long-term effect.

The collision of so many tragic elements in this case made it stick in our
minds: the pregnancy from the rape, the survivor's silence about being
raped by her sister's boyfriend, the little girl who came to be because of this
violence, the interviewer holding this baby with the discomfort of realizing
this could have been her, the fate that separated two women of the same
age—the interviewer and the survivor—into two very different life
courses. All but three of the interviewers talked about this case in their own
exit interviews. I suspect many of us harbored some guilt for feeling
relieved that we weren't the one who had to do that interview. We admired
this interviewer's strength to get through this case, and we found comfort
in her resilience. We also felt deeply for this rape survivor and her child.

A second story also showed us how the smallest details can separate "us"
and "them." In this story, the survivor had done something that each of us
had also done many, many times without incident. It's something most
women have done at some point in their lives. Some may escape harm; this
particular woman didn't. For the interviewer who talked with this survivor,

this story hit home literally and figuratively. The assault happened in the interviewer's neighborhood at a place she walked by every day. The victim was at a bar—a bar the interviewer had also frequented—when a man came up to talk to her. She wasn't interested in him but was trying to disengage herself politely from the conversation. She decided to step outside of the bar for some fresh air, but he followed her. According to the interviewer:

> It's a very busy neighborhood, lots of people around. She went outside for a minute, and he followed her out there. He started talking to her. She was trying to be nice—she didn't think to be scared of him—but wasn't interested. Then he grabbed her and shoved her into a car and took her to a hotel and raped her repeatedly. He sodomized and vaginally penetrated her.

This rape was extremely brutal. The victim was beaten and torn vaginally and anally. The rape went on for hours. What was even more difficult to hear was how this woman managed to escape from the rapist. She was scared he was going to kill her, so she did whatever it took to get out of there alive. She pretended she was having a good time with the rapist. As her interviewer recalled:

> She figured she'd act as crazy as he was to get out of it. So she told him she had a great time, so he'd let her go. She was really bleeding though, so she told him he should take her to the hospital so she could get it cleared up, but other than that, things are great. He said he wouldn't take her to the hospital, but he would drive her back to the bar. Before he drove her back, he asked for her phone number, and get this, he checked it before he took her back to make sure it was a real phone number—her phone number and not bullshit. She somehow knew to give her real phone number just in case. There was no way in hell she wanted to give him her phone number. I guess she figured she could get it changed if she got out of there alive. He might have killed her or started all over again if he realized she lied to him. But she faked him out to get away. I can't believe how smart she was, how she figured out how to get away.

For the interviewer, the extreme violence of the assault, the reality that she too had tried to avoid men in bars by walking outside for fresh air, the fact that this woman was abducted—in front of other people—in the interviewer's home neighborhood was almost too much to bear:

> Her and I were very similar, you know: from the same age group and educational level, from the city, similar interests as far as social

interests and things like that. And it [the rape] happened in my neighborhood. . . . It was so close. Physically close to me. And that I thought I lived in a pretty safe neighborhood. It was in my neighborhood. She could be any one of my friends or me. I was just thinking how many times have I stayed outside of a bar to get some air, and how many times have I walked by that hotel? We've all done things like that. It can just happen, and that's what really struck me. Nowhere is safe and no one is immune. I'm not safe. I realize that it gets to you anywhere. The violence does.

This interview blew my whole world right out. Blew me away and blew my safe space within the world. I mean, I knew the reality that it could. I guess, in theory, I understood it could happen to anyone. This time it did, you know? My safe place was ruined. What also got to me about this case was that I guess in my head I figured that mostly I would be hearing date-rape stories. That's what a lot of rapes are. Then I heard this abduction rape story, and it just really blew me away. I didn't really think that I thought only white college girls get date raped, but maybe I was living under that assumption. Anyone can be date raped, anyone can be abducted.

I don't know if I would have known what to do to get out of that situation. I have such respect for this woman for being able to pull it together and get out alive. Who would think that the safest way out would be to pretend to be okay with it? I am in total awe of her survival instinct. In some ways, I guess what shook me up so badly about this interview was that I felt so similar to this woman, which made me realize how it could have been me or anyone else I know in that situation. And I don't know if I would have been as smart as she was about how to get away. That made me even more scared. We're really similar, and this could have happened to me, but I don't know if I would have figured out how to protect myself.

When our research team heard about the case of the baby conceived in the rape, it stunned us into silence. But this interview jolted us into frantic conversation. When this interviewer finished telling this story in our staff meeting, she was in tears. We first responded with comfort and support, then we launched into discussion: Oh my God, how many times have each of us blown off some guy in a bar? How many times have each of us stepped out of a bar to get some air? That could have been us. That could have been anyone. What stymied us was how this victim eventually got away from the rapist. I wrote in my field notes that night:

It was very interesting because so many in the group didn't feel okay about what this woman had done. They said things like, "I can't believe she did that." "She was lucky that worked." "Why did she do that?" "He must have believed her, but that's bad because now he thinks raping women is okay. He thinks she enjoyed it." After we spent so much time in training about victim-blaming, people were trying so hard not to blame her or judge her escape strategy. It was just so foreign. I tried to pull this conversation out by saying, "Look, I know we're trying not to blame the victim here, but what is it about what she did that's so upsetting to us?"

They were all quiet for a few moments, then another member of the team [not the one who conducted this interview] said, "You know, I can sit here and talk about how dangerous it was, how it might have reinforced his twisted, fucked-up ways, but the God's honest truth is that I don't think I would have thought of it. I could have been in her situation, I could have been her, and I don't think I would have known to pretend everything was okay. And because of that, I probably wouldn't have gotten out alive. We can be defensive and get judge-y, but that's about our own fear. We know that could have been us, and we know we might not have been smart enough to escape. That scares the hell out of us."

At the end of the project, other interviewers who didn't do this interview still felt compelled to talk about it because it pressed so many buttons. It hit close to home for many of us because we had done the very same things that preceded this rape. What happened was not the victim's fault, but it was just so damn scary to think about how she had no control over the situation. We also felt for the interviewer who heard this story firsthand. As another member of the team described:

I went home that night and I felt so bad for [this interviewer]. She has to walk by that hotel where the rape happened everyday. To get back and forth from work to home, she's got to go right by there. How do you glue yourself back together after that? I prayed for [this interviewer] that night and I hope she felt my love and respect for her. . . . It's so unfair. We all realized we could have been in the same situation as that victim. But the rest of us don't have to walk by a reminder of our own vulnerability every single day.

We *knew* at the beginning of the project that rape can and does happen to women from all walks of life. We knew the prevalence estimates. We still needed to believe that rape happens to others. I suppose one could argue that we should have known better, but that's exactly the point. We did know better, and we still felt otherwise. We needed to feel protected and we may have clung to this belief precisely because our perceived risk went up after every interview. Our futures were uncertain. And we not only knew that but also felt it.

These Rules Will Protect Me

We know the rules virtually by heart: don't walk alone at night, don't park your car in dark places, be wary of strangers, learn self-defense, carry a whistle, learn to yell loudly, don't live on the first floor, walk confidently, be assertive. These are the safety rules women in this society are supposed to follow. We start learning these rules as little girls and grow up in their shadow. These recommendations seem to offer reasonable advice, but such rules are fraught with problems because they create the impression that women can control whether they are raped. Because rape is unwanted, forced, sexual contact, it is by its very nature not within the control of the victim. Believing in the utility of these safety rules seems harmless enough, until you hear a rape survivor beat herself up, blaming herself over and over again for walking home from work. There is no crime in walking home from work. We run the risk of blaming ourselves for things that are not criminal, but day-to-day, activities that we have every right to do as members of society. The risk for self-blame is only part of the picture. By having rules that dictate our daily lives, enforcing some behaviors, forbidding others, rape becomes a method of social control. The fear of what could happen limits the choices many women make in this culture. The fear of rape constricts our movements, like the too-tight clothing we're also not supposed to wear. It's such a trap.

The fear of rape permeates women's lives. It is something we learn, and learn to live with. In the most comprehensive study of the fear of rape to date, Margaret Gordon and Stephanie Riger (1989) interviewed women in three major metropolitan areas—Chicago, Philadelphia, and San Francisco—and found that the fear of rape was central to the daily concerns of about one-third of the women they interviewed, a sporadic concern for another third, and of little concern to another third, but even those women took precautions to avoid rape. Women said they feared rape because of the possibility of being killed in the assault, and if they did survive, of being humiliated and stigmatized. In addition, Gordon and Riger noted that the fear of rape is different from the fear of other crimes because "women know they are held responsible for avoiding rape, and should they be victimized, they know they are likely to be blamed" (p. 2). Unlike other crimes, society's response to this form of trauma is often revictimizing in its own right (Campbell, Sefl, Barnes, Ahrens, Wasco, & Zaragoza-Diesfeld, 1999; Campbell, Wasco, Ahrens, Sefl, & Barnes, 2001; Martin & Powell, 1994; Williams, 1984). To survive rape, a woman has to live through the attack, cope with the emotional aftereffects (e.g., anxiety, depression) and the physical aftereffects (e.g., sleep disturbances, gastrointestinal ailments, gynecological problems), and withstand the blame of society more generally. There is a lot to fear about rape.

Because women fear rape so strongly, we take numerous precautionary measures to reduce the likelihood of victimization (Gordon & Riger, 1989, Stanko, 1992, 1993). Women drastically limit their activities, particularly at night or times when they are alone. In a review of women's fear of rape, Kristin Day (1994) enumerated the various strategies women use to avoid rape. The sheer number of items on this list is staggering: installing extra locks at home, installing security systems at home and in the car, refusing to open the door to strangers, taking self-defense classes, being accompanied by others at all times, checking the backseat of one's car, checking the closets and "hiding spaces" at home, wearing clothes that don't hinder running away, avoiding eye contact, leaving indications of a male partner, avoiding potentially dangerous public spaces, limiting drinking in public, strategizing about travel routes/methods, monitoring one's physical surroundings, avoiding hitchhiking or picking up hitchhikers, walking confidently/sending confident body signals, carrying a whistle, not living alone, not living on the first floor. There are so many things we choose not to do to try to protect our safety.

These precautionary strategies do work from time to time, but they miss the point. As Kimberly Lonsway (1996) argued, "[these] strategies can only protect individual women (albeit with no guarantees), but can never reduce the vulnerability of women as a group" (p. 232). Like Lonsway, Elizabeth Stanko (1992) and other feminist scholars have also been sharply critical of this focus on women. Many rape "prevention" programs teach women how they can "avoid" rape, as if the victim, not the assailant, has control over the assault. Victims don't cause rape; rapists cause rape. Prevention programs targeted to women miss the target audience and do not address root causes. A disproportionate number of rape prevention programs address possible perpetrators (Lonsway, 1996). In addition, these precautionary tactics are largely focused on the threat of stranger rape. Public safety campaigns that focus on changing women's behavior and architectural design (e.g., lighting, doorways, etc.) to reduce the possibility of street assaults completely overlook the danger posed to women by people they know and trust. Stanko (1992) suggests that this focus on public safety may derive from public officials' concerns about their own culpability: they could be held responsible for what happens to women on the streets, but what happens in the privacy of their own homes is merely a personal, domestic problem. Women do not fear their friends, family, and partners nearly to the same extent we fear strangers. These men, after all, are our friends. Why would they harm us? But it is this very violation of trust that makes acquaintance, date, and marital rape so devastating to victims.

These precautionary recommendations create an illusion of safety. We start to think that if we do what we're supposed to do, and don't do what we're supposed to avoid, we'll be safe. But what we heard in two interviews in our research project deeply challenged our faith in these safety rules. Although we knew women are at risk for attack by both strangers and those close to us, we had no idea the lengths rapists will go to to harm their victims. What we wanted to believe, needed to believe, was dismantled right before our eyes. We cling to these safety rules—don't go out alone at night, don't live alone, and so many more "don'ts"—even though they unfairly curtail our freedoms, because we hope for their helpfulness. Yet in our research we heard from rape survivors who had played by the rules. They did what they were supposed to do, and they were hurt anyway. We expect some protection in return for our acquiescence. What some get in return is rape.

One of the rape survivors who participated in our study followed the rules as much as she could. She lived alone, but on the fourth floor of her apartment building. She had to work long, odd hours in her job, but she carried herself with conviction and toughness. She was the last person you would ever think would be assaulted by a stranger. But she was. The circumstances of this interview raised more fear within us than virtually any other interview. The violation was so egregious that it left us wondering why we even bother trying to follow the rules at all. As one of the interviewers (one who didn't even conduct the actual interview) recounted:

> One of the cases that stands out the absolute most in my mind is one I didn't even do myself—I just remember hearing about it and being so completely freaked out I couldn't sleep. . . . It was the one where the woman lived alone in an apartment in the city, and she had a place on like the third or fourth floor—something high up and supposedly safe. But some guy had been following her and watching her and he used a ladder to get into her window at night to rape her.

The assailant had indeed been stalking this woman, tracking her comings and goings. He waited until she returned home from work very late one evening, and used a ladder to scale the outside of her building up to her fourth floor apartment and crawled through the open window in her bedroom. He put a pillow over her face so she couldn't see him. So strong is the belief that a woman would be safe from such attacks on the fourth floor that the police did not even believe this survivor. The police would not go searching for a ladder; they would not even consider this as a possibility. Despite the survivor's persistence, the police did not pursue this case, and the assailant was never caught or prosecuted.

This woman had followed the rules as much as possible. She had to live alone. She had to keep odd hours because of her job. She didn't live on the first floor; she lived on the fourth floor. She had her windows open because it was hot, but she lived on the fourth floor. Who would think? It's telling that the "rebellion" of opening the windows on the fourth floor of an apartment building qualifies as a risk. The survivor did absolutely nothing to bring this attack upon herself. There is no crime in wanting fresh air. It is a crime to crawl through that open window to commit a rape. What happened to this survivor was so disturbing that over half of the interviewers on the project also discussed this case in their exit interviews. As another recalled:

> There was another one [interview] that really stuck out in my head. The guy used a ladder to get into her third floor [sic] apartment. That's just one of those things I always thought—if you're on the third floor [sic] you're fine. Logic would say that somebody would see you with a ladder and call the police. . . . You can be around 500 people, and no one is going to do a damn thing. That's personally terrifying.

Another interviewer discussed how this case hit close to home for her and made her angry because she too had gone to such lengths to choose where and how she lives:

> I could not sleep when I got home [from the research group meeting] that night. I live on the fourth floor of my building. And you know, I live on that floor because that's what we're supposed to do as women. Yeah, the apartment on the first floor had a better kitchen and bathroom, but no, I took the one on the fourth floor because it's safer for women. But he used a fucking ladder to get in. Where are we safe? I must have double-checked all my windows to make sure they were locked for weeks after that. I still won't go to sleep with the windows open. It makes me so damn mad. I am roasting my ass off in fear. I can't enjoy a cool breeze at night because I'm a woman. . . . But I will. In the long run I will open my windows again and I won't live like a caged animal. . . . Doing these interviews just reminds me of all the stuff I try to ignore and need to ignore to get through day-to-day life.

We worry about those strangers—the ones in the bushes and now, the ones with the ladders. Although the epidemiological data clearly suggest we should be more afraid of our acquaintances, friends, and romantic partners, we aren't.

We heard plenty of date-rape stories in our research, which served as constant reminders that we *should* fear those we know. But the safety rules are all about stranger rape. The safety rules don't provide "protection" from our friends and partners. Another interview highlighted this point and sparked profound anger and fear within us because it showed just how cruel people can be, even those we trust. As the interviewer who heard this story firsthand recalled:

> She was gang raped on a boat. And what made it even worse, she was lured there by her ex-boyfriend. She was getting ready to go out with some friends, but they had to cancel on her at the last minute. But then her ex-boyfriend called and asked to see her. She didn't think anything of it. It was his revenge. He lured her out to a boat where his friends were waiting. She thought she was going sailing with some friends. They got her far out in the water, and then gang raped her. She kept talking about how there was nothing she could do about it; she was so trapped. I could have fought them, I could have run, but I couldn't've swam six miles back to shore. This one stuck with me because there was nothing she could do. She was so completely trapped, by the betrayal of her boyfriend and by the boat and the water. There was no way she could have got out of that. It was so thoroughly unfair.

This case made me angrier than virtually any other I heard about in this project. It was shocking, absolutely appalling, precisely because it played by none of the rules of rape. When I was discussing this case with the interviewer who heard this story, I shared with her how I was affected by what happened to this woman:

> I don't know why I should be so surprised by this. It's not as though I don't think some men in this society are capable of such things. I actually do believe they are capable of this, and even worse. Perhaps I need to believe there are some rules that dictate and govern this completely unfair injustice women must endure. I want to believe that there are some rules, guidelines, about what is and is not fair in the unfair business of rape. Being lured to a boat, with no escape, as an act of revenge, is completely outside the boundaries.

Another interviewer also reflected upon this case in her exit interview, examining rape as a type of hate crime that enforces the control and oppression of women:

> I remember the case where the woman was gang raped on a boat. Everything was used against her. She had no reason to believe that her ex-boyfriend harbored such hate. He took advantage of her kindness. Talk about being blind-sided and not seeing something coming. . . . What is it saying that her ex-boyfriend's idea of revenge

is punishment by rape? I don't think I heard another story over the course of this whole project that so completely captured just what rape is. It's an act of power and control, and hatred against women. We lock ourselves up in our homes and are all afraid of the bogey-man. I don't want to think that I live in a world where I have to be afraid of all men—like the ones I date or used to date. . . . Rape is a method of social control of women. It's all that, and it's about oppression and hating women. This son of a bitch hates women. His idea of "punishment" is gang rape. No one could have ever done anything to merit that punishment. . . . I am so scared to think that I live in world with people who hate me and members of my gender, and carry out that hate with rape.

The fear of rape and the crime of rape isolate women, boxing us into smaller and smaller quarters. Although we fight against this "victim mentality," most women nevertheless alter our behaviors in response to this threat. We don't do some things we are entitled to because we fear being assaulted and then blamed for that crime. Rape is an isolating crime. Women are usually attacked when we are alone or when we are unable to reach out to others for help. The shame that is then inflicted upon survivors furthers this separation. That one of the women we interviewed was literally isolated on a boat serves as a poignant reminder of this isolation.

The Social Systems of Society Will Help Me

We need to believe that rape can't happen to us, but if all else fails and we are assaulted, we want to believe that we will be helped and supported. Our legal, medical, and mental health systems are empowered to punish and help, but in the case of rape, too often it is the survivor who is castigated. When women go public with their stories of rape, they place a great deal of trust in our social systems as they risk disbelief, scorn, shame, punishment, and refusals of help. How these interactions with system personnel unfold can have profound implications for victims' recovery. If women receive the services they need and are treated in an empathic and supportive manner, then our social systems can work as effective catalysts for healing. Conversely, if victims do not receive the services they want and are treated in an insensitive manner, then interactions with community personnel can magnify feelings of powerlessness, shame, and guilt for rape victims. These negative experiences have been termed "secondary victimization" or "the second rape" (Campbell & Raja, 1999; Campbell et al., 1999; Madigan & Gamble, 1991; Martin & Powell, 1994; Williams, 1984). Throughout our project, we heard seemingly countless instances of secondary victimization.

Unfortunately, a growing body of research suggests that survivors are often denied help by their communities, and what help they do receive often leaves them feeling revictimized (Campbell, 1998a; Campbell & Bybee, 1997; Campbell et al., 1999; Campbell et al., 2001; Frohmann, 1991; Madigan & Gamble, 1991; Martin & Powell, 1994; Matoesian, 1993; Spencer, 1987; Williams, 1984). For example, most rape survivors never get their day in court. Only 25% of reported rapes are accepted for prosecution, 12% of defendants are actually found guilty, and 7% of all cases result in a prison term (Frazier & Haney, 1996). Yet a small proportion of rape victims do have their cases prosecuted, but it is unclear whether this assistance is actually helpful to survivors. For example, both Greg Matoesian (1993) and Lacey Sloan (1995) concluded that many of the procedures of prosecution are harmful to women's well-being. Similarly, Patricia Cluss and her colleagues found that rape victims whose cases were prosecuted were more distressed than those whose cases were not prosecuted (Cluss et al., 1983). By contrast, Patricia Frazier and Beth Haney (1996) reported that survivors held positive attitudes toward investigating officers, but were frustrated by the overall response of the criminal justice system. These findings suggest that the type of help offered to some rape victims by the legal system may not be perceived as "help" and instead is experienced as stressful and traumatic.

Rape is not only a criminal event but also a health risk. As a result, many rape survivors turn to the medical system for assistance (e.g., a physical exam to detect/treat injuries, forensic evidence collection, screening/ treatment for sexually transmitted diseases (STDs), and pregnancy testing/prevention) (Campbell & Bybee, 1997). Despite these diverse medical needs, current research suggests that many survivors are not receiving adequate care. Over half of female rape victims are not advised about pregnancy testing/prevention, and only 40% are given information about the risk of STDs (Campbell & Bybee, 1997; National Victim Center, 1992). Even if rape survivors are able to obtain needed medical care, there has been some concern in the literature that the services themselves may be quite traumatizing. The physical intrusiveness of the rape exam procedures often leaves many women feeling violated and reraped (Parrot, 1991). The services provided by the medical system, like those offered by the legal system, may provide assistance to some rape survivors but for others may actually increase trauma.

Due to the trauma of the rape, mental health workers are also called upon to help victims and those close to them who are also traumatized by the rape (e.g., family, friends, and/or marital/relationship partners). A variety of successful clinical interventions have been supported in the literature (e.g., Foa, Steketee, & Olasov., 1991; Frank et al., 1988; Resick & Schnicke, 1992; Rothbaum, 1997) suggesting that mental health services are quite beneficial to rape survivors. However, not all mental health providers use these established successful techniques, and some feminist therapists have argued that traditional psychotherapy can be victim-blaming (e.g., Brown, 1994; Wyche & Rice, 1997).

The pervasiveness and detrimental impact of secondary victimization was one of the key substantive findings that emerged from our interviews with rape survivors (see Campbell et al., 1999 and Campbell et al., 2001). Consistent with the findings of other studies, we found that, overall, rape victims receive little help from the criminal justice system, and this victim-blaming contact tends to be quite distressing for survivors. This effect was far more pronounced for victims of nonstranger rape (i.e., acquaintance rape, date rape, marital rape), who were at particular risk for secondary victimization. However, it was the stories of secondary victimization behind the statistical findings that so moved us. As described in the preface of this book, one of the interviews I conducted was saturated with instances of victim-blaming from social system personnel. The police officer would not even take a report of the gang rape, instead favoring his erection from the pleasure that this woman's pain brought him. The doctor would not perform an exam on this survivor because she had bathed prior to coming to the hospital. This example was not all that uncommon. Other interviewers heard similar stories of secondary victimization that flamed our emotions.

The sheer frequency with which we heard about women being denied justice and assistance nearly numbed us to our anger and rage, but two cases broke through to capture our collective frustration. In these stories, the survivors were raped by police officers, making their rape by the system both literal and figurative. The legal system, which has such a difficult time handing down punishment to any rapist, was particularly ineffective in prosecuting some of its own. For example, one interviewer described one survivor's experience of being gang-raped by two cops:

> She was raped by two cops. I know that a lot of police don't take their job to help rape victims seriously, but this was so far beyond that. It wasn't that they just wouldn't help her, no, they were the ones doing the rape. It was like they were thinking, "I can do whatever I want to do."

> The fact that she was a prostitute—they took such advantage of her. Told her no one would believe her anyway. It was hard to hear. It really was. She was hungry. She was trying to get something to eat. The cops pulled up and told her, "Oh, we'll take you to get something to eat," so she went with them. Then she realized they weren't taking her to a restaurant. She was out in the middle of nowhere—in no man's land. That's when they gang-raped her. Out there. They told her no one would believe her. She was just a whore. This is what she wanted. She deserved it.

That this woman was trying to earn a living by working as a prostitute made her particularly vulnerable to these police officers. Where could she turn? She could have been arrested for prostitution, but instead they assaulted her. The survivor's analysis of the situation stunned her interviewer and the other members of the research team. As the interviewer recounted:

> What really shocked me is she [the rape survivor] said, "I was pissed off because I was working and I wasn't getting paid for it." Inside I was saying, "But they were raping you. They could have killed you. You're worrying about not getting paid." But see, I guess I have never lived in her shoes, and I don't know what it's like. . . .

> But this woman knew she had been raped by the police officers, so it wasn't like she was saying it was trick that she didn't get paid for. No, she knew it was rape, but she was also saying that working in prostitution is all about getting raped and getting paid hush money to keep it quiet. She just wasn't paid by the cops; they could take advantage of her to get their rape for free and because they're cops, she will have no chance for justice.

> So after the cops were done with her, they threw her out, and she had to walk back to town. She went into a bar to get a drink—I mean who could not need some numbing after that—and some guy came up to her in the bar and told her she looked like she really needed a friend. She talked to him, and he bought her dinner. He told her she looked tired. They went to his room, and instead of letting her sleep, he raped her. Three times in one day. She was raped three times in one day, and she said to me, "I was raped three times in one day, and no one paid me for it."

> I was completely stunned by this one. I'm trying to take all of this information in, and not get my own feelings all mixed up in it. It was really hard doing these interviews. I knew my job was to listen and ask questions that would help me understand her. So I know she knew she was being raped and that prostitution was rape with money. But it was so hard because it doesn't matter that she's a prostitute; she didn't deserve to be raped. The cops knew she couldn't do anything about it, so they took advantage of her.

A number of elements made this case hard to digest: the first two assaults were committed by police officers (agents of the legal system itself), the survivor was working as a prostitute, she had no legal recourse, she was raped again that same day, and the victim herself emphasized how mad she was about the lack of financial payment from her assailants. It was absolutely bewildering to many on the team. For example, another interviewer described how she felt hearing this story in our staff meeting:

> I was so confused by that one interview, the one where the woman was raped by the police officers, but she was a prostitute too. That one really made me think. On the one hand, it's almost easy to dismiss her because she's a prostitute and she kept complaining about not getting paid. Not a sympathetic victim. But she's actually really a very sympathetic victim, and I went home that night and cried for her because she had nothing and nowhere to go. She's working as a prostitute to try to survive, and the system literally fucked her over. The cops raped her. She has no hope of getting the case prosecuted because of who she is, and she wasn't paid for her silence. It was so upsetting for me to hear about how this woman defined being a prostitute: getting raped, but getting money for it. The money is for silence. God, is that what it's like to be a prostitute? What does that mean about rape? What does that mean about sex?

Other interviewers found this case very troubling for what it suggested about how our society in general and our social systems in particular define who is and is not eligible for justice. Women in general don't seem to qualify all that often, but women working in prostitution definitely do not. The extremeness of the case made it difficult to sort through, but as one interviewer described:

> That one was one of the hardest to hear because it was so shocking, but once you sifted through all of it, you realize so many of those things are like background noise. I don't mean any disrespect to this survivor. I just mean that the fact she was a prostitute and talked about money is not the issue, but you can get hung up on it. Her case was really about how the legal system can be so harmful to rape survivors. Not only was she literally raped by the system— those cops—but she had no way of getting what happened to her punished, and she knew it and we all knew it. To me, this case just showed how unfair our justice system really is because in practice it dictates who can qualify for help. She doesn't because she's a prostitute, but that's just the more extreme case of what we heard over and over again in all the other interviews. So many other survivors couldn't get their cases prosecuted either, and they weren't prostitutes. Because this one was, it was like a smokescreen, all smoke and mirrors, but it's really the same thing for so many victims.

In fact, another story we heard in this project underscores this point. A different young woman was also raped by a police officer. She was not working in prostitution, yet the end result was the same as it was for so many women in this study. Virtually no help was provided by our social systems, and what "help" was offered was not healing but hurtful. The interviewer described her experiences interviewing this other survivor:

> She was maybe 19 or 20, and she had been assaulted in the back of a cop car. I was pretty upset. Upset as in angry. My anger was directed at the cops. Her case was embedded in a whole other host of corruption cases, and just thinking about the way in which corruption gets portrayed and kind of glamorized . . . [it was] upsetting to me because I kept seeing this girl. I kept thinking about how young she was and how deeply affected she still was and what happened to her. I was pretty angry about it. I think that perhaps that reaction is because that's one of the things that most flies in the face of our expectations. Assuming that we have some kind of expectation that survivors' experience with systems will be bad or negative. But nowhere in there does that leave room for a woman to be raped by a cop and to have that interaction with a cop. That's like . . . it's sort of like removed from the picture when you think about social systems and contact with social systems. Wait a minute . . . that it's really horrible to be raped by a cop and to go to the cops. So because that didn't fit into the prepackaged model of this project, I think that perhaps went through me the most. Maybe I would have been similarly upset had a woman said, "Oh, I was raped by a gynecologist." Or "I was raped by a lawyer."

Another interviewer also reflected on this story:

> I remember [interviewer] talking about one [interview] she did with that really youngish woman who was raped by a cop. It made me think about all the ways our vulnerability is exposed. . . . She was so young and naïve and literally fucked over by the system for it. It made me so angry. I've never felt the same about the police after hearing this story. You know, what that damn badge will allow them to do and get away with.

We began this project with some skepticism about whether our social systems would in fact assist rape survivors. The academic literature and personal experiences some of us had had as rape victim advocates had already gone a long way in disabusing us of the hope for protection. Yet the sheer frequency with which we heard about secondary victimization was stunning and infuriating. Two survivors in our project were assaulted by police officers, and their cases made secondary victimization all that more explicit: although some rape survivors are helped by social systems, for many more, the assault is continued and sustained by system personnel.

Recovery from Rape Is Possible

Finally, we need to believe in women's survival, their capacity to survive rape. Most do, but only after prolonged pain. Rape survivors suffer a myriad of problems postassault. It is not uncommon for victims to experience psychological distress, including depression, posttraumatic stress, fear and anxiety, anger, diminished self-esteem, social adjustment problems, and sexual functioning difficulties (see Goodman, Koss, & Russo, 1993a; Herman, 1992; Koss, 1993; Koss et al., 1994; and Resick, 1993, for reviews). Similarly, sexual assault survivors also have high levels of physical health distress, including injuries and/or STDs sustained in the assault and varied somatic complaints (headaches, gastrointestinal problems, gynecological symptoms, neurological problems, sleep disorders, eating disturbances, and chronic illnesses [e.g., hypertension, diabetes, arthritis]) (Beebe, 1991; Golding, 1994; Kimerling & Calhoun, 1994; Koss, Woodruff, & Koss, 1991; Murphy, 1990). In general, these symptoms remain elevated for the first few weeks postassault, but then gradually decrease over time (Koss et al., 1994). Several researchers have found dramatic improvements in psychological symptomatology within the first two to six month postassault but minimal additional improvement beyond that point (Calhoun, Atkeson, & Resick, 1982; Cohen & Roth, 1987; Frank & Stewart, 1984; Kilpatrick, Resick, & Veronen, 1981).

Although many symptoms stabilize within a few months postassault, others do not entirely disappear. Many victims exhibit chronic reactions to the trauma of rape that persist for years (see Resick, 1993). It is not uncommon for rape survivors to experience long-term problems with fear, anxiety, and sexual functioning (Becker, Skinner, Abel, Howell, & Bruce, 1982; Cohen & Roth, 1987; Siegel, Golding, Stein, & Burnam, 1990; Steketee & Foa, 1987). In addition, some victims make major lifestyle changes postassault, including changing jobs or residences, dropping out of school, and/or terminating friendships or romantic relationships (Becker et al., 1982; Burt & Katz, 1988; Ellis, Atkeson, & Calhoun, 1981). It also appears that while psychological symptoms improve within months, physical health symptoms may take much longer to dissipate. Mary Koss and her colleagues found that the greatest increase in medical service utilization occurred during the second year postassault, suggesting that somatic problems may persist longer than psychological distress (Koss, Woodruff, & Koss, 1991).

For both scientific and practical reasons, researchers have sought to identify factors that differentiate survivors with more or less successful recoveries, but definitive answers remain elusive. For instance, there is mixed evidence linking demographic characteristics and recovery outcomes (see Koss et al., 1994; Resick, 1993, for reviews). Some researchers have found that older survivors and those from lower socioeconomic statuses have more difficulty recovering from rape, but others have found no association at all. What actually happened during the assault also has varied effects on outcomes. A few early studies in the literature found that stranger rape victims were more traumatized than non-stranger rape victims, but more recent work suggests no differences at all. The actual degree of violence during the assault is not nearly as predictive as the perceived threat of violence—survivors who feared more for their physical safety during the assault have more difficulty recovering from the rape. Post-assault events also impact recovery outcomes. As discussed previously, experiencing secondary victimization (negative, victim-blaming treatment from social system personnel and/or refusals to provide assistance by social system personnel) significantly contributes to posttraumatic stress (Campbell et al., 1999). Yet receiving quality, sustained support from informal sources (e.g., friends or family) or formal outlets (e.g., mental health services) appears to buffer the negative effects of the assault and promotes healthy recoveries (Campbell et al., 1999; Ullman, 1996abc).

In our project, we interviewed women who were raped very recently (within weeks) and some who were assaulted long ago (over ten years). No matter how long ago the assault happened, it was difficult for women to discuss their memories. Indeed, for some, their recoveries were evident. For others, we left the interview wondering if recovery was ever going to be possible. We had read the academic literature and understood that recovery is a long-term process, but this did not necessarily prepare us for the emotional experience of talking with women who remained deeply affected by the assault. It was shocking to see how badly some women were hurting from the assault. Moreover, we found that the long-term devastation of rape can be much more severe than what is typically communicated in the academic literature. We interviewed women who were permanently disabled from the assault, which shook our faith in the absoluteness of recovery. We realized that recovery does not necessarily mean returning to the same preassault levels of psychological and physical health. Rape is a transformative event, emotionally and physically, for everyone touched by its effects.

For one interviewer, the most emotional case was her very first interview. Her assumptions and beliefs about recovery were shattered from her very first day, leaving her confused and depressed. In this case, the long-term effects of the assault were permanent and life-changing. To try to escape from the rapist, the survivor jumped off the balcony of her apartment building. As the interviewer recalls:

> My very first interview is one that stuck out the most, because I saw the side effects. I mean, well, what happened afterward—because

she feared for her life. I couldn't believe that someone would actually scare someone to the point where they would make them
almost commit suicide. To me, that was a suicide attempt. Because
when you jump . . . how did she know that she would just be paralyzed? That she wouldn't end her life? She feared for her life. . . .
To make it so bad that—the assailant was her husband—that's
hard for me to deal with. But I did.

She jumped off a four-story—four stories or five stories. There was
nowhere for her to go. If she went out in the hall, he would have
met her at the door. So she went out the balcony. That was one that
really stuck out. Now she's paralyzed from the waist down.

But by this being my first one, and seeing how a rape survivor . . .
she's actually surviving what happened. That really hit me hard. I
said to myself, "Will they all be like this? That traumatic?" I just
prayed. I hope the next one is not this bad. All of them were though.

This interviewer sat with a woman in a wheelchair and heard how the rape
put her in that chair. The interviewer saw exactly what rape can do, and
how long and how permanent its effects can be. It was not at all abstract;
it was a wheelchair, and the interviewer saw it and touched it. As another
member of the team recalled:

I know one of the first cases I heard about in the [team meetings]
was the one where the woman was paralyzed from the assault. I
think she had jumped out of a window to get away from the rapist.
I remember that I felt like the air in my lungs just went totally still
when I heard that. I couldn't believe it. It was so outside anything I
could imagine. I guess I must have been hoping to hear all the positive, uplifting, made-for-TV-type endings where the survivor would
stand up triumphantly and declare her survival and strength. Well,
there was no way this woman could ever stand again, and from
what [the interviewer] described, it didn't sound like this woman
was feeling any sense of recovery or closure. I guess I wanted every
case to wrap up nicely so I could feel good about it, and feel good
for the survivor. It was unbelievably sad and frightening to realize
that this wasn't going to be the case a lot of the time.

The end of the project closed with a similar case where the survivor was
permanently disabled from the assault. Although she was not paralyzed,
the victim had been so severely injured by her attackers that she could
barely walk, and was unable to work. She had been in and out of hospitals
for months. As the interviewer recalled:

I would say this one will haunt me for a little while. . . . Each time you go to interview a woman, you try and anticipate the story she's going to tell you. But every time you go, it's a surprise. It's a different twist. It's not what you thought. Not that any interview is worse than another or any one story is worse than another. But this woman . . . the torture that they performed on her, to me, made it seem like maybe there are some worse cases—worse than others. Although you don't want to minimize anybody else's trauma.

She was abducted off a city street. . . . They told her that they had killed three other women that night—Chopped them up and threw them in the Chicago river. Psychological torture to start with. . . . Then they assaulted her with sticks and batteries and anything else they could find. Tortured her with cigarette burns from her neck down to her feet. And then they kind of said, "Well, do you think she's had enough or should we kill her?" And for whatever reason, they decide not to directly kill her, but leave her for dead. So they wrapped a shirt around her head and put her in an abandoned automobile. When the one guy was pulling her into the car, the other guy took a box cutter and cut her legs into shreds, leaving her to bleed to death. Then she . . . I think the most remarkable thing at this point is that she got the shirt off of her face, untied her hands and looked up out of the car before they left, and got the license plate number. But she was at this secluded kind of out-of-the-way place—factory building or something. [She couldn't walk because her legs had been cut so badly so] she crawled on her hands and knees in the gravel. . . . It was seven blocks that she crawled in order to get help for herself. She got to the gate of a taxi dispatcher garage, and the dispatcher came to the gate. She told him I need help. This is the license plate, and just passed out.

The other thing that was kind of . . . one of those things that you notice during an interview: she only cried . . . when she was telling me her story, she only cried when someone performed some act of kindness toward her during that evening. She didn't cry the whole time she told me this horrific stuff. She told me, well, I was kind of conscious when the police got there, and the police officer gave me his coat, and that was it. She started crying. Another time when someone else showed her the slightest bit of kindness, that was it too. She started crying again.

[Q: Why do you think that was?]

I don't know. I wonder, if I want to get way off course, I wonder if someone who's assaulted starts to immediately devalue themselves.

They just completely in order to . . . they just devalue themselves while the assault is happening. They're being devalued. For somebody to come and say yes, you're worth something—even in the slightest way—unfortunately, calling them back to the level they should be. I think that's traumatic—ironically.

It made me extremely frustrated [how her case ended up]: the two guys were caught, but they only got 25-year sentences. Half time or good time. Basically for torturing and almost killing her, they got 12 1/2 years, which is terrifying that these men will be out on the streets.

At the staff meeting in which we heard this story, there was utter silence—arms crossed tightly against our bodies, eyes staring off into space. We couldn't stand what we were hearing, and I later learned that many felt guilty for the relief they were experiencing because they were not the one who had to do that interview. No one wanted this story in their life. No one wanted to hear it. It was so bad that we never were really able to fully discuss this case as a group. Over the next few weeks, I spent a great deal of time privately with the interviewer who talked with this survivor—to process, to vent, to discuss what, if anything, we could do for this woman. This was a research project, not a service program, and it was clear to both the women we interviewed and all of us on the team that the interviews were designed to be one-time experiences for reflection and sharing. But we could not get this case out of our heads. We were concerned that this woman could barely walk, was not receiving physical therapy, could not work or support herself, and was still so severely traumatized and symptomatic several months postassault. In her interview, we learned that this survivor owed over $10,000 in hospital bills stemming from her post assault medical care that she was unable to pay. She was in danger of being sued for lack of payment and losing her home. She had not been hooked up with a hospital social worker or any other type of advocate who could help her navigate the system to seek medical cost reimbursements or file for social security disability compensation.

We had all left interviews worried and concerned about the future well-being of the women we had just spent so much time with discussing such private and painful things. We had developed a referral packet that we were proud of for its completeness and user-friendliness. It was not uncommon for interviewers to spend some extra time with women after the interview to go through the referral packet and help them plan out how and where they might go for further assistance. In this particular case, we knew our limits and that we could not help her fight the system, but we decided to do more extensive follow-up. We identified specific advocates throughout the city with specializations in the types of problems this woman was facing, and the interviewer recontacted the survivor and helped her connect with these advocates, who then stepped in to assist.

This case got under all of our skins. For the interviewer who heard this story firsthand, it helped her understand her own beliefs about rape and the seriousness of rape:

> This interview rattled my sense of security, because I think . . . maybe a coping mechanism that I've been using in my life to go somewhere where you might feel insecure is to think, I'm aware. You know what I mean? I know this area. I can handle myself. All those things. I'm streetwise. You know what I mean? So, I think that's kind of a coping mechanism to get through where you need to go and things you need to do. [This interview] shook me a bit. It made me think, Well, you know, you're just not so immune. What are you going to do if somebody just snatches you off the street?
>
> Right after the interview, I was thinking I can't wait till my next interview because then it won't be my last interview. But then, the next one could have been even worse. Or equally worse in a different way.
>
> Now, I'm kind of glad that it did turn out to be my last one, because I think if I had interviewed someone who, say—I hate to say this because I don't want to minimize this—someone who was date-raped, it would have been easier for me to focus on that and say, "Okay, this is how most rapes are. There's not so many of these really traumatic ones."
>
> But I think it's important to keep the traumatic ones in mind long-term. This is also what rape can be.

What we saw and heard in many of these interviews was often worse than what we expected. These stories were a violation of our own beliefs. We had all read studies in the literature, but that didn't provide much insulation from how it would feel to sit across from a survivor and bear witness to the telling of her story. It was shocking and surprising, sad and depressing, anxiety-provoking and scary, and sometimes uplifting and empowering. But regardless of the specific emotions each interview stirred within us, what was most striking was the very fact that we were feeling. The eight stories described in this chapter were flashpoints, moments of emotional awakening for members of the research team. It hurt too much. Rape was something we had been thinking about, but not necessarily feeling. The actual lived experiences of the women we interviewed jolted us from that security of comfortable thought. Over time, many on the team found their ways to balance thinking and feeling, but it was still shocking to have our emotions so present in a research setting. And more often than not, the emotions themselves were painful.

Feeling

The Emotions of Researching Rape

T his is the chapter I dreaded writing, but it is the very core of this book. This is what it felt like to study rape, up close and personal. It hurt—a lot—a great deal of the time for most of the project staff. Yet interspersed with overwhelming anger, fear, loss, and pain was undeniable hope. The rape survivors we interviewed entrusted us with their stories, which were indeed devastating to hear, over and over again. But in witnessing the telling of these stories, we also felt the incredible strength and resiliency it takes to survive rape. More often than not, we could walk away from an interview feeling good about our work and having something uplifting to remember about each woman. In fact, I must note that two of the interviewers did not describe negative feelings at all. For them, this experience isn't remembered as painful but as empowering.

It is tempting for everyone's well-being—mine, the writer; yours, the reader—to focus on these positive emotions of researching rape. But to do so would betray the day-to-day reality of nearly every interviewer in this project. It would also run the risk of trivializing the pain each survivor endured in the rape and in the telling of her story of the rape. It would be nice to walk away from this chapter, and this book, feeling good. And as noted, positive emotions do grow in this unlikely medium, and I will describe them in this chapter. But to understand—no, to feel—why we came to treasure our feelings of hope, we must delve into the grittier emotions. This is what is absent from so much of our academic discourse on rape.

In the second chapter of this book, "From Thinking to Feeling: The Stories That Bring Feeling to Researching Rape," I described eight of the hundred-plus stories we heard that stood out in our memories and made us feel rape. But there were 90-plus other stories that we also heard that are not shared in this book. These others are by no means unremarkable. The rest include other stories of stranger rape, plenty of other instances of date and acquaintance rape, other gang rapes. In fact, I know that some of the most painful are not retold here; more time and distance are needed to lift their burden. I also know that many of our more "straightforward" cases are not described here. I say this with great trepidation because there really is no such thing as an easy, or straightforward, case of rape. They are all horrible violations. But, I can't deny the fact that it is much easier on the researcher to interview a survivor who has indeed survived the assault with composure and perspective.

What we felt in this project, therefore, comes from all of these stories. Whereas individual cases may have shocked or surprised us, unleashing specific bursts of fear or anger, it is the cumulative effect of hearing *all* of these stories that defines what it feels like to study rape. It is far more than the sum of its individual parts. This chapter describes the negative and positive emotions—loss, pain, fear, anger, and hope—that our research team felt throughout this project across these hundred-plus stories. Not all emotions were experienced by all members of the team, nor were any emotions felt with uniform intensity. There is no tidy summary that conveys what all of us felt. This chapter presents the range of what different people on the team felt throughout the project, and together these pieces begin to tell the story of how it feels to study rape in the manner in which we did for this research. In addition, this chapter describes how we coped with these feelings, particularly the painful ones. It is not impossible to hear stories of rape over and over again. But it does take a certain amount of resourcefulness to figure out how to hear this information and respond to one's emotional reactions to that information. This topic of coping was regularly addressed in training and weekly staff meetings, but it is a fundamentally individualized activity. This chapter provides a window into how that personal process unfolds. But first, we have to go where we'd prefer not to be.

Loss

Rape steals so many things: safety, identity, well-being. A survivor's life is never the same. She may heal, learn to cope with this event, grow stronger, but she is never the same. The recovery process evokes mourning for one's innocence and former self. As the rape survivor must mourn for what was lost within herself, those of us who bear witness to the crime of rape also experience loss. No amount of preparation can completely mitigate that loss. Our innocence is also sacrificed. We mourn for the survivor's losses, but we also mourn for our own. The losses are not the same by any means, but there is some common ground. Interviewing rape survivors challenges researchers' beliefs about safety and justice; we learn, because we hear it over and over again, that the world is not safe for women. We can no longer cling to our hope that we can be safe. We know that we cannot. But even if we already knew that, it is still disturbing to come face to face with all the details.

Without a doubt, the hardest day for me throughout this entire project was the last day of interviewer training. The loss I felt that day far exceeded the peaks of anger, fear, and pain I felt at other times in this work. This was the last day rape would be abstract; thereafter, it would become specific and probably quite painful. Even those who had interviewed before, had worked with rape survivors before, had never done anything quite like this. After that last training meeting, I made this entry in my field notes:

> Today was the last day of interviewer training. [In the coming days] each will sit down with a rape survivor to witness what it means to tell the story of rape. Each will complete her first face-to-face, in-person interview with a rape survivor. Starting tomorrow, rape will never again be abstract. It will no longer be the subject of an independent study undergraduate course, or a "program of research" in graduate school. Rape will have a face, then multiple faces; it will have a name, then many names. The interviewers will hear their first stories, and then many more thereafter. But tonight, their minds don't know many details, their realm of possibilities is still narrow. I mourn for this unfettered space within each of them because I know it will soon be spoiled.

> Women in this culture know rape. We know what it is, and our fear is well conditioned. In this sense, the innocence of the interviewers was lost long ago, and it had nothing to do with me and this project. Yet it is one thing to know rape happens, and quite another to hear about it in painstaking detail. It is one thing to know a handful of stories scattered across one's lifetime of acquaintances and friendships or even through one's work as a volunteer rape victim advocate, and quite another to hear scads of stories in rapid succession. It is the difference between dunking your feet in the shallow end of the pool, and plunging head first into the deep end. You don't develop the same understanding of the properties of water.

> We have prepared the interviewers as best as we know how—swimming lessons of sorts. We have walked through the interview protocol in great detail—every question, every section, every transition. I have assigned readings that try to communicate the prevalence and impact of sexual assault. Over the past several weeks, they have conducted mock interviews to learn how to complete the protocol. They have interviewed each other, my friends, and myself. They have gone through the interview from start to finish many times.

We have role-played difficult situations and discussed how to handle
them. We have reviewed, over and over again, the safety rules and
procedures every interviewer must follow. We have discussed the
project's confidentiality policy so many times that I believe they
could all recite it by heart.

We have discussed the emotions they may experience when interviewing rape survivors. I have shared my own emotional experiences of ten years of volunteer advocacy work and research
interviewing. I have gone over and over how important it is to be
human to these women. It is not okay to "move on to the next
question." We must pause, affirm, support, and encourage rape survivors. We must answer their questions. If we can provide validating,
normalizing information to the survivors, we must do so. Move
through the interview at the survivor's pace. When in doubt, I have
told the interviewers to follow their instincts of human decency—
don't sacrifice the woman's well-being for the sake of the research.
Our mantra: do no harm. Plenty of harm has already been done.
Our hope: this experience of talking about the assault in a supportive environment will be empowering and healing for the survivors.

It takes a special kind of conditioning to be able to hear over and over
again just how bad one person, or persons, can hurt another. To see
it, to hear it, to smell it, to feel it—over and over again. We have done
what we can to prepare the interviewers. We have put mechanisms in
place to try to take care of them once interviewing is under way. We
will meet weekly as a group to discuss what we have heard, to vent
the emotions, and to garner support from the research group. I have
encouraged them to draw upon each other in between these meetings. I have given my office and home phone numbers, and encouraged them to call me as well. We have set up a schedule that will
rotate them off interviewing periodically to give them a break. I have
developed a time line that can withstand an unexpected delay in data
collection if any of them need additional breaks.

All I have at this point is hope—hope that the safety net of group support will be enough, hope that they will be able to withstand the pain
of what they will hear, hope that none of them will have too many
"really bad cases" in a row, hope that they will experience more anger
than fear, more optimism than pessimism. But it worries me what
they'll see and hear. Once these words and images are in your head,
you can never get them out. Once the filth of rape has saturated your
skin, you can never really be clean again. No amount of scrubbing
can get this out of your life. I have tried to explain as clearly as I could

what it could be like: they might have nightmares, difficulty sleeping, unpleasant thoughts, increased fear. That, in short, this would be difficult. They all nodded and said they understood, but I doubt anyone can really understand until they have done it.

Yet it will not always be painful. The interviewers will have moments of incredible warmth, connection, and healing. They will bear witness to both incredible pain and incredible strength. They will feel, perhaps more strongly than ever before in their educational experiences. They will feel the power of connecting with other women, and feel the support women can provide to each other. They will become united with many other women in the struggle to end violence against women. But the only way for them to get to this good is to pass through a lot of bad. I hope that they will grow from this experience. I hope they will not long too strongly for their innocence. I hope that they can all find a way to live with what they are about to learn.

The guilt and sadness I experienced that evening was almost unbearable. I knew we had done everything we could to prepare the interviewers, but it would still not be enough to spare them a great deal of pain. There is no way to do this kind of work this way without emotional sacrifice. Later on, at the end of the project, one of the interviewers commented on this last training meeting as she sensed my sadness:

I remember our last training meeting, the one right before we all started interviewing. We were all really hyped up, you know, scared and excited. You [Becki] were also really up. Your voice was really enthusiastic and full of energy. I also remember that you also looked really sad. It's hard to describe. It's like there was something really sad around your edges. . . . Later that night I was going over the interview again, getting ready for my first interview the next day, when it really hit me. I was gonna be filling in *answers* to all of those questions. That hit me like a ton of bricks. Up until then, I had been totally focused on getting the *questions* right, and I hadn't thought about the *answers* all that much. I remember thinking that night that I bet that was what was making you sad. You knew what the answers were going to be like.

Another interviewer also reflected upon the last day of training and how it marked a transition for her from what she lost to what she found:

I think about that last day of training as the last day of being unaware, you know, going through life with my eyes closed. Ever

> since that day, I haven't been able to look at things the same again.
> I can't look at men the same anymore. I can't think, I wonder what
> he's like, I'd like to get to know that guy. I think, I wonder if he's
> the one I just heard about. I wonder if he's raped a woman, or
> when he'll rape a woman. . . . I feel like I lost something that day
> [last day of training]. I lost my old self, the self that was so trusting
> and naïve. I lost believing everything was OK in the world. Now I
> know better. . . . I'm not angry or upset about this, and I wouldn't
> do anything different, and I don't think there's anything you could
> have done for us that would have prepared us better. We were well
> prepared. It's just still a jolt to have all the lights snap on and to see
> the world as it really is, you know, to see all the danger in it.

I have heard this metaphor many times, from many interviewers, over
many projects. To learn about rape is to see things for the first time, to open
one's eyes and to see the world in a completely new but unfortunately scary
way. It's a tremendous loss, because once you see it, you can't go back. A
switch gets turned on and can never be turned off. We long for when it was
dark, when we couldn't see, when we were unaware. I believed we would
get through the process of interviewing, and we did. Our training program
laid the foundation, and the ongoing support and mentorship senior graduate students provided other members of the team carried on long after
training ended. For some, their losses were gradual; for others, it was an all-
at-once awakening. Although we were hardly naïve, we still had vestiges of
innocence. Despite extensive preparation, that innocence could not be
totally protected.

Pain

We have good reason to want to be unaware of rape and what it does to
women's lives. Telling what it has done hurts. Watching that telling is also
going to hurt. Asking survivors to tell their stories in their own words, as we
did in this research, means that the listener will bear witness to the survivors' pain. No two stories are alike in what is said or how it is said. Some
cry, some sob, others recount the events in emotionless journalistic prose.
Some whisper, some yell, others can really *talk* about it, have a conversation about what happened and what it did to them, because there has been
enough healing to provide perspective. But more often than not, this is
very painful to witness. It hurts to see someone suffering. It hurts to think
about what has happened to them and to feel for them.

We were entrusted with private information, allowed to enter very personal spaces within the survivors' lives. We heard about the rape and sometimes about other significant events—other abuse, strained relationships,
illness, death—in their lives. The act of telling shares the pain between the

survivor and the listener. We then carried around within us these stories and the pain of these stories. Many of the interviewers described a "fuzzy zone" that they slipped into after completing an interview, awash in the sadness and pain of what someone was unfairly forced to endure. I can recall how I tried to go grocery shopping after one of my interviews. I shuffled up and down the aisles, absent-mindedly blocking all traffic around me, and finally gave up mid-task, abandoning my half-full cart. I wanted to be alone for a while to let myself come to terms with what I heard that day, and allow the sadness to pass. Over the course of the project, we had to absorb the impact of each individual interview and the cumulative impact of hearing all of the interviews.

This is not easy to talk about either. To talk about it is to feel it again. When I asked each of the interviewers how they felt doing these interviews, what emotions they experienced, there was usually a noticeable pause before answering. I suspect there was some deliberation about what to reveal and what to keep private, what was safe to refeel and what was best left untouched. One interviewer shared with me what she was experiencing:

> What emotions did I experience? What didn't I feel? Mostly, it just hurt. You know, I heard your question, and knew the answer, right away, but it took me a second to answer because I felt reluctant to open it up again. It gets easier to live with it to talk about it, but there's also a part of me that wants to just forget about it. What did I feel? Pain, hurt, ugliness, sadness. I've been just soaked in it. It's impossible to get away from. Yeah, we can talk about how she survived and how she's doing good in her life, and don't get me wrong, I live to hear that. I really hope with every interview I hear something like that because I know that no matter what, I'm also going hear something really ugly. It adds up over time, the ugliness. It gnaws away in your stomach.
>
> But it's not like hearing something inspiring really takes away the pain. It's not a zero-sum game. One doesn't undo the other. Yeah, it was incredible to hear from one of the women that she's now involved in volunteer work at a rape crisis center and is really just solid. Really together and together so much that she can actually give something back now. But as great as that is, it doesn't take away what was done to her and it doesn't take away what it felt like for me to hear both parts of her story. I heard both. One doesn't make the other not exist. It doesn't work like that.

Another interviewer described how much it hurt to do a specific interview, but also noted how the pain of feeling that interview was not uncommon. The stories run together, making a fairly continuous stream of hurt.

Moreover, this interviewer noted, as did others, that she didn't ever really hear anything uplifting and never felt much relief from the pain:

> She was sobbing—I mean crying so hard at times she was almost choking. It was horrible. I remember feeling like I didn't know what to do. Part of me wanted to reach out and give her a hug, but then again, I'm not really a touchy person. I knew if I did that, it was going to seem a little awkward. It wasn't going to feel right. I wasn't going to feel comfortable, and she would know that, but then I didn't. But to sit there while she was sobbing, without hugging her, it's strange. It sticks out in my head not so much because of her story as my own ineffectiveness—my own inability to really be there for her the way I'd like to have been.
>
> [Q: How did you feel after the interview?]
>
> Pretty numb actually. I kept thinking about it all day. . . . I think what I remember most is her sobbing just because I remember this has got to be so painful. Watching the pain she was in. . . . It hurt.
>
> I'll just be honest: this [the project overall] was depressing. The stories have been more sad than uplifting. It wasn't like, "I've overcome this, I'm a survivor." That kind of thing. I haven't gotten that here [in these interviews]. I mean some were easier than others, but there's none that have been terribly inspiring.

Similarly, as another interviewer recalled:

> I think I thought I understood a lot more about rape than I really did when I first started this. . . . But there's no way to know how much this hurts. What you think it's going to be like, and what you actually feel are totally different. It's really painful, you know, it just seeps into you. . . . I'm trying to consume all of this information, but it's impossible. You can't get your feelings too mixed up with what's going on, but you can't not feel. It was very hard doing these interviews. Extremely hard.

What do you do with this? What makes it possible to endure such constant hurt? We had weekly staff meetings to discuss our interviews, and it was not uncommon to talk with each other in between meetings. A regular supportive outlet for venting was critical. But what about during the actual interview? What do you do when it's just you—the interviewer—and the survivor? No supportive team of researchers right there at the moment? The interviewers used different words to describe what they did: numbing, blunting, checking out for a moment, filtering, selecting. These words speak to a process of regulating the pain by limiting what you take in. You don't feel all of that pain right there and then—maybe because you've made yourself go numb to it, sometimes because you've been able to sift through it and focus on only certain parts of it. What do you do with this? You don't try to do anything with *all* of it.

For example, these two interviewers described how they just shut down emotionally during the interview, numbing themselves to what they were hearing:

> When I was interviewing this woman, she didn't have any chairs in her apartment, so we sat on the floor, and she pulled up her pants leg and showed me the scars on her leg [injuries from the assault], which were unbelievable. And she told me her story, and there was a point where I swear I don't remember asking her some questions. I felt like, you know, I just need to regroup before I can be of service again. But I went on with the interview. I just wasn't processing what I was hearing for a while.

A second interviewer described:

> There are certain things you can block out, just put in the back of your mind and keep going. So bad you can't react right away. You have to wait till later, react later. If you reacted now, the survivor would be taking care of you in the interview. . . . We're here to be there for them—to listen to her story. You do whatever it takes within you to be able to do that. Sometimes that means you go numb for a while. . . . Seems ironic, I guess, you have to go numb to keep on being present in the interview, and feeling and support-ing the survivor. It's not disingenuous, I think. You just can't per-sonally react to what they say, so you can go on showing warmth, and concern, and compassion, and support her strength. It's weird I guess—you can't feel so you can feel.

Another interviewer described how numbing is a conscious, deliberate process. In addition, it is interesting to note how *thinking* becomes a useful mechanism for not *feeling*. In other words, coping with the pain of researching rape can involve intellectualizing the issue as a means of numbing the pain:

> It's an emotional removal. For me, I know what I'm doing. It's defi-nitely a coping thing for me. . . . I get analytical about things when I don't want to be in touch with my emotions. I'll just think about them. I'm thinking about my emotions. I'm not feeling them. I think

that's what I do with a lot of these stories. I think about them a lot but I don't think I'm always feeling them. And then there's the ones I've actually felt.

[Q: So some are felt, some are not. What happens to the distress?]

I don't think I feel it. I think as they [distressing emotions] start to turn on, there's almost like a switch in my head that I can feel going off. Like I always know exactly when I'm doing it. As it starts happening. I really feel like I'm taking a step over, or something's clicking, or I'm going to a new perspective and thinking about things instead. And analyzing them. And dissecting them. And thinking about the implications of them.

[Q: Is it that you don't feel right then or don't feel later on either? What happens in the interviews that are salient to you—the ones that you said get under your skin?]

Try to turn it off—can't. It's a habit to intellectualize, and then something happens with the women just sobbing, and it kind of gets moved back over into the emotional side of things.

For other interviewers, coping with the pain of this work didn't involve growing numb to that hurt but, rather, trying to select what they would feel. Similar to numbing, this selection process is a highly *thinking* enterprise. Intellectualizing becomes a useful coping device:

After a while, it just hurt too much, so I was like, well, how am I going to get through this? I can't dwell on everything that I've seen and heard. It's just too much. So, I had to put up a filter. You know, only let certain things come through. I decided to feel only certain things. Mostly, I would try to feel the good. Remember the interviews that went well, when the survivor was really strong and was really surviving. I just couldn't think about or feel any of the other interviews.

I didn't want to shut down completely, but I couldn't deal with everything that was coming in. I wanted to pick and choose what I felt. It sounds impossible to do, but I guess I figured out a way to do that in my own mind. It was like a conscious choice whether I would listen to different things and feel different things. I had to select what I would let in.

And another interviewer:

> This may sound bad, but one of the best days for me was the staff meeting where I was hearing everyone else talking about their cases and I was just thinking about them. I couldn't visualize the survivor, I couldn't feel what she was feeling, I couldn't feel what the other interviewer must have felt. I felt nothing, and it felt great. Well, I felt a little guilty. But, it was a relief to sit there and think, hmm, I wonder how this case will fit into the data analysis—seems like an outlier. I wonder what that will do to the analyses. . . . I felt really happy when I could do this without getting ripped up inside. When it became interesting in an academic sort of way. But, at the same time, I knew it wasn't real. What's real is when you feel it, but it gets harder and harder to feel it as time goes by. I just needed to filter the pain out for a while by thinking about something else. Make it abstract and academic.

This balancing act of feeling/not feeling, feeling/thinking was often described as the remedy to the enduring hurt of feeling rape. Our feelings of loss and pain were difficult to talk about, and not even hearing more positive endings to some stories could take that away. As one of the interviewers described, this is not a zero-sum game. The positive does not undo the pain of the negative. We often had to rely on our cognitive abilities to "check out" from time to time to get some relief. We were grateful that thinking helped ease the pain of feeling.

Fear

Hearing about other people's traumatic experiences is enough to provoke fear; we don't actually have to experience a dreaded event to fear it. The power of fear lies, in part, in what is hidden and what is revealed. Fear is created by what little is revealed: we see enough to perceive danger and be afraid. Fear is maintained by what is not revealed: we haven't seen enough to understand it, so we continue to fear. The fear of rape is also constructed through this balance of known and unknown danger. Women learn to fear rape in this culture, and this fear is often based on personal experience. Approximately one in four to one in five women are raped in their adult lifetimes, giving 20 percent to 25 percent of the adult female population first hand knowledge of the devastation of rape. And because of this, the other 75 percent to 80 percent also learn to fear rape. Some women fear rape because they lived through it; some fear it because they don't want to have to live through it. The ugliness of rape is revealed in full to some women and, in doing so, is revealed in part to many, many more.

We had prolonged, intense exposure to rape as we studied sexual assault in an urban area. We were constantly reminded of our own risk as we heard story after story of victimization and then had to go about our daily lives in a major metropolitan city. Throughout the first several months of the project, this fear was about interviewing itself. For many of the less-experienced interviewers, there was considerable anxiety about what they would hear during the interview and their ability to manage their own emotional reactions during the interview. For all of us, there were also concerns about our physical safety traveling throughout the city to conduct the interviews. However, as the project progressed, we had to cope with the fears generated from what we were hearing in the interviews. The content of the interviews heightened our awareness of the risk of rape, and we feared that we too may be harmed in our lifetimes.

The initial anxiety for some was rooted in their perceived unfamiliarity with the topic. Interestingly, even after completing training, which consisted of several months of reading about rape, talking about rape, role-playing interviews, hearing from rape survivors, and so on, most of the undergraduate interviewers felt they didn't really know much about rape. They wouldn't know rape until they did their first interview; the academic literature and practice interviews just didn't communicate the reality of rape. These fears dissipated when they had each completed their first couple of interviews; for example, as two interviewers described:

> I had no idea whether I would be able to do this. I mean, would I be able to hold it together? Would I be able to get through the interview and not freak out the victim or freak myself out? I was scared to death that I would lose it—cry, panic, I don't know, just not be able to do it.
>
> [Q: Do what?]
>
> Do the interview, go from start to finish, hear everything she had to say, not mess up, not say the wrong thing to her. I knew you [Becki] had a lot of faith in all of us and believed in us and told us over and over that you believed we could do it, and that helped. But honestly, I didn't know if I should believe you, because I didn't know if I could do it.

And another:

> I didn't really calm down until I had my first couple of interviews, till I had proved, to myself, I guess, that I could handle it. They were hard, but they weren't as bad as I thought they were gonna be. I was surprised at how composed and strong these women were, and I found a lot of my own strength in that. If she can get through being raped and be here today to tell me about it, then I can damn

well get through hearing about it. It was a good feeling—getting rid of all that fear and feeling strong.

Perhaps our biggest fear, which touched all of us—undergraduate, graduate, and postgraduate researchers alike—was a concern for our physical safety while interviewing. Although we had addressed these issues in training and developed safety protocols for project staff, the unknown safety of the neighborhoods into which we traveled to conduct interviews continued to be stressful, particularly for myself and the interview coordinators. During the staff exit interviews, team members asked me what I feared and why; my responses always focused on their physical safety when conducting the interviews. For example, as I said to one interviewer:

> Regarding issues about physical safety, that's something that I think primarily was my biggest stressor of all . . . my fear day in and day out was that something was going to happen to an interviewer. . . . We had gone over safety planning so many times, and I felt from the beginning of the project to its very end that we had taken the appropriate steps to ensure the safety of the interviewers, but I still worried about it. I know we had planned responsibly, but you never know. . . . I paid an incredible amount of attention to who I asked to be interviewers. That I got women who I perceived as "streetwise." I know that all those things can't prevent harm, but I think they can prevent some things from happening. So I tried to pick women to do this project who had good safety skills, who were streetwise, who would be able to walk with some confidence to try to deter some of the crime that could have been sent their way. Then we added even more training. But you know, I lived in constant fear that something would happen to someone. I tried to manage the risk as best as possible. That's why we spent so much time on these issues in training. I feel very fortunate that no one was hurt.

One of the interview coordinators harbored similar concerns about the safety of the members of the research team:

> Before [we] started the interviews, I should have gotten in my car and driven around Chicago. I felt there was a lot of weird tension going on with where the interviews were going to take place. I felt strange for myself when I was sent out to interviews, and also sending other people out to interviews, not knowing where I was sending people. . . . There were a couple of times I was sent off to areas that were probably the projects [Chicago Public Housing Projects], and I had severe anxiety about doing it. It would keep me up the night before. My God, is this going to be okay. Again, I'm sure if I

was there at 9:00 at night . . . but 10:00 in the morning it was perfectly fine. So there was a lot of anxiety for myself, and the project
itself, that was unnecessary.

Most interviews were conducted at our university or in some safe public
space. Interviews in "risky" neighborhoods were done only during the
morning and early afternoon. The survivors themselves were proactive in
providing us with "neighborhood safety tips" when setting up interviews
in their homes. Fear of the neighborhoods in which we would be interviewing was indeed a source of great tension on the project, and it sparked
painful discussions about racism and classism. Many of the white interviewers feared being sent into the public housing projects to do interviews,
and many of the women of color were deeply offended by their fears. From
my field notes:

> [T]here was an awkward silence when [one of the African-American
> interviewers] told the group that she "lives in the projects. You're
> talking about my home." Her teeth were clenched and her hands
> were balled up into fists. She told the group that all of the white
> interviewers had no reason to be afraid there. It was fine during the
> day. And it wouldn't matter anyway; they were safer as white
> women. She said to the group, "I have more to be afraid of there
> than you do. They won't mess with you, but they'll mess with me."
> I told the group that we would all have to confront going to places
> that made us feel uncomfortable, whether it was because of our
> gender, race, or social class. And we would all have to work on
> understanding those feelings of discomfort because those feelings
> were showing us our own prejudices. I wanted to be respectful of
> the fears many on the team were having, but at the same time, I felt
> like some of their fears were about issues of racism, not rape. So I
> did my best to try to engage the team in a discussion about racism
> because I also have a responsibility to the anger of the African-
> American women in the group.

At the conclusion of the project, all of the African-American interviewers mentioned these struggles as key experiences defining their participation. As one summarized:

> I realize all of us were scared. We're all afraid. We didn't know what
> was gonna happen or what we would find when we got there. But
> it really hurt when the white women in the project seemed to get so
> scared about going into the projects. You know, they'd act like it
> was all about being afraid of rape, when it was more about being
> afraid of black people. It was like it was an excuse. You know, say it's
> about rape and being safe when really it's about being racist. And

some days it was like they thought their safety was more important than ours, or at more risk, when it really wasn't. But it was good for them to have to go there. I'm glad you [Becki] made all of us go, no matter what. No one could get out of it, black or white. I think everyone learned a lot. I think many of them [white interviewers] learned that "black" doesn't always mean "poor and in the projects," and the projects don't always mean you're not safe. By making all of us go there [the projects], you made people learn more about racism. I don't think people planned on learning about their own racism, but I'm glad you made them learn about it. I would have been really angry at you if you hadn't done something about it. So I'm glad you did. But it probably was hard for people to have to come to grips with their own racism at the same time as all of us had to deal with being afraid of rape.

The anxiety of learning about rape brought many issues to the table. We all had to identify, however implicitly, what we were afraid of and why. We became acutely aware that we could just as easily be on the other side of the interview. We no longer feared doing the interviews; we feared what we were learning about in the interviews. What is remarkable about our fear of rape is that we never talked about this fear directly. I was struck by the infrequency of the phrase "fear of rape" in my field notes and in our interview transcripts. We talked about being afraid, but we rarely talked about being afraid of rape. I suspect this is because it never needed to be said; it was assumed and shared by the group as a whole. We feared being harmed. One of the interviewers talked about the pervasiveness of the fear:

It can't really even be named — it's just fear.

[Q: Fear of what?]

It's not really about fearing this or that. It's like living in a constant state of fear. There is no "of what" because it's everywhere. . . . Do I fear being raped? Of course, all of us did. Did I fear men? How could I not? Total strangers, people in my life? Sure. You can't name it or pinpoint what it is, or where it comes from, because it's everywhere. It's so on our minds that we never get away from it. We're so far into it and have seen so much, that we know it's all around us. . . . It's not about the specifics anymore; it's not about fearing this or that, for this reason or that reason. What I'm talking about comes after that. It's when it's so general, so global, that it's just fear — fear of existing because existing is dangerous.

Similarly, another interviewer described how working on this project heightened her concerns for her safety:

I've never been so afraid in my life. I feel like I'm afraid of everything. Even before I did this [participate in this project], I would be
afraid if I was alone at night or if I could hear someone walking
behind me. But now I'm afraid a lot more. . . . I'm afraid when I go
to the grocery store or am doing my laundry or going out on a
date . . . and I feel it too. My heart races, and my breathing
changes and gets really shallow and fast. I'm real shaky. I feel like I
could scream at the drop of a hat.

All of us experienced moments of intense fear throughout the project,
but for some of us, our fears broke through in visceral displays of emotion.
It just came out, all at once, with incredibly intensity—a pure, unadulter-
ated expression of fear, fueled not by the unknowns of rape, but by all the
known details. More specifically, these outbursts were triggered when we
were startled by men. For example, one interviewer described how she was
waiting for her boyfriend outside of a restaurant, and when he came up
behind her,

I whipped around like I was ready to do something. He was like,
"are you okay?" I was like, "don't do that. I was going to lay you out
in the street right here." He was going to get clawed or kicked or
something.

[Q: Why do you think you had this reaction?]

. . . because you think for a split second that it's your turn now. Your
number's been called. And you scream at the thought of having to
endure all that anguish. . . . I don't think it's an accident that this
was started off by being startled by a man, whether it's your
boyfriend or whoever. He's the reminder that you could be next. A
symbolic rapist.

Similarly, from my field notes:

I was down in the basement of my building today doing laundry. I
had my head in the washing machine, fishing out the last sock,
when a man opened the door. I jumped and screamed very loudly.
It turns out that he was another tenant of the building, who had
every right to be there too. I didn't register who he was or why he
was there. I was afraid. He was clearly shocked, and said, "I'm sorry,
I didn't mean to scare you." I suppose I was nearing my limit of san-
ity because at first I honestly thought he said, "I'm sorry, I didn't
mean to rape you." This constant day-in and day-out exposure to
rape is wearing on me and, I think, everyone else.

In addition to experiencing these startled responses, our fear of rape was also exhibited by the degree to which we tried to plan for our safety. The motive to avoid rape is very strong, and as a result, most women, including all of us in the research team, follow some safety precautions in their lives. For us, because we knew so many specifics about rape, our safety planning was incredibly detailed. The constant exposure prompted more elaborate planning, as two interviewers described:

> After I heard all these stories that took place in Chicago at places I knew of, at places near me, it started making me more nervous. I mean, there were many nights where I'd go to sleep and I'd hear noises and I'd be convinced someone was breaking into my house. I'd literally get up to go check. Or I'd be lying in bed and I'd create this, like, escape plan. Okay, if somebody broke into my house right now, what would I do? How would I get to the phone? Which window could I jump out of and not break my leg? This was all the plan . . . I'm looking around corners. I'm looking behind bushes. If I see a dark alley, I'm constantly looking. And I think I did it somewhat before, but [it's] very much heightened [now]. My awareness is very much heightened. . . .

And another said:

> I plan as best as possible for my own safety, try not to take as many risks, have safety plans, really try to think through every scenario, be really careful about who I am around. I look at men in the workplace—my mailman, everyone. How would I escape if this one, or that one, came after me? You know, it's like, use these stairs if X, use that door if Y. I've actually planned an "escape route" for every major place that I spend time in—different classrooms, different rooms where I work, my neighborhood. Sometimes I get angry that I've spent all this time planning, but it really does help me sleep at night.

No one expected to be quite so afraid, but fear was the most frequently discussed emotion in staff meetings and in my individual interviews with team members at the conclusion of this project. Interviewing rape survivors put us in touch with our own vulnerabilities and reminded us that very little really separated "us"—the researchers—from "them"—the rape survivors we interviewed. We walked down the same urban streets, lived in the same neighborhoods, and also spent time with male friends and partners. We were studying something that we are very much still at risk for experiencing in our lives. With every passing interview, the list of what to fear grew longer and longer.

Anger

It made us mad that we became afraid of our own shadows. Over the course of the project, we found ourselves avoiding certain streets, looking at our male friends and partners with suspicion, and sleeping with doors and windows locked through even the hottest weather. And it made us mad, very mad, to see how rape was controlling our lives and the lives of women more generally. It made us angry that there were so many women to interview. Over time, the very fact that our project phones kept ringing—that there were new women coming forward every day to talk about what happened to them—frustrated us. It made us mad when during an interview we noticed that we were checking off item after item after item on a list of postassault health problems. We got angry when we saw how thoroughly rape messes up women's psychological and physical health. When we heard, yet again, that a police officer, doctor, family member, friend, or significant other had chosen not to help or support a rape survivor, the pool of anger deepened. As one interviewer summarized, "We have a lot to fear, but we have even more to be angry about."

It is not at all surprising that this anger bubbled up and spilled over into our lives. At times, friends, colleagues, and our partners bore the brunt of that anger. Somebody was going to pay for all this injustice, even if occasionally it was the wrong person, someone we actually liked and cared about. Unfair, yes. Excuse, no. But yet another instance of complete unfairness of rape. Although we often felt guilty about these spillovers, we also found odd comfort in our anger. "As long as I can still get mad, I know I'm still doing OK," one interviewer recalled. To cope with what we were seeing and hearing it was useful to grow a bit numb, to block out emotion, and to try to feeling nothing. This is risky because it makes rape abstract, and it's not at all abstract to rape survivors. If we could feel anger, then we knew we could feel something, and feeling brought us closer to understanding the experiences of the survivors we interviewed. It is a useful emotion, anger, as it bridges feeling and thinking. Why are we angry? What are the implications of that anger? Anger provides a political analysis of rape that had been drawn upon by researchers and activists long before we started this project. Being this close to rape is a consciousness-raising experience.

Over the course of this project, anger arrived a bit later than some of the other emotions, like fear. It took a while to tap into those feelings. For example, these two interviewers described how anger was not an immediate reaction, but something that grew from earlier feelings of fear:

> I remember really clearly the first day I really felt mad. It was weeks into the project, which now seems like it took forever before I got mad, but it did take a while. I was swimming in feelings, and it took a while to get ahold of each one and identify and label it. . . . I was

walking to my apartment from the El [public train] stop [on my way home from doing an interview], and I noticed I was walking really fast, looking all around me, and I practically ran up my stairs and locked the door behind me. I remember standing there looking at my locked door for a second, thinking I had locked out everything bad and nothing could touch me, and then I got mad, really mad.

[Q: About what?]

That I was so afraid, I was practically running home and then realizing that I still wasn't safe . . . so angry realizing that no matter what I did, I was still at risk.

And another comment:

You know, all my life I've been told I can't do this or that because it's not safe for women. I've lived so much of my life in fear. It's gotten even worse after hearing all these stories. You know, that a rape happened literally just down the street from where I live. The only thing that makes that fear manageable is that I've finally gotten mad about it. I'm really angry that I choose to limit my life in so many ways to try to be safe and that I'm not alone. Lots and lots of other women do the same damn thing. And you know what? It doesn't even work! What a load. It doesn't even help because you can still be raped, and it's still seen as your fault. Such a trick, such a dirty trick played on women. . . . I still feel afraid—I think it's impossible not to—but now I feel angry and afraid. The anger is easier to deal with than the fear because it helps me understand the fear.

Given the effects that bearing witness to rape had on the interviewers, it is not surprising that there was some negative spillover into personal relationships. Interactions with male partners were at times strained throughout the course of the project. One interviewer described how this work had a negative impact on her relationship with her male partner:

It was building up, listening to so many stories. It was really affecting my relationship with my lover. He was misunderstanding how . . . he was like, do you hate men now? I'm a man. What does that mean? Do you not love me? I don't understand what's going on. . . . That just blew me away because I love him more than anything. . . . We had to sit down and really talk through this. He told me that I had been double-bolting the door [to our apartment] consistently through the whole project. And I never used to. I just would close it. That's one thing he was really taking personally. He was like, "I

thought you were locking me out, figuratively and literally." I didn't
even realize that I was doing it [double-locking the door]. I was
doing it automatically. I don't stop myself [from double-locking the
door] because I need to do it right now. But I let him know it wasn't
him I was locking out.

Many of the other interviewers could resonate with her experience, as this
was an issue with which many were struggling. Over time it became
increasingly difficult to interview women about acts of male violence during the day, and come home at night to one's male partner without some
displaced emotion. As another interviewer described:

I don't lock my windows and door anymore now than I did before,
but on more than one occasion during this project, I've lashed out
at my boyfriend during my sleep. I actually kicked him—sometimes
I would scream in my sleep too. I would wake up, realize what I had
done, and just start crying and apologize. He's a gentle, nonviolent
man. He doesn't deserve this. . . . This [my involvement in researching rape] really put a strain on our relationship. . . . I think he felt
very defensive about being a man. He has said stuff like, "What the
hell am I supposed to do about it? I can't apologize for this. I can't
apologize for being a man, or for all the things other men have
done." It was really hard trying to take care of myself and work
through all this fear and anger, and respond to his needs. It's not fair
to either of us that my work got all tangled up in our relationship,
and I do feel bad about that.

It got really tough because you want to believe and really need to
believe that your boyfriend or husband is different. You know, he's
the kind that wouldn't do this. But you know, when I hear all day
long about the boyfriends women thought were OK and would
never hurt them, and then they turned out to be rapists, well, it gets
hard to tell which end's up. . . . I understand that my boyfriend gets
upset and angry when I take things out on him. He says things like,
"Not every man is a rapist. Stop treating me like one." But I also
know it ain't just one lone rapist out there in the world creating all
of these victims and survivors for me to interview. Somebody, some-
bodies are doing this and how can you tell, I mean really tell, who
is and who isn't? Of course I don't want to believe that my
boyfriend is a rapist, but then again, none of the women I've interviewed ever did either. I guess sometimes I act so guarded with him
[my boyfriend] because, it's like, how can I not?

Interviewing rape survivors heightens one's awareness of the risks, which
unfortunately also means taking a second look at the people already in our

lives. This work provides a nearly daily reminder of what some men do to women, and there are days when it is easy to forget about the "some" and let anger fuel overgeneralizations. At the same time, men live very different lives with freedoms women don't know.

Our anger also spilled over into nonromantic relationships with both men and women. One of the interviewers said she felt like she had become the mythic Greek character, Cassandra, and shared her curse of seeing the future and speaking the truth that no one wanted to hear. We found ourselves warning our female friends about the risk of rape, and pushing our male friends to do something about violence against women by challenging other men. For some of the interviewers, speaking out about what they saw and learned through this project strained their friendships:

> I've been saying things more lately, speaking out against all the hatred of women in the world. I think it's good because I'm saying things and not being part of the silent majority, but I don't want to alienate people that I don't think are necessarily bad people. . . . So, it's also affected my friendships in that a lot of my friends have ideas about this, and I don't know how to reconcile this. My male friends. It was my male friend that asked, "Do you think women make it [rape] up?" It was a male friend that said, "Do you think your ideas are changing about this because of this project?" They make it sound like it's brainwashing. So with my male friends, this has been difficult. How do you stay friends with someone that says he wants feminist friends, but really treats feminism as the enemy?

And another said:

> I've gotten into a lot of arguments since I've been in this project. Everyone's like, why are you so hostile? Why are you so angry? It just got clearer that I thought about things differently than other people did. . . . I may have lost some friends because of the way I felt.

> [Q: How do you feel about that?]

> Probably better to know what they stand for, and know that that's not okay for me. It's been a little sad, but also really a strong growing thing. To stand up for what I believe, and speak out no matter what. I'm okay with that.

It is interesting to note that although interviewers described these spillovers with some guilt, there was also a sense of needing to speak out against rape, regardless of the risk to personal relationships. One of the interviewers described this delicate balance:

I don't feel any regret for anything I've said to my friends or boyfriend [throughout this project]. For the first time in my life, I feel like I've actually seen the world as it really is—all the blinders came off, you know. I felt compelled to speak out against all this violence and to educate others about it. I know I've become "more difficult" but I tend to see it more as, I've become more aware and more outspoken. . . . I don't feel I've really risked any of my relationships with others. I feel like I'm a better judge now of who I want to spend time with and be with. So what if some people are mad at me because I got on their case about something? That's good to know about them, tells me that I don't necessarily want to be around them either . . . my close relationships didn't suffer, they got stronger.

What does this anger mean? What are the implications of this anger? I asked these kinds of questions at staff meetings and in the end-of-project interviews. I felt it was important to talk about the anger project staff were experiencing and to locate those feelings within a broader political context. Equally important to me was that I did not force-feed any such analysis. But I didn't have to. All I had to do was ask these kinds of questions. The interviewers filled in the rest on their own. I didn't have to spell out the meaning of the concept "rape culture," nor did I have to explain how other feminist researchers and activists have found anger a mobilizing call to action. For example, after two months of interviewing, I made this entry in my field notes:

I can see the interviewers getting angry about violence against women—it's a politicized anger. They see the political ramifications of the culture of rape, where women live in a constant state of fear that they will be raped, and then blamed for it. It's a real turning point when the cases stop becoming individual cases, but examples of a larger societal issue. Even among the graduate students, who already had a more feminist political analysis, I see their anger deepening and sharpening as they explore the societal implications of living in a rape culture. . . .

Would they still have these realizations if I weren't the project director? Did I "brainwash" them? Did I make them think about this the way I think about it? Just because I have a political analysis of rape, did I explicitly or implicitly encourage them to adopt it too? I see this kind of critique in all sorts of feminist scholarship. I have seen so many of my senior colleagues under attack and I hope I've learned from them about how to respond to these criticisms. This "critique" tries to put feminists on the defensive. It also seems to imply that

students are passive vessels, capable of being filled up with anything. I just don't think that's the case. In many respects, I really
hold back on my politicized feminist analysis of rape, so much so
that some of the graduate students have criticized me for keeping
quiet early in the project. My experience suggests that they'll get
there. I've seen it in rape crisis center training and in other research
projects. The process of acquiring a political analysis of violence
against women happens slowly over time—I don't need to encourage it or pull for it or demand it. I try to encourage students to
reflect on what they feel and consider the broader implications of
what they feel.

How does this political analysis come about? I suspect it varies consider-
ably, but at its core is the realization that we live in a rape culture, a society
where violence is gendered. Rape is not the individual problem of a particular victim or particular assailant. It is a pervasive threat to women's psychological and physical health, and it goes largely unchecked. One of the
interviewers could recall when and how she began to understand rape as a
political problem:

I went home and cried [after a particular interview]. I was just so
sad, thinking about this woman and all she went through, and worried, really worried about what was going to happen for her. Wondering if she was going to be OK. Then it hit me. This was no
different. I could cry for this one, and the next one, and the next
one, and the next one until I was out of tears. I don't have enough
tears to cry for each rape survivor. I don't have enough. No one has
enough. I was just furious . . . this is happening to so many women,
all of the time. And all the sadness doesn't do any good. My tears
aren't going to help that woman and they're not going to help anyone. . . . And that fucking rapist isn't home crying about what he
did . . . no more tears. I got cold that day, cold with anger when I
stopped seeing this as an individual thing. This is about harming
women as a means of sexism and oppression. It's no accident that I
have so many women to interview. We're supposed to take it, keep
quiet. I can't anymore. I won't. No more.

Another interviewer described her frustration with how others may challenge such a political analysis of rape:

I can imagine what others would say, I can think of what some of
my other professors might say or critics could say: "But of course
that's what you'd think. You have such a biased perspective. Of
course you'd think rape is all around you, you're doing a project on

rape and have heard all these stories. That's what feminists want
you to believe. They want you to think you're a victim or could be
a victim." It makes me angry to think that others could think the
problem of rape is anything but political. I have heard all these stories. I'm in a better position than most to really know that rape happens to all kinds of women and has a really horrible effect on their
lives. And because I've heard so many stories, I know this is not an
isolated event or individual problem.

Feeling angry about rape can be paralyzing at times—you're so mad you
don't know what to do. But more often than not, anger was a mobilizing
emotion for project staff. You're so mad, you have to do something. Interviewers described how their feelings of anger helped them find ways to
speak out against sexism and violence against women. They found their
voice. For example, these two interviewers described how their anger gave
them the power to speak their minds:

> I found my voice in all of this. I learned how to really speak my
> mind, and that's had such a positive and profound effect on my life.
> I wouldn't give that up for anything. I'm glad I've learned what I
> learned, even though it's uncomfortable and painful. . . . I am really
> angry. I am really mad about how many women are harmed every
> day by this. I know this sounds strange, but I'm really happy to be
> so mad. I'm glad I'm mad because I know it means I'm seeing the
> world as it really is—unsafe for women. All this anger and frustra-
> tion is useful . . . it keeps me speaking out and doing something for
> women.

And another:

> I remember one day when I was getting into it with one of my male
> friends. He was just being stupid, and I got in his face about it. So
> he comes back at me and says, "Oh, such the angry feminist. You're
> all such man-hating feminists." This wasn't the first time I've ever
> heard that kinda crap, but it was the first time I said back, "So
> what?" It was like I was reclaiming that anger—you know? You
> can't hold this anger against me and other women. We have a right
> to that anger, you know? We have a right to be mad. For the first
> time, I really saw comments like that a way of trying to silence
> women. So I'd run and hide and be ashamed of my feelings or that
> label "angry feminist." Hell yeah, I'm angry. Women have a lot to be
> angry about, whether they're feminist or not. This is nuts what we
> live in, all this violence around us. . . . I wouldn't let [this male
> friend] take this away from me that day. I wouldn't let him silence

me. I told him straight up, "Yeah, I'm an angry feminist. Yeah, I hate what a lot of men do to a lot of women. And I have every right to be angry. You can't take that away."

[Q: What did he say?]

He was silent. For once, he was silenced! He shook his head and just walked away from our conversation. I have never felt so proud of my own voice.

Over the course of this project, many of the project staff had been or were currently involved with feminist social change organizations, like rape crisis centers. For almost half of the staff, such involvement stemmed from participating in this research project. Being involved with direct service work with survivors, or doing public education presentations, or conducting rape prevention programs provided a constructive outlet for these feelings of anger. We were mad enough to try to do something about the problem of rape. We wanted to take what we had learned and try to make a difference by helping a survivor or preventing another rape from ever happening in the first place. Research was not enough; we needed to be doing something more about the problem of rape. It hurt to be so mad, and it was frustrating to see how rape touched everything in our lives—our sense of safety, our relationships with our friends and partners—but it was also possible to harness these feelings and channel them into doing something about the pervasiveness of rape.

Hope

Feeling rape—at all, or to this degree, or with this range—was not something many of us completely expected in this project. This was a research project, and it was somewhat surprising to have this work stir our emotions so intensely. And it was the "negative" emotions that predominated: loss, pain, fear, and anger. These emotions were discussed more frequently and in more depth during team meetings and in the end-of-project interviews. For instance, in these interviews I asked: "How did participating in this project and interviewing rape survivors affect you? What emotions did you experience?" In all but two cases, interviewers' answers focused on loss, pain, fear, or anger. Yet, as already noted, interviewers still found some positive aspect to each of these negative feelings. The loss of innocence hurt, but the knowledge gained was useful. Witnessing the trauma of rape in each and every interview was incredibly painful, but that pain also showed the tremendous strength and resiliency women have to survive rape. The anxiety of living in fear of rape was exhausting, but the heightened awareness was protective. Anger at the injustice of rape was frustrating, but it brought a call to action, to speak out and become more involved in stopping rape.

But there was also something uniquely positive in this work, something beyond just finding the good side of the negative emotions. It's hard to get an exact label for this—it's certainly not "happiness," "joy," or "gladness." It's about connecting with other women, feeling pride in their strength and in our collective strength, helping someone in ways you didn't expect, feeling part of someone's life. Having those experiences nurtures hope—for the survivor, for yourself, for women, for a future free from violence. For two of the interviewers in this project, this perspective was the defining aspect of their work. For example, one summarized how she experienced this work:

> This didn't affect me in a negative way. I mean it hasn't brought me down or anything, which is good. I mean in some ways it felt good to be involved. . . . [We were] helping these women to some degree. Even though we don't really expect the outcome of this study to help these particular women, they seem to have gotten a lot out of participating. I think in the beginning I would be kind of nervous [about conducting the interviews], but I definitely found that [I liked talking with the women]. I don't know if "enjoy" is the right word, but I didn't hate them [the interviews]. They weren't horrible things. People say like, "Oh, they must be so depressing," and that kind of stuff. It definitely wasn't. It was never that . . . because I really do get to care about the women. Sometimes I leave with little tears in my eyes. But not even so much like sad, but touched that they would share stuff with me.

For most, hope had to coexist with more difficult feelings, but it broke through with the greatest clarity and intensity during interviews in which there was a real connection between the interviewer and the survivor. This is even more remarkable when we remind ourselves of the inherent strangeness of interviewing. In a manufactured setting, two strangers (usually) come together and one shares with the other some personal, perhaps painful, aspect of her life. Sometimes the other stranger will share some information as well, but the interview is typically a temporary relationship, created and dissolved within mere hours. That anything real, binding, and connecting comes through is somewhat surprising. But it does happen, and it did happen many times in this project. Despite the artificiality of the research environment, the interviewer and survivor sensed that they would like each other and would enjoy being around each other outside the interview room. For example, these four interviewers described such connections and the positive effect it had on them:

It was really more like a conversation I'd have with a friend. That felt very good. And I think it felt good for her to have somebody who knew something about the topic to be doing that. . . . I felt like it was validating for me; it was validating for her. I think it was based much more on anger than anything else. We started getting angry together.

We really connected . . . it just clicked. She gave me a big hug. She said she felt comfortable already. . . . It was like we were just two friend there talking; we were vibing.

And I felt good because she felt confident in me. She trusted me even though I was young. We got along really well. She said she liked to talk to me. She was interested in who I was. She didn't ask too many questions. She was curious about what I was doing, how I got into this. It was nice to be able to talk with her.

At the end [of the interview], when I was saying thank you for being willing to share all this with me and especially a stranger, she said something like, "Well, I hadn't really talked to anyone about it before and I decided to talk to [named interviewer] about it." We definitely, we connected really well. We had good rapport.

This last quote in particular captures how in the course of these research interviews, the interviewer and survivor can break through the strangeness of the setting and connect in a genuine way. The survivor didn't tell anyone until she decided to tell this interviewer her story. She didn't tell her story to a stranger; she told it to someone she now knew and trusted.

These connections may have formed because many survivors found participating in this research project helpful in its own right. We were very clear with ourselves and the survivors we interviewed that we were not clinicians, and that this project was not an intervention designed to help rape survivors. Nevertheless, participating in a study where survivors had the opportunity to tell their stories in their own words, and to have someone listen to and bear witness to that telling, was powerfully healing. There was something helpful to these survivors about being able to tell their stories in the context of a research study—not to be analyzed, picked through as in therapy; not to be reacted to, revenged, as in telling someone like a friend or boyfriend. But to be heard—listened to and documented. As one interviewer recalled: "She [the survivor] was like, 'Oh my god, that's a good question.'" The research interview asked questions survivors may never have thought about, and provided an opportunity to reflect on something in a new way, or helped them piece together what has happened to them. We were privileged to share in that discovery, and it brought hope and meaning into our lives as well.

Sometimes a specific section of the interview provided a space for the survivor and interviewer to connect. For example, the interview protocol contained an assessment of the survivor's physical health postassault, which several women noted was surprisingly helpful to think about. It felt good for us to have provided useful information and normalized women's reactions and experiences. For example, one interviewer recalled an exchange she had with one of the survivors she interviewed:

> In particular, talking about dramatic back-and-forth weight changes that she experienced. She was wearing a pair of overalls and she was showing me how much weight she's lost. It was like a circus tent; these overalls were gigantic. At some point in the interview, I made the comment that I made in almost every interview—that it's very common for women to experience different physical health symptoms [postrape]. She was so struck by that. Whether it was a function of her age or a function of the lack of information she'd gotten from system contacts. I could see a lightbulb go on in her. Wow, this is universal. This happens to other women. She was very touched by that. And I was very touched by her reaction.

Similarly, from my field notes after the first interview I completed:

> We had just started the health section, and she stopped for a second and paused, then said: "I've never really thought about this. This is interesting." I asked her what was interesting about it, and she said she hadn't thought about how the assault may have impacted her physical health, but hearing herself answer my questions and hearing herself list off all the health problems she was having and how frequently she was experiencing them really made her realize how big an effect the assault had on her life. Whether it was causal or not, it didn't matter. She noticed a connection; her health had declined—a lot—since she was raped. She told me then, and again at the end of the interview, how helpful it was to be asked those questions. It was helpful to be asked about things she hadn't thought about. I felt really proud about this work then. Proud that we [our research team] had put together something that was useful.

For other survivors and interviewers, there was no one specific section of the interview that allowed for an emotional connection; it was the overall process of coming together and sharing in the experience of talking about rape. For example, two interviewers recalled how survivors told them how much they benefited from participating, and how hearing that filled them with hope, pride, and optimism:

There were a few of them [survivors] that remarked they felt really good afterward [after the interview], so I thought that was a really good thing. If they got anything out of it. They got one more place that they vented and they feel like they've examined it thoroughly. That was what made me feel good about an interview. When the woman said that the interview process itself was helpful.

I can think of at least five women I interviewed who told me at the end that it was really helpful to them to talk to me—to just talk it through with someone who would just listen and support them while they told what happened to them. . . . I have been very moved and actually really humbled by how powerful this really is. Just being there to be present for someone telling something meaningful to them. . . . I am struck by how helpful this seemed to be. . . . I had no idea this was going to be so healing and meaningful to so many women. Just to listen, and listen well. It brought something good into my life, too, to have been a part of that. It's been humbling and empowering to be a part of it. I feel very proud to have been a part of this project and part of these women's lives.

We felt good because we were listening, helping discovery, providing information, destigmatizing, and normalizing survivors' experiences. The role of researcher established us, to some extent us, as experts, so we were in the position to be validating in ways we may have never expected. That we asked and documented what being raped meant to them and did to them legitimated these survivors' experiences—and legitimated our feelings of hope. As one interviewer said at conclusion of her end-of-project interview:

I felt like I did something really worthwhile. I always felt like that. I felt like I did something really good, and that she did something really good. It was the best experience I've ever had in my education. That's it. That's all I have to say. The end.

four

From Feeling
to Thinking

The Insights Feeling Rape Bring to Researching Rape

hinking about rape became a refuge from feeling rape. It was oddly refreshing to return rape to its more abstract academic form. In the end of project interviews, when I asked the members of the research team what they learned about rape through this journey, the tone and mood of the conversations almost always perked up, like a rope thrown down for rescue.[1] But these reflections were informed by a different set of knowledge bases. What was learned came through "different" means, different sources of information. Bringing feeling and thinking together altered each. The thinking provided useful coping, blunting some of the more difficult emotions. But it was what feeling did to thinking that was so striking. These emotions of feeling rape made us think about rape in new ways, prompting useful questions about much of what we had learned from the academic literature. It was as if nothing could be taken for granted anymore. We didn't look at our day-to-day social worlds the same, and we didn't look at research the same either. It looked different; it felt different. What was feeling rape teaching us? How was our thinking being informed by our feelings?

In this project, our research team interviewed over one hundred rape survivors, providing a supportive environment for women to tell their stories and for other women to bear witness to that telling. In chapters Two, "From Thinking to Feeling: The Stories That Bring Feeling to Researching Rape," and Three, "Feeling: The Emotions of Researching Rape," I described some of these stories and how they affected the members of our research team. It did hurt a lot a great deal of the time to study rape in this way. The survivors' stories became part of our individual and collective memories. There are images we don't want to remember, but they are a part of us and define what it meant to do this work. We learned to cope with our anxieties, hurt, and fear. Emotionally disengaging was an often-useful strategy for getting through the negative parts, which helped us cherish the positive connections we formed with these women. Through the pain of talking about rape, we felt how the burden of this violence can be lifted. The power of rape to silence and blame dissipates in the emotional connection of sharing experiences of loss, pain, fear, anger, and hope. It has been personally meaningful to us and to many of the survivors we interviewed, which I believe is reason enough. But there is more to it than that. In the first chapter of this book, "Creating Difference—Thinking versus Feeling: The Role of Emotions in Research," I argued that emotions can be a useful resource for intellectual discovery. Studying our own emotional experiences of doing social science research can yield useful insights into the phenomenon of interest. Researching the researcher creates another perspective; what we feel and why we have those feelings provide additional data about the subject of study. Attention to emotion in research can provide intellectual gain. In this chapter, I will explore what feeling rape suggests for future research. In the end-of-project interviews, I asked team members to reflect on what they had learned about rape through their participation in this study. My aim here isn't to summarize specific lessons each person learned, but to present my analysis of the collective implications feeling rape brought to thinking rape.[2]

By studying our teams' emotional reactions to this work and reflecting on those emotions in the context of research, I gained a different perspective on two emerging issues in the rape victimology literature. First, the group's emotional experiences suggest that the trauma of rape extends far beyond its victims. Although there is growing interest in documenting how rape affects the family, friends, and intimate partners of victims as well as the professionals and paraprofessionals who assist victims, there is scarce attention paid to if, how, and why researchers may also be affected. Barring a few exceptions, researchers have implicitly or explicitly excluded themselves as potential secondary victims of rape. The results of this work reveal that we had emotional reactions similar—parallel perhaps, but not identical—to those of survivors: shock, surprise, betrayal, hurt, fear, anger, and hope. The intensity and duration of our distress was not as strong or long-lasting as what the survivors we interviewed had to endure. In this chapter, I draw upon compassion fatigue theory and emotion work theory to explore how and why our research team was emotionally affected through of our study of rape.

This finding is a novel contribution to the literature in its own right but, more important, it suggests that the academic literature has underconceptualized the trauma of rape. To date, researchers have focused much of their attention on the victim, and rightly so. The dominant themes in this literature examine who is assaulted, how sexual assault affects victims' psychological and physical health, and which treatment protocols are more

effective in alleviating postrape distress. In other words, rape is traditionally studied as an affective, cognitive, and behavioral problem affecting
individual women. Less than 5 percent of the studies in this literature
examine the effects on others (e.g., family, friends, partners, helping professions) or how extraindividual factors contribute to such trauma (e.g.,
how the community response to rape could be exacerbating trauma).[3] Yet
the extent to which this field characterizes rape as a problem of the victim,
researchers are underconceptualizing the gross impact of sexual assault. The
results of this researching-the-researcher project indicate that the harm of
rape extends beyond the cognitive/behavior emphasis that dominates literature. Specifically, the rape victimology field has tended to underrepresent
who is affected by rape, how they are impacted, and what effects rape has
on all of its victims. The scope of the problem is worse than what much of
academic research suggests.

The second issue raised by this researching-the-researcher project concerns the degree to which the academic literature is fully communicating
what rape means to women and how it affects our lives. Everyone on our
research team read journal articles, books, and book chapters in preparation for this project, and as one of the interviewers summarized:

> I read it. I read that stuff, and it didn't prepare me for this work. So
> much of what's written doesn't capture what really happens to
> women when they are raped. . . . It's written in this cold, distant,
> professionalized language that doesn't convey or connect with the
> actual experiences of survivors.

There was a marked mismatch between what we heard from survivors, our
own experiences of empathizing with those experiences, and the written
texts that document this problem for the academic world and general public. In other words, studying our emotional reactions provided some insight
into what may be problematic about not only the scope of this field, but
also its tone and content. In this chapter, I examine the extent to which the
language of rape research conveys the emotionality of rape.

This is a stickier issue to examine. This is, after all, research, not fiction,
not poetry. To what extent should research and the language of research
even try to convey emotionality? This debate must be framed within its
historical context: the academic study of rape has been around for only 30
years. Raising the issue of *how* rape is described means that early leaders in
the field fought and won the fight over *if* rape should be researched in
academia. But now that there is a place for the topic of sexual assault in
academic discourse, it is important then to consider how much congruence
there is between the findings in the literature and lived experiences of rape
survivors. Let me be very clear here: I am not calling into question the
empirical accuracy of existing studies in this field. I have great trust in the

methods of science and the peer review process such that when I read scholarly works, I am generally inclined to accept the veracity of researchers' findings. Instead, my experiences of feeling rape in this project and studying how it affected our research team makes me question whether what I read, and indeed what I have helped produce as a contributor to this field, in the academic literature conveys, in an emotional way, the impact rape has on women's lives. I question the emotional accuracy of academic research on rape. It now strikes me as too clean, too sanitized, and too distant from the emotional, lived experiences of rape survivors. What is the "rape" portrayed in academic discourse? To the extent to which academic discourse frames rape as an individual problem of individual survivors, devoid of emotionality, it may miss the mark in representing the problem of rape in women's lives and our society.[4]

Redefining the Scope of Rape: The Ripple Effect of Trauma

It is to be expected that survivors would be traumatized by sexual assault. Three decades of research has refined the details—how much trauma is typical, why such trauma occurs, how such trauma can be treated—but the basic effect is immutable. Rape has a deleterious effect on survivors' psychological and physical health (see Goodman, Koss, & Russo, 1993a; Herman, 1992; Koss et al., 1994; Resick, 1993 for reviews). But the scope of rape extends far beyond its primary victim. A growing interest in the field is documenting and explaining the ripple effect of trauma, defining the "secondary victims" who are also adversely affected by this violent crime (Ahrens & Campbell, 2000; Davis, Taylor, & Bench, 1995, Holmstrom & Burgess, 1979). It is not unreasonable to assume that the significant others, family members, or friends of a victim may also be harmed by an assault. Furthermore, it is also reasonable to infer that trauma counselors may be troubled by extended work with rape survivors (Astin, 1997; Brady et al., 1999; Schauben & Frazier, 1995). There have even been a few hints in the field that rape researchers may not be immune to the trauma of rape (e.g., Dunn, 1991; Kelly, 1988; Stanko, 1997). This researching-the-researcher project takes this work to the next level by providing direct empirical evidence of how and why the ripple effect of trauma can reach out to touch the supposedly untouchable realm of science.

To understand why studying rape was upsetting for us—the researchers—we need to first consider the origins of the trauma by examining how sexual assault affects its primary victims. Rape is a traumatic event that has destructive effect on women's health, and within psychology, this trauma is typically viewed as a manifestation of posttraumatic stress (PTS) (see Goodman, Koss, & Russo, 1993b; Herman, 1992). Posttraumatic stress disorder (PTSD) is a clinical diagnosis that captures the psychological sequelae of both chronic and one-time violence and trauma (American Psychiatric Association, 1994). Although there is considerable debate in the field as to whether the PTSD diagnosis indeed captures the full experiences of rape survivors (see Wasco, 2000 and Weaver & Clum 1995, for reviews), existing research reveals that rape victims constitute the largest single group of PTS sufferers (Foa, Steketee, & Olasov, 1989). These psychological reactions occur because the traumatic event is outside normal human experiences (e.g., war, violent crime). Virtually anyone would find such occurrences distressing, hence PTS is viewed as a normal, albeit distressing, reaction to abnormal events.

Victims respond to these traumatic experiences through alternating sequences of intrusions and avoidance. Intrusions are the reliving of the trauma: flashbacks, nightmares, repeated thoughts that won't leave one's mind. Avoidance refers to how victims isolate themselves from reminders of the traumatic event to prevent becoming emotionally overwhelmed: emotional numbing, withdrawal from others, intellectualizing. Other responses common with PTS include dissociation, increased arousal, irritability, angry outbursts, hypervigilence, sleep disturbances, and other physical health problems. In my experiences interviewing rape survivors, I have found that providing victims with basic information about PTS can be very comforting. For many survivors, learning that there is a name, or names, for what they are going through is normalizing. Learning that other survivors also suffer from these problems provides solace. In addition, for practitioners, the PTS model can guide effective treatment approaches.

Yet, despite the utility of the PTS framework to survivors, practitioners, and researchers, feminist scholars have raised important questions about the broader implications of this model (see Brown, 1994; Goodman, Koss, & Russo, 1993b; Wasco, 2000). The PTS clinical framework is based on the assumption that this psychological distress is a normal reaction to an unusual event. Violence against women is not an out-of-the-ordinary experience in our culture; it is frighteningly common. This suggests that we are mislabeling a societal problem as an individual one—that is, the victim's problem, because after all, she is the one with the clinical diagnosis. The PTS framework depathologizes victims' responses, but it depathologizes them only to an extent. I say this not to diminish or aggrandize the magnitude of distress victims endure, nor to question the very real utility of psychological intervention, but to concur with other feminists who have argued that the trauma of rape is a psychological problem with societal roots. Nevertheless, whether the PTS framework is wholly accurate, there is substantial evidence to suggest that rape indeed has a profoundly negative effect on women's health.

This focus on victims' well-being has been a central theme in the rape victimology literature. Yet a growing body of work suggests that rape also harms those close to the survivor, termed "the secondary victims." Research in psychology, nursing, and social work has demonstrated that husbands/significant others, family, and friends of rape survivors are also detrimentally affected by sexual assault (see Davis, Taylor, & Bench, 1995; Holmstrom & Burgess, 1979; Remer & Elliott, 1988ab). For example, Courtney Ahrens found that rape stresses victims' friendships with others because their friends often have difficulty understanding how and why survivors cope as they do with the assault (Ahrens & Campbell, 2000). Quite simply, it is upsetting for friends to learn that someone they care about has been harmed. This effect is magnified for male partners of female victims. Robert Barkus's (1997) case study of a therapy group for male partners of female victims of abuse found that these men exhibited symptoms that mirrored the experiences of female partners of war veterans. Specifically, men felt isolated, confused, angry, powerless, and frustrated living with their partner's extreme emotional reactions, which ranged from depression to withdrawal to rage. Other studies with larger samples of men have found similar results: partners of rape victims have significantly higher distress symptoms than partners of nonvictims (Veronen, Saunders, & Resnick, 1989).

Similarly, when rape survivors turn to community systems for assistance, service providers are also emotionally touched by this crime. Therapists, counselors, and social workers who treat rape survivors experience many of the same reactions as do victims: anxiety, fear, exaggerated startle response, difficulty sleeping, nightmares, and on and on. For example, in Laura Schauben's and Patricia Frazier's (1995) study of 220 female counselors, they found that as the percentage of therapists' caseloads devoted to treating sexual assault victims increased, counselors reported more posttraumatic stress symptoms (see also Brady et al., 1999; Chrestman, 1995; Kassam-Adams, 1995). Consistent with these findings, Millie Astin (1997), a sexual assault therapist, noted that it was working with rape survivors as opposed to victims of other forms of violence against women, that was so difficult for her:

Although I have worked with several types of trauma survivors including battered women, childhood sexual and physical abuse survivors, and various other crimes . . . vicarious traumatization never seemed to be an issue for me. Despite hearing the sad and frightening stories of many women who were brutally beaten by their partners, I never took their stories home with me. . . . When the main focus of my work shifted to working with rape victims, that bubble was burst rather quickly. Suddenly, I found myself experiencing nightmares of being raped. Or I would turn a dark corner in my home and imagine a rapist coming toward me just like one had for my client. (pp. 102–103)

As I thought about it, I came to realize that with other victims [battered women, child abuse survivors] I had been able to set myself apart from them and maintain my sense of invulnerability. . . . With rape, I could not maintain my distance. . . . I was just as vulnerable as anyone else. That

realization made me more susceptible to symptoms of vicarious traumatization. It also has brought me closer to the struggles of my clients. For
that I am grateful. (p. 108)

Patricia Tyra (1979), Linda Eberth (1989), and Sharon Wasco (Wasco &
Campbell, in press) have found that volunteer rape crisis counselors/rape
victim advocates also reported behavioral, somatic, and psychological reactions to their work.[5] Even providing medical care to rape survivors can produce secondary stress, as Carol Hartman (1995) documented that nurses
who work with victims of violent crimes, including rape, experienced
increased health complaints.

This trauma of treating survivors of violence is most commonly referred to
as secondary traumatic stress (STS) (see Figely, 1995a, b; Dutton & Rubinstein,
1995) or vicarious traumatization (VT) (McCann & Pearlman, 1990a, b, 1993;
Pearlman & MacIan, 1995; Pearlman & Saakvitne, 1995a, b; Saakvitne &
Pearlman, 1996). STS/VT is the mirror image of PTS: intrusive imagery,
numbing or avoidance of efforts to work with traumatic material, somatic
complaints, addictive or compulsive behaviors, physiological arousal, impair-
ment in day-to-day functioning. Charles Figely (1995a) offered an explanation for why STS/VT occurs in trauma workers: the DSM-IV (American
Psychiatric Association, 1994) diagnosis for PTSD clearly allows for indirect
effects of trauma. Learning about unexpected or violent death, serious harm,
or threat of death or injury experience by a family member or other close
associate can produce posttraumatic stress symptoms (Diagnosis Criterion
A1). This emphasizes "that people can be traumatized without actually being
physically harmed or threatened with harm. That is, they can be traumatized
simply by learning about the traumatic event" (Figely, 1995a, p. 4). Laurie
Pearlman and Karen Saakvitne noted that VT produces a "transformation in
the inner experience of the therapist that comes about as a result of empathic
engagement with clients' traumatic material . . . we view it as an occupational
hazard, an inevitable effect of trauma work" (p. 31). Thus PTS reflects the
effects of trauma on primary victims (e.g., rape survivors), and STS/VT refers
to the impact on those close to the victims (e.g., partners, family, community
service providers). STS/VT is a set of parallel emotional reactions, diminished
in intensity and less likely to require formal psychological intervention, but
also a component of trauma work that should not be ignored.

Yet the STS/VT explanatory model may not sit well with some trauma
workers. Just as PTS has been criticized as pathologizing victims' responses
to a violent, criminal event, STS/VT can be seen as pathologizing the experiences of trauma workers. Yet, as Pearlman and Saakvitne argued, trauma
produces undeniable devastation for victims and undeniable stress for
those who work with victims to rebuild their lives. Trauma therapists experience episodes of sadness and depression, sleeplessness, general anxiety,
and other forms of suffering. But if these reactions are not indicators of

pathology, then what are they and why do they happen? In response to these challenges, Figely (1995a) argued for an alternative conceptualization of this distress, compassion fatigue theory, which was first suggested in the nursing literature (see Joinson, 1992). He writes, "There is a cost to caring. Professionals who listen to clients' stories of fear, pain, and suffering may feel similar fear, pain, and suffering because they care" (p. 1). The key element of this theoretical framework is the meaning of compassion: a feeling of deep sympathy and sorrow for another who is stricken by suffering or misfortune, accompanied by a strong desire to alleviate the pain or remove its cause.[6]

At the conceptual heart of compassion fatigue theory are the concepts of empathy and exposure, not intrusion and avoidance. Empathy is a major resource for trauma workers, who use it to assess victims' problems and develop treatment approaches. Thus: "the process of empathizing with a traumatized person helps us to understand the person's experience of being traumatized, but in the process, we may be traumatized as well" (Figely, 1995a, p. 15). Repeated exposure to this pain, and the need continually to empathize with survivors' suffering produces psychological distress reactions in trauma therapists. Similarly, Saakvitne and Pearlman define VT as the "cumulative *transformative* effect on the helper of working with survivors of traumatic life events" (p. 17, emphasis not in original). The compassion fatigue model further depathologizes the experiences of trauma workers by postulating that such distress is not only a normal part of this work, but also essential. The very things one must do as a therapist to be effective put one's psychological well-being at risk. By its very nature, the role of trauma therapist requires empathic exploration of painful material. Counselors must personally endure repeated exposure to distress and use their own feelings of sorrow as tools for therapy. As such, it is impossible to escape this kind of work without personal consequences. Consistent with the depathologizing philosophy of compassion fatigue theory, Figley and others argue that self-care, not psychotherapy, is the solution for practitioners (see Munroe, et al., 1995; Pickett, et al., 1994). With opportunities to vent and process their feelings with others, trauma therapists can buffer themselves from the ill effects of their work.

Although traditionally used to describe the experiences of trauma therapists, compassion fatigue theory provides one framework for understanding the impact of researching violence against women. Dutton and Rubinstein (1995) even mentioned "applied researchers" in their conceptualization of trauma workers who are susceptible to STS. In our project of interviewing rape survivors, we too were touched by the ripple effect of trauma, and it was these reactions that emerged as the most prominent finding of this researching-the-researcher study. In varying degrees, research team members felt fear, grief, pain, and horror as the crime of rape intruded into our lives and thwarted escape. Many of us had difficulty sleeping and were haunted by nightmares in which we relived the stories of rape we heard about from the survivors. We were afraid to go out at night, and sometimes even in the day. We were afraid to stay home after hearing so many stories of rape committed by friends, boyfriends, and husbands. We barricaded our doors at home and work, and snapped at the slightest startle. Yet it should be remembered that the key aspect of secondary trauma is its similarity with, not its exact replication of, the victims' experiences. What we encountered was not nearly as bad as what the survivors went through.

Discovering that researchers can also be affected by secondary trauma is a significant finding in the rape victimology literature. Compassion fatigue theory provides a compelling model for understanding researcher's reactions, as we certainly had sustained, repeated contact with trauma. Yet there are some potential problems with such an application. Compassion fatigue is useful to explain therapists' distress because it stipulates that the very things that allow them to do their jobs—empathy and exposure—are exactly what cause them distress. But researchers do not have the same roles as therapists. The researcher is "supposed" to be objective; thus the critical element of empathy in compassion fatigue theory may not apply. In other words, the very things that define our roles as researchers do not necessarily heighten our risk for distress. It is entirely possible that researchers can be emotionally unaffected by their research. This was not, however, my experience or the experience of our research team. Nor has it been the experience of other rape researchers.

We were emotionally affected by witnessing rape because, as feminist scholars, we did empathize with our research participants. The empathic method of imagining yourself in someone else's situation means that we were reminded—constantly—that we too are at risk for rape. We could just as easily be the interviewee as the interviewer. The critical elements of empathy and exposure were commonplace in our work, but they may not be so for all social scientists. Compassion fatigue theory provides a useful model to characterize our emotional experiences but may not apply for other researchers. In our case, the very things we did as researchers did indeed put us at risk for distress. They also afforded us a deeper understanding of rape.

A compassion fatigue model interprets the emotional reactions of fear, anger, and sadness as normal reactions to working with trauma survivors. Yet as normal as these reactions may be, it is important to keep in mind that they are indeed *emotional* reactions. What does it mean for researchers to experience emotions in research? Does that feel normal? In our case, it did not always feel so normal. We were hurting, and although we validated such reactions for rape victims, we had difficulty normalizing them for ourselves. We often felt conflicted about our feelings. Compassion fatigue theory can account for what we experienced—a parallel reaction to the posttraumatic stress experienced by the rape survivors we interviewed. This model can also explain why we experienced these emotions: through repeated exposure to empathizing with victims, the very nature of our work put us at psychological risk. Yet the CF/STS/VT models were developed to explain what trauma therapists experience. To some extent, therapists expect some type of emotional carryover from their work. The norms of research do not typically provide for such effects. By and large, the culture of research does not allow for emotional reactions. As a result, even though we were deliberately challenging those norms, most team members still felt conflicted about possessing these emotional reactions. Thus, drawing upon emotion work theory sheds some light on how we experienced our feelings and why often we felt conflicted about them.

Emotion work theory was developed by Arlie Hochschild in her classic study, *The Managed Heart* (1983; see also 1975, 1979), which articulated how and why people regulate their emotions as part of their employed jobs.[7] Typically, emotion work is described in the context of service professions: flight attendants (Hochschild, 1983), supermarket clerks (Tolich, 1993), clerical workers (Davies & Rosser, 1986; Rogers, 1995; Wichroski, 1994), nurses (Aldridge, 1994; James, 1989, 1992; O'Brien, 1994; Rose, 1998; Small, 1995; Smith, 1989, 1991, 1992; Staden, 1998), and physicians/medical students (Smith & Kleinman, 1989).[8] These jobs require attending to the emotions of others: to provide comfort, patience, and compassion (nurses), cheerfulness (supermarket clerks), tact and discretion (clerical workers), and physical/sexual attractiveness (flight attendants). These jobs require employees to respond to other people's feelings, creating and maintaining desired emotional states.

This situational mandate to help others feel a certain way can run amok with what one actually feels. Hochschild notes that there are culturally bound "feeling rules" that dictate what we are supposed to feel in different situations, as well as "display rules" that govern how emotions can be expressed given certain audiences. The feeling rules and display rules of many service jobs require that the workers' real feelings be squelched. For example, even if they may feel like yelling, being rude, or dumping hot coffee in passengers' laps, flight attendants must be courteous, smiling in spite of their true feelings. This balancing of genuine and manufactured feelings is called emotion work. Employees must manage their own reactions, sometimes to the extent of making them invisible, if they are inconsistent with the norms of the job. Only the role- and setting-prescribed affect should come through. If your work requires attending to others' emotions, you must work on your own feelings to uphold that responsibility. Doing this kind of repeated emotional labor can create within workers a sense of "emotive dissonance," as they are unable to distinguish between their true emotions and the emotions that they have artificially created as part of their job.

To date, emotion work has been examined in the context of emotionally stressful jobs outside academia. But what if the difficult job was being a researcher who studied an emotionally charged topic? Sherryl Kleinmann and Martha Copp (1993) were among the first researchers to note that emotion work theory may also apply to social scientists. For example, in their monograph on field research, they noted that:

> As members of the larger discipline, fieldworkers share a culture dominated by the ideology of professionalism or, more specifically, the ideology of science. According to that ideology, emotions are suspect. They contaminate research by impeding objectivity, hence they should be removed . . . fieldworkers, then, do emotion work (Hochschild, 1983), molding their feelings to meet others' expectations. (p. 2)

With respect to the job of researcher, the norm is not to express emotions. The feeling rules are that there are no feelings. The display rules are that no emotions are displayed. Therefore, to the extent to which such role-violating feelings develop, the researcher must find ways to cope or manage those feelings to make his or her internal and external states consistent with expectations.

In the context of our research interviewing rape survivors, emotion work theory provides a useful framework for understanding how we felt about feeling rape. In a word, conflicted. The feeling rules of science were deeply ingrained in all of us, even the undergraduate interviewers who had less time in the academy than other members of the research team. Yet feminist methodologists have explicitly challenged the feeling and display rules of research (see Bergen, 1993; Fonow & Cook, 1991; Mies, 1991; Oakley, 1988; Reinharz, 1992). The relationship between the researcher and the researched can be nonhierarchical, characterized by the sharing of information, resources, and experiences—including emotions (see Jaggar, 1989; Oakley, 1988). Inspired by the writings of Raquel Bergen (1996), Ann Oakley (1988), and Shulamit Reinharz (1992), we tried to bring these ideas to life in our project. It can be done, but I was largely unprepared for what it would feel like to try to change such norms. What I discovered in this researching-the-researcher project is that the feminist methodology literature provides a template for change but little warning about what it might *feel* like to actually try to reconceptualize the research setting in this way. It felt very confusing. Even when deliberately and consciously trying to establish new feeling rules, there was a great deal of emotion work necessary to negotiate such conflict.

Although no one in the research team reported the emotional dissonance Hochschild describes (i.e., we could distinguish between what we thought we should feel and what we did feel), we engaged in emotion work before, during, and after the interviews we conducted with rape survivors. In preparing for an interview, we had to pull into ourselves, blocking out the rest of our lives (temporarily) so we could give a hundred percent of our attention to the rape survivor. Over time this became easier to do, and we

needed less emotional setup time to get ready for an interview. Nevertheless, we had to manage the uneasiness of anticipated interviews.

It was during the actual interviews that our need to regulate our emotions was at its strongest. As feminist interviewers, we planned on engaging
our participants, sharing information and feelings. We would not sit there
showing nothing, revealing nothing. If we were upset, then our project's
ethic dictated that we could show those feelings. But only to a point. The
interview should always be about the victim; she is the focus, not us. To
gauge what we should and should not reveal, I offered this guideline in
training: if you think your reaction would prompt the survivor to stop talking about what happened to her so she could attune to your feelings, that's
too much emotion revealed. No one got close to that point in an actual
interview because we were all quite successful in roping in our feelings and
managing what we revealed. But it was hard work. One of the interviews I
conducted, which I describe in the preface of this book, provided the greatest challenge I had ever faced in controlling my feelings. I felt physically ill,
so I had to check out emotionally until the interview was over. Then I
found a restroom so I could, finally, get sick. If the pain of hearing a victim's story was just too great for us to bear, we would shut down and work
on emotional autopilot. Yet we did not pretend to the survivors that we
were unaffected, because we did show emotional reactions but we almost
always muted them.

Outside the context of the actual interviews themselves, the emotion
work continued. Many team members felt that they did not have legitimacy to their feelings of distress because they were not the victim, nor were
they trauma therapists. We were feeling too much for what our role as the
nonvictim dictated. It was difficult breaking the feeling rules of research
and trying to create new rules. So despite the fact that we followed a feminist approach to interviewing, many of us still worried that we were feeling
too much. We were concerned that we had violated the norms of research
too much. Yet, others on the research team worried that they felt too little,
less than they should have, in deference to the role of a researcher. They
worried they should have showed more feeling. If we felt too much, we
found ways of numbing ourselves, selecting specific emotions to feel and
not feel. If we felt too little, the solution usually wasn't to try to feel more,
but to intellectualize the process of feeling.

Throughout this project, we were constantly barraged with feeling—our
feelings, the feelings of the rape survivors, the feelings of those close to us
who we were witnessing this process. Our research team met weekly to discuss our experiences, but many chose to keep some of their feelings private.
It was only in the end-of-project interviews that many felt ready to talk
about the impact this research had had on their lives. To some extent, we
continued to manage our emotions by controlling what we did and did not
reveal to each other. I believe that such privacy is needed. Just as a rape sur-

vivor controls what she reveals, to whom, and when, we also selectively
disclosed. What is contained in this book is what was ready to make public. The emotion work continues.

But as difficult as this was, as stressful as it was trying to negotiate new
feeling rules for research, this emotional journey raised important substantive questions about how the scope of rape is currently defined in the literature. This researching-the-researcher project clearly indicates that there is
a ripple effect of trauma, and the negative aftermath can extend further
than what is typically considered. Yet it is also important to note that our
findings do not suggest all researchers would necessarily feel traumatized
by studying rape. Compassion fatigue theory argues that the key element
for experiencing secondary traumatic stress is empathy. The extent to
which researchers redefine their roles and activities to empathize emotionally with the populations under study determines if and how they
too may be traumatized. Under these circumstances, the distress we experienced is a normal reaction to this work. The empathy we needed to do
our jobs as feminist interviewers put us well within reach of the ripple
effect of trauma. Even so, it was difficult to accept at times that we were
being affected. Consequently, this project also demonstrated that emotion work is not limited to jobs outside academia; the process of doing
emotionally charged research can instigate emotion work as well. Emotionally involved researchers will feel and will be emotionally affected.
It's hardly wasted emotion. Only by locating ourselves in that emotional
space were we able to see that emotion work does indeed occur in
research and that there are many more kinds of secondary victims of rape
than previously acknowledged.

But if ill effects of rape can reach that far and wide, then the scope of
rape is much broader than what is suggested by much of the victimology
literature. This cannot be the problem of individual survivors—rape cannot possibly be just the affective, cognitive, and behavioral problem
depicted in much of the academic literature. It touches too many people
too deeply for such an individual level of analysis to be wholly accurate.
Rape is a cultural problem. It affects both the survivors themselves and all
those within reach. In fact, other research suggests that the ripple effect
extends into society as a whole. In the 1980s psychologists Margaret Gordon and Stephanie Riger found that the fear of rape is widespread among
women, and such fear limits women's daily activities and choices. The
scope of this problem is wide enough that fearing rape is enough to cause
distress. In the 1990s, Emilie Buchwald, Pamela Fletcher, and Martha Roth
emphasized in their book, *Transforming a Rape Culture*, the need for societal-
level reforms because we live in a "rape culture." Consider the number of
women who are raped in this country; then add the trauma of these vic-
timizations; then add the distress experienced by secondary victims; then
add the impact of living in fear of rape; and then add the violence-laden

media and culture in the background. That sum total is the rape culture that Buchwald, Fletcher, and Roth argue must be dismantled. Rape is not only what it does to its primary victims—that's only one part of the problem. To the extent to which rape research defines the scope of rape as the immediate effects on survivors, this narrow view is reinforced. Yet, in all fairness, no single study, nor even a strong series of studies, can possibly capture the range of what rape is and what rape does. But as more research moves beyond an individual level of analysis, the scope of rape can be better understood.

Recapturing the Emotionality of Rape: The Lived Experiences of Survivors

In this project, we followed the rape survivors into the uncomfortable places of feeling rape. By documenting this process for research, we saw that under certain circumstances and contexts, researchers could also be secondary victims of rape. And once there, once in that space of feeling rape, we could look back to that vacated zone of abstract thinking. Our position had changed, creating new vantage points—everything looked different from where we now stood. In the middle of feeling rape, we had a new perspective on thinking about rape. What did the academic literature look like from this view?

In the end-of-project interviews, several of the interviewers reflected on this issue, noting that they felt a disconnection between the experiences of the survivors they interviewed and the academic articles and book chapters they had read in training and throughout the project. Of course, none of us has read the entire literature, every single thing ever written about rape, but all members of the team were well read on issues of prevalence, impact, treatment, and prevention. The concern wasn't factual accuracy; at issue was whether the writing communicated the emotionality of rape. As one of the interviewers summarized:

> I don't know if we're even talking about the same thing. . . . I went back and read those overview articles assigned at the beginning, and there was no connection. I didn't feel like those researchers and I could possibly be talking about the same thing when we said "rape." I mean no disrespect to them, the research is first-rate; it just didn't feel like anything I have witnessed lately.

Indeed, from the position of feeling rape, academic texts on sexual assault can appear distant and devoid of emotion, and as such, they may not be capturing the reality of rape from the survivors' perspectives. As researchers, I believe our first reaction is to defend such an approach in the name of science and objectivity. It is not an appropriate job of scientists to convey feeling regarding their subject matter. Thus I ask that we temporarily suspend those notions and consider what may be lost by not tackling the emotionality of this subject. What does it mean that several of the interviewers in this project noted that the academic writings assigned in training didn't seem to connect with what they were hearing in their interviews with rape survivors? What does it mean that throughout my own field notes, I too noted marked disconnection between what I heard and saw from rape survivors and what I was reading in the academic literature? From the position of feeling rape, much of the published literature didn't feel emotionally accurate. It may very well have been scientifically valid, but it often didn't convey the lived experiences of rape survivors. I believe it is important to ask why that is and what we may be losing—scientifically—by not feeling rape.

Why is it then that when in the world of feeling rape, so many academic writings appeared disconnected from what we were experiencing? Why do I now question the emotional accuracy of much of this discourse? To answer these questions, it is important to examine how rape has been defined in academic work. As a developing discipline, a primary task for the field has been to define what constitutes rape. To study sexual assault, we must know what it is, how to define it, and how to operationalize it for research purposes. But defining rape also sets the tone for the field—how the boundaries have been drawn around this topic reveals a great deal about how rape has been viewed and discussed in academic writing. Psychologist Seymour Sarason (1974) noted that academics may have a tendency to define problems in ways that are ultimately familiar and convenient to them as researchers, but such definitions may not be grounded in the experiences of those suffering from the problem. He wrote:

> If, as academic disciplines, they made the mistake of transforming problems in ways that made dealing with them more compatible with their own pasts and traditions and in doing so rendered themselves insensitive to the basic problems of social living, it should be no cause for surprise. (p. 277)

The process of defining rape has served multiple purposes, and through an examination of the definitions in the literature, we can trace what has become of rape in academic research. These definitions show how emotional aspects of this crime have been neutralized. What happened when the visceral, violent crime of rape was moved into the academy? Consistent with Sarason's observation, I argue that "rape" as a topic of scientific inquiry took on the values and norms of the academy itself. Settings have a profound effect on individuals, and the setting of academic science has had a constraining effect on how rape is defined and studied. I don't believe that the "rape" conveyed in academic writings is at all the same "rape" that is experienced by rape survivors. What happened in between?

When rape emerged as a topic of scientific inquiry in the 1970s, many scholars turned to the law to guide their definitions: What legally defines rape? What they found were definitions based on English common law, which placed extreme emphasis on the victim. For example, Cassia Spohn and Julie Horney (1992) noted that: "historically, rape was defined as 'carnal knowledge of a woman, not one's wife, by force and against her will'" (p. 21). These laws were so heavily biased against the victim that they often required an unreasonable demonstration of nonconsent. The victim had to prove that she:

> did everything she could under the circumstances to prevent the defendant from accomplishing his purpose. If she did not do that it is not rape . . . [the jury] must find that she was overcome and overpowered, and that resistance must have continued from the inception of the case to its close, because if she yielded at any time, it would not be rape. (People v. Murphy 145 Mich. 524, 528 108 NW2d 1009, 1011 (1906), cited in Spohn & Horney, 1992)

In response to these kinds of laws, a key goal of the early antirape movement was the reform of federal and state rape statutes (Berger, Searles, & Neuman, 1988; Fischer, 1989; Searles & Berger, 1987; Spohn & Horney, 1992). The legal emphasis on the victim was deemed unacceptable as it institutionalized victim-blaming and all too often let the behaviors of the rapist go unpunished (Brownmiller, 1975; Schechter, 1982). Through grassroots organizing, feminist activists and scholars were successful in legally redefining rape (see Spohn & Horney, 1992 for a review). For example, consider the current U.S. Federal Code:

> The definition of a sexual act in the U.S. Federal Code: a) contact between the penis and the vulva or the penis and anus, for purposes of this subparagraph contact involving the penis occurs upon penetration, however slight; b) contact between the mouth and penis, the mouth and vulva, or the mouth and anus; or c) the penetration, however slight, or the anal or genital opening of another by a hand or finger or by any object, with an intent to abuse, humiliate, harass, degrade, or arouse or gratify the sexual desire of any person. (Federal Code 18 U.S.C. 2245)

In the current legal definition, rape is broken down into its constituent parts: the equipment (penis, vulva, anus, mouth); the act (contact or penetration); and the reason (abuse). The actors (rapist and victim) are undefined, as is the impact.[9] All of the context is stripped away to focus upon the act of rape itself.

Because academic rape researchers have heavily drawn upon legal conceptualizations, it is not surprising that many social science definitions of rape follow current legal trends. Although some early characterizations of rape mirrored the old, victim-blaming laws (e.g., Amir, 1971; Kanin, 1957), most social science models have developed in the tradition of the reformed legal statutes (e.g., Bachman & Saltzman, 1995; Kilpatrick, et al., 1987; Koss, Gidycz, & Wisniewski, 1987). In other words, academic research has been guided by the legal conceptualization of rape, giving rise to behaviorally based definitions of rape that emphasize the actions of the rapist. Although there is still considerable variation in exactly how researchers define rape (see Bachar & Koss, 2001, for a review), most national prevalence studies and smaller-scale projects inquire about specific behaviors: sexual intercourse or other sexual contact attempted or completed through the use of force, threats, coercion, administration of drugs/alcohol. This is a social science interpretation of the law, with definitions firmly rooted in the legal elements of the crime, but with the jargon translated into examples and situations that are more familiar to victims: nonconsent means when you didn't want to; use or threat of force means someone threatened or used some degree of physical force (twisting your arm, holding you down, etc.). Such behavioral specificity has provided more accurate estimates of the prevalence of rape, but it is important to note that all of these definitional models emphasize the exact *behaviors* of the *rapist*.

Where are the *emotions* of the *victim* reflected? Not in the legal definitions of rape. Not in most social science definitions of rape. Making the legal definitions less victim-blaming and the social science prevalence surveys more behaviorally accurate are good things, necessary things, representing major accomplishments for the antirape movement. But for all their improvement and utility, it is also important to acknowledge what these definitions lack: the voice of the victim, the feelings of the victim, the emotions of surviving rape. Granted, it has not been the intent of the law or the scope of most social science research to reflect this perspective. That these definitions did not capture what they did not intend to assess is hardly a founded criticism. Rather, my concern is how we're going to be able to hear the voices of victims within this predominately legal/behavioral paradigm. To do so, I believe we must focus on the emotional experiences of what it feels like to survive rape, and move away from the academic precision afforded by the law and by social science methodology. A total rejection of these traditions is hardly necessary, but an in-depth look into the alternatives may provide helpful guidance.

"Emotion-focused" definitions do exist, although they are not "definitions" in the traditional sense. More descriptive in nature, these writings convey the ungodly mess of what rape is and what rape does. For example, in her classic work, *Against Our Will: Men, Women, and Rape* (1975), Susan Brownmiller offered her definition of rape:

To a woman the definition of rape is fairly simple. A sexual invasion of the body by force, and incursion into the private, personal inner space without consent—in short, an internal assault from one of several avenues and by one of several methods—constitutes a deliberate violation of emotional, physical, and rational integrity and is a hostile, degrading act of violence that deserves the name of rape. . . . What remains is the basic male-female struggle, a hit-and-run attack, a brief expression of physical power, a conscious process of intimidation, a blunt, ugly sexual invasion with possible lasting psychological effects on all women. (pp. 376–377)

Brownmiller's definition of rape stands in sharp contrast to the dominant themes in the academic study of rape. Her definition is not based upon the legal elements *per se* (although there is certainly some overlap) or upon the precise behaviors that constitute the act of rape, but rather on the emotional experiences of the victim. Rape is what it does to the victim. The dirty, invasive nature of this crime is conveyed in Brownmiller's definition. Her tone is visceral and emotional, like the crime itself. The cool objectivity of the law, and social science, is traded for the raw emotionality of the victim's experience.

A similar victim-based, impact-based definition of rape was suggested by feminist legal scholar Catherine MacKinnon:

Politically, I call it rape whenever a woman has sex and feels violated. . . . To me, part of the culture of sexual inequality that makes women not report rape is that the definition of rape is not based on our sense of our violation. . . . The crime of rape—this is a legal and observed, not a subjective, individual, or feminist definition—is defined around penetration. That seems to me a very male point of view on what it means to be sexually violated. And it is exactly what heterosexuality as a social institution is fixated around, the penetration of the penis into the vagina. (MacKinnon, 1987, pp. 82, 87)

MacKinnon unearths the contradictions between the legal definitions of rape and women's experiences of rape. They don't match. The sense of violation that so essentially defines what it *feels* like to be raped is not legally important or relevant. A law defined by a woman's sense of violation may not be practically feasible, but MacKinnon suggests it would be more experientially valid.

Perhaps the clearest "definitions" of rape are those provided by the survivors themselves. In 1998 and 1999, four remarkable books were published by survivors of sexual violence: *After Silence: Rape and My Journey Back* (1998) by Nancy Venable Raine; *Telling: A Memoir of Rape and Recovery* (1999) by Patricia Weaver Francisco; *Lucky* (1999) by Alice Sebold; and *Working with Available Light: A Family's World after Violence* (1999) by Jamie

Kalven (an account of how a rape impacted the family of a rape survivor). As first-person narratives, these memoirs define rape by how it felt and continued to feel in the months, years, and decades after the assault. Defining rape is to describe it, which is a full story, not a short, portable quote or excerpt. That said, I wish instead to call attention to language that these authors use in their narratives. These examples, though not fully capturing how these survivors define rape, do reflect the kind of tone and emotionality that is largely missing in academic discourse:

> He threw me on the bed facedown, his knee in the middle of my back. He pressed down with his full and great weight so that I thought he might snap my spine in two, like a twig. (p. 10) . . . Over the next three hours he raped me and tormented me with descriptions of how he would kill me with a knife, telling me exactly where he would cut me. Or maybe, he said, he would smother me with my pillow. He seemed undecided about the method. (p. 11) . . . In this detachment, a state I reached at the moment I knew I could not physically escape, I experienced his rage as if it were a separate entity, a shadow self to his physical being. I understood that this entity was hungry and that it was feasting on something from me—my terror, my physical and psychic pain. (p. 13) . . . [In the hospital emergency room after the assault] [t]he doctor cuts off the overhead lights and holds an ultraviolet lamp between my legs. She names parts where she has found semen, which glows from its bacteria in the eerie light . . . I see the sperm in my mind, the size of maggots. I shudder and feel I am curling up, like a worm that has been cut in half by a trowel. (p. 28) (Raine, 1998)

> I actually remember little in my thoughts and feelings about the physical experience of being raped. I remember in my body the subjugation of my body. *Just get through this,* I tell myself. I know I might be killed, but at this point, I believe I will survive. *All you have to do is get through this.* It is so dark, and I am so tired and afraid. The easiest thing to do is to leave. Let my body stand in for me. As I write this, it sounds like a decision, but it happened instinctively, as one swerves just soon enough to avoid the crash. These are not willed acts of survival. We are in some way assisted, led away from what can only harm us. I remember this moment from a spot up near the ceiling, through a consciousness separated from the bodies below. As a result, my memory has a quality of dreamy calm that I want at times to rip away. Only years later, when I learned to retrieve a bodily memory of this night, did I finally experience some of the details. (p. 28) (italics in original) (Francisco, 1999)

> As I tried to hide my nakedness—at least I had my underpants on—he looked down at my body. I still feel that in that gaze his eyes lit up my

sickly pale skin in that dark tunnel. Made it all—my flesh—suddenly horrible. *Ugly* too kind a word, but the closest one. "You're the worst bitch I ever done this to," he said. It was said in disgust, it was said in analysis. He saw what he had bagged and didn't like his catch. No matter, he would finish. (pp. 16–17) . . . [in the hospital emergency room after the assault] I saw my face in the mirror. I reached my hand up to touch the marks and cuts. That was me. It was also an undeniable truth: No shower would wipe the traces of the rape away. . . . The shower was small and made of white tile. I asked [my friend] to turn on the water, "As hot as you can," I said. . . . I wished I had a wire brush but even that wouldn't be enough. (p. 29) (italics in original) (Sebold, 1999)

It's as if a deep wound, long buried, has been laid open. Lying beside my wife, I'm confused by my maleness—so hard, so insistent—and feel somehow implicated in her wounding. Every caress feels coercive. (p. 11) . . . When I arrived at the emergency room, I was met at the door by a woman doctor. "Your wife has been assaulted and badly beaten. She needs you to be calm. Can you do that?" I nodded. . . . I took her hand and tried to comfort her. She released a sob and began, in discontinuous fragments, to tell me what happened. I didn't know what she was feeling, only that it was overwhelmingly powerful. (p. 14) . . . Flooded by feelings I haven't the words to speak, I stand by her savaged body and hold her hand. A man looking on. (p. 15) (Kalven, 1999)

Contrast the language that is typically used to define rape—"contact between the penis and the vulva," "forced or coerced to engage in unwanted sexual activity," "anal or oral intercourse or penetration by objects other than the penis"—with the passages above. Survivors do not tell their stories with these words. The assaults are instead described primarily through feelings—afraid, terrified, determined, emotionally detached, dirty, violated, confused, ashamed—less so by acts or events. Rape is what it feels like. These differences in language weighed heavily on me throughout our research project. After conducting my own interviews, listening to the audio tapes of those done by other interviewers, and hearing how we talked about rape in our research team, I became more and more impatient with academic science. Yet I have not lost confidence in the methods of the social sciences to inform our understanding of the social world. I realize that there is no reasonable way to assess the prevalence of sexual assault with emotionally based definitions. I also realize that such a focus on the emotionality of rape carries personal and political costs for researchers. Nevertheless, I raise the issue of how we can describe rape in ways that are more consistent with victims' lived experiences. As an exercise for myself, I tried to close this gap and see if I could write about rape in a way that more closely matched what we were hearing in our interviews. This is what I wrote in my field notes:

What is rape?

Rape is being held down, pinned down, immobilized by the weight of another body on top of you. It is the hardness of the floor, the concrete, the ground, the bed beneath you, digging into your back, or into your stomach. It is the scraping of your body against that floor, concrete, ground, or bed, over and over again, as you are rammed into it by the weight of another body on top of you and inside of you.

It is so close, it is stifling, smothering, and suffocating. It is having to breathe the same air as the rapist. It is his skin on yours, rubbing against yours, leaving traces of it behind. He is leaving behind bits and pieces of himself and his act on you, and in you. It is all over you. The debris of violence is all over you. It is sweat, it is tears, it is blood, and it is semen. And it, too, is on you and in you. It is the grabbing of your arms and your hands, and holding them down. It is the bruising of your flesh, the biting of your flesh—be it with his teeth, with his penis, his hands, or whatever other object was handy.

It is fear, so concentrated that it is almost unrecognizable. It is the fear of death. You are going to die; you are going to be killed. If he can do this, what is to stop him from killing you, or rather, finish killing you. It is the lifelong torment—why didn't he just finish me off, kill me, so I wouldn't have to live with this? Because you do live with it—every day, in varying degrees of memory, in varying degrees of conscious thought. But the debris is left, and it clings. No amount of showering, no amount of bathing ever really gets rid of it.

It is a detached state of consciousness. It is the dissociation that comes after fear and panic. It is the numbness that takes over, waiting for the rape to be over. It is the distancing of one's self from the filth being spread over and into one's body. It is leaving yourself, trying to leave behind what is happening, only to have to gather it all up later and bring it home.

It is sometimes in a state of altered consciousness—being drunk, stoned, or high. Of "coming to" with the weight of another being on top of you, holding you down. It is rubbing up against you, and in you, spreading debris and filth. It is trying to comprehend what is happening to you, when there really should be no part of anyone's mind that has space and a mechanism for understanding what this is.

And it is penetration—of the mouth, of the vagina, of the anus, of the mind, and of the soul. It is penetration with a penis, or several penises. It is penetration with a hand, or several hands. It is penetration with an object, or several objects. It is whatever is on hand, whatever is available. And it presses into you, forces into you— unprepared and unwelcomed. It is the tearing of soft tissue. It is the stretching of delicate tissues, but stretching them too quickly and without permission, so they break, rip, and tear. It is bleeding and soreness, and a burning, searing pain. It is the bruising of the cervix as it is beaten, rammed into, over and over again.

It is the debris, the skin, and the semen that is rubbed into you and all over you, again and again. It is spilled on you, dumped on you, and into you. It is the bacteria and the viruses that could be being mixed into you. It is the diseases, curable and incurable, that might be forced into you. Mixed into you, stirred into you—the semen into the blood, stirred by the force of a penis.

That is what rape is.

I wrote this "definition" within two months of the interview I conducted with the rape survivor described in the preface of this book. I was working on another manuscript at the time, which prompted me to review the standard definitions in the field. I could not find anything that came close to capturing what I had seen and heard in that interview, or any of the interviews before or since, and my own published work in this area was no exception. There was a remarkable lack of congruence between what I was reading in the academic literature and what I had been experiencing talking with survivors. This entry in my field notes was an exercise for myself in trying to reflect what is experienced by rape survivors.

What I hope may be helpful in Brownmiller's and MacKinnon's definitions, the stories of Raine, Francisco, Sebold, and Kalven, and my field notes essay is the implicit challenge this language issues to academic researchers to describe and understand rape as it is experienced by survivors. Brownmiller's and MacKinnon's definitions tap into the emotional experience of being raped, which is largely missing from the legal definition and all of its derivatives. Yet when these legal/behavioral and experiential/emotional definitions are viewed side by side, they demonstrate the social construction of rape in academia, the social construction of thinking versus feeling. In academic research, rape is traditionally defined and described in cold, distant language: "contact between the penis and the vulva," "forced or coerced to engage in unwanted sexual activity," "anal or oral intercourse or penetration by objects other than the penis." Rape is not described emotionally, and its impact is not described emotionally. Yet rape is emotional—highly emotional—to its victims.

It took nearly 30 years of this field's history to debate and refine a definition of rape and of how to measure its impact. As a result, such work has successfully raised public awareness about rape (and acquaintance rape in particular), by demonstrating with specific, behavioral measures just how common rape really is and how it negatively affects women's psychological and physical health. And in doing so, I believe it is also fair to ask how well we have communicated to fellow researchers and to the general public what rape really is.[10] Our efforts in this regard have not been entirely unsuccessful either—our books and articles are often sprinkled with very powerful, very emotional quotes from survivors, judges, prosecutors, and others. The words of others are used by proxy to convey emotions; our words—the words we select to join the quotes—often do not. As a whole, this literature does not convey the emotionality of rape—rape has been sanitized. This is not necessarily an issue of style or semantics. The "crime" here is not that we have written about rape for the past 30 years from a less-than-emotional vantage point. The problem, I believe, is our field's underlying ambivalence about what to do with the emotions of rape and researching rape. I suspect that rape has been described so neutrally as a means of conveying objectivity and appearing unbiased and rigorous, which is not at all a bad strategy for an emerging controversial area of research.

But today, sexual assault has all the markings of a legitimate field of inquiry: specializations of topics, even subspecializations; at least three peer-reviewed victimology journals as primary outlets for research on violence against women; publishing houses with book lists on violence against women; federal, state, and local funding resources for research.[11] It is to the credit of the founding scholars that new generations of rape researchers rarely even have to fight for the legitimacy of this topic. Again, raising the issue of *how* rape is discussed means rape *is* being discussed. Rape has become a (more or less) acceptable subject for academic research; it is now an established discipline within social science. It is not, however, without controversy, stigma, or backlash. It has, and continues to, inspire all three. Nevertheless, rape has become part of academe.

In many respects it is highly ironic that rape has emerged as a topic of science, because the reality of rape and academic science have very little to do with each other. There is nothing academic about rape. It is an ugly crime, which could easily soil the pristine ivory tower. It has been *made* into a topic suitable for academic research. It has been cleaned up enough to pass muster within the academy. We—the collective group of rape researchers—have, perhaps unknowingly, taken something that is, at its very core, emotional, at its very core, painful, and essentially stripped it of its emotion. We have operationally defined "rape" and "sexual assault," learned how to ask about rape in ways that are respectful and supportive to survivors. We have assessed how often rape happens, to whom it happens. We have created different interventions to assist survivors. And we engage in scholarly debates about all of these issues. But violence is not something to be debated; rape is not something to be debated. This is not a problem to be debated, it is problem to be ended. Social problems such as violence against women cannot truly be understood from a position of emotional neutrality, of academic "objectivity" because these problems are, at their core, emotional. They are, at their core, painful. The conflict here runs quite deep. Social problems like rape are inherently emotional, but science is not supposed to be emotional; it is supposed to be logical and objective. For rape to qualify as a legitimate field of inquiry, it had to become something other than what it really is. The academic study of rape is necessarily different from the actual lived reality of rape; it is the social construction of rape in an academic setting. Rape has become a topic, a specialization, a debate, and a discipline.

A dividing wall between intellect and emotion has been constructed to make the study of rape quite separate from the experience of rape. Propping up this wall on one side is the argument of objectivity: such discussions of the emotionality of rape are not needed, maybe even undesirable. Raw emotion will only obscure the truth, create bias, encourage advocacy that will interfere with objectivity. These arguments are based upon a positivistic view of science. Recent thinking in constructivist epistemology (see Gergen, 1985) contends that science never was, nor will be, an objective enterprise. It is only through understanding the subjectivities of the world that "truth" and "truths" can emerge. But on the other side of this divide is the world of emotion, and in many respects, it is in the best interest of the researcher to maintain this separation between feeling rape and thinking about rape. The researching of rape, or any topic in social science, requires a substantial investment of concentration and commitment. Given the amount of time and energy that we must invest in rape to study it, we would be absolutely tortured by it if we didn't think about rape in the abstract. No one wants to feel rape—not the survivor, not the researcher. It is easier, though not easy, to think about rape. But it is the researcher who has the luxury of thinking about rape; the survivor does not—she has no choice but to feel it. As researchers, we must challenge ourselves with difficult questions: Just how good is our science if it is not known from the experience of the rape survivor? How good is it if we characterize it one way, but it is experienced as another? How good is our research if we maintain, however explicitly or implicitly, that rape can be about logic, intellect, and objectivity, when it seems to be about emotion? In an intellectual culture that hierarchically separates thinking and feeling, scientific validity takes precedence over emotional accuracy. But then again, what does it mean if something is scientifically valid but not "real?"

Moving Forward: Suggestions for Researching Rape

Where can we go from here? If the scope of the problem of rape is wider than the literature generally reflects, and if this literature doesn't often convey the emotionality of rape, then what does this mean for research on violence against women? What could be different? Based on this researching-the-researcher project, I propose three interrelated strategies for the field that begin to address these issues: to expand what we study—the topics—how we study it—the methodologies—and how we report the findings of these studies—the writing itself. The past 30 years of research has built a solid foundation of replicable findings. We could continue to replicate and refine, but I am hopeful that the field can push into new terrain.

First, in terms of what is studied, rape researchers have tended to concentrate on a handful of topics (e.g., prevalence, psychological impact, treatment, etc). Yet this field is quite young, and I argue that there is still much surveying to be done to find out what needs finding out. There is a strong tradition in psychology of emulating the physical sciences by establishing a set of hypotheses and methods and then working through numerous variations of this research paradigm. The same ground is covered very thoroughly in hopes of isolating and understanding "the effect" and the circumstances that make "the effect" happen, happen to varying degrees, or not happen. This approach is systematic, programmatic, and thoughtful. And it can also limit the topical diversity of research produced.

In 1999, psychologist Mary Koss directly challenged the narrow scope of the field in her address to the American Psychological Association, "Rape Research in the Year 2000 and Beyond." Key among these issues is investigating the prevalence of rape. There have been at least four major national-scale prevalence studies in addition to the National Crime Victimization Survey.[12] Koss questioned the utility of this "number's game" when she asked, "do we really need more studies of rape prevalence or is this a strategy to resist change?" (p. 1). Prevalence rates indeed vary somewhat from study to study and population to population, but they do converge on a common range of 15 percent to 36 percent, which is simply far too common. Koss argued that there are other, more pressing issues that receive far less attention, among them understanding vulnerability to victimization, assessing the accessibility and effectiveness of community services for rape victims, and developing theoretically based rape prevention programming.

I echo this concern and add to this list my call for more research on the secondary victims of rape. The prevalence of rape may range from 15 percent to 36 percent, but these numbers, I believe, vastly underrepresent the harm of rape in our culture. If one in three to five women has been assaulted, then for each one, there may very well be an additional set of secondary victims who have also been touched by this crime: friends, boyfriends, girlfriends, partners, lovers, fathers, mothers, siblings. There are emotional costs for counselors, therapists, advocates, and health care providers as well. The ripple effect can even extend into the research setting, reaching interviewers, transcribers, and other members of a research team. Investigating what rape does to families, friendships, service providers, and researchers shifts the conceptual focus from individual victims to a broader contextual perspective. In their book, *The Rape Victim: Clinical and Community Interventions*, Mary Koss and Mary Harvey (1991) outlined an ecological model of rape trauma that calls for research on not only person-centered (i.e., victim-centered) variables, but also event and environmental constructs. Such work is critical in accurately assessing the scope of this problem and its costs to our society.

Second, as research continues along established paths and expands into these understudied topics, I also argue that the field would benefit from greater methodological diversity. As noted previously, much of the rape victimology literature, particularly in psychology, is steeped in a logical positivist, quantitative framework. This hypothesis-testing approach has served us well, but it has its limitations. It is harder, though not impossible, to capture the "rape" victim's experience through standardized, closed-ended scales and research protocols that are designed to test the experimenters' hypotheses. There just isn't much room in that framework for diversity— the closer the fit between victims' experiences and researchers' expectations, the more likely that version of "rape" will be reflected in academic discourse. This doesn't mean that this kind of research isn't capable of detecting varying points of view—it can indeed, in the form of error variance and/or disconfirmed hypotheses. Such results are often viewed as quite interesting, as they stir debate and bring new ideas to the surface for further investigation.

My point here is not to single out this kind of science unfairly but rather to issue a call for greater methodological variety in how we study violence against women. Heeding the advice of Toby Jayaratne and Abigail Stewart (1991) to move beyond the oversimplified quantitative/qualitative dichotomy, I am not suggesting that the "solution" here is simply to do more qualitative research. The appeal of such methodological traditions is their potential for personal connection between the researcher and the research participants, which can contribute to a setting of open disclosure and dialogue. However, qualitative methods are not without their problems. For instance, Lynn Weber Cannon, Elizabeth Higginbothan, and Marianne Leung (1988) note that because it is primarily white, middle-class individuals who typically volunteer for these in-depth, self-reflective studies, qualitative research is quite susceptible to racial and social class biases. But it certainly isn't the case that narrative methods won't work in communities of color or with women of different social classes. Research by Luciana Ramos Lira, Mary Koss, and Nancy Felipe Russo (1999) provides a thoughtful example on how to use qualitative techniques with nonwhite, non-middle-class samples on sensitive topics such as sexual violence against women. With careful attention to issues of diversity, qualitative techniques can provide opportunities to hear survivors' stories in ways hypothesis-driven research cannot match. I believe it is important that we focus greater attention on those stories because I am concerned the "rape" reflected in academic discourse may be too clean and emotionally disconnected from what survivors actually experience. If we can provide opportunities for survivors to talk about what has happened to them—either orally in interviews and focus groups, or written in questionnaires and surveys—we can bring their experiences to light.

It may be common in research studies to include such open-ended assessment, but I also suspect the data generated go largely unanalyzed. It is difficult to analyze textual data, but with recent advances in techniques and software for qualitative analysis (e.g., Q-NUDIST, Ethnograph), this kind of work is more accessible to researchers of various training and backgrounds. Similarly, there are a number of beginning texts that provide specific instruction for planning qualitative projects (e.g., Huberman & Miles, 1994; Miles & Huberman, 1994; Strauss & Corbin, 1990). An excellent resource for concrete, completed example projects is Ellen Kimmel's and Mary Crawford's (2000) book, *Innovations in Feminist Psychological Research*. This collection is based on two volumes of *Psychology of Women Quarterly* on innovative feminist methods.

Nonquantitative research also has the reputation of being unfundable, but that is changing. The National Institute of Justice, through the Violence Against Women Grants Office, has issued requests for proposals (RFPs) that specifically include qualitative research. For example, the RFP for the national evaluation of the domestic violence victims' civil legal assistance program stated that: "A multi-method evaluation, including both quantitative and qualitative approaches, is required. Evaluating impact and capturing the voices of the victims will be essential components."[13] Furthermore, violence against women researchers has an excellent track record for successful advocacy. In less than 30 years, millions of dollars for research have been obtained, three journals have been created, and new generations of researchers have been trained. Supporting research of varying methodological traditions is no greater or smaller a challenge.

Finally, I raise the issue of how we write about rape. Academic discourse is highly standardized and regulated: the existing literature must be thoroughly reviewed without bias or exception, empirical findings should reported with minimal interpretation, and throughout, advocacy is traditionally kept to a minimum. The overall effect is to communicate a thoughtful, rational, objective account of a given reality. And more often than not, the resulting text may be clear but is not often linguistically vivid and engaging (Richardson, 1994). Yet there is growing interest in how scientific writing is itself a highly subjective process whereby collective norms are created and reinforced (see Richardson, 1994). Termed the "ecology of writing science" (Howarth, 1990), styles of reporting are a key ingredient and process through which research findings are socially constructed (Charmaz & Mitchell, 1997; Hunter, 1990; Richardson, 1994; Sandelowski, 1994). For example, sociologist Laurel Richardson (1994) asked: "How do we create texts that are vital? That are attended to? That make a difference? . . . How we are expected to write affects what we can write about" (p. 517, 520). Her recommendation is to break free from these traditional forms and styles of writing to create text that is both intellectually and emotionally engaging.

How can this be done? Richardson (1994) and Kleinman (1997) have presented several examples of alternative writing formats: "experimental representations," "evocative representations," "ethnographic fictional representations," "essaying the personal," "realist tales," and so on. The specific differences between these kinds of writing are perhaps not as central as what is similar about them: they reflect different criteria for the construction and evaluation of writing research findings. Scientific writing is judged for its accuracy and clarity. Narrative writing is evaluated for its coherence, verisimilitude, and interest. Richardson argues that vivid social science writing is a balance of both. Margarete Sandelowski (1994) noted that it is often the voices of the research participants, shared through quotations, that provide the real interest in a piece of writing. However, she cautions against just simply adding more quotations to our writing as a means of making it more affectively cogent. She encourages researchers to select quoted excerpts based upon their scientific utility (e.g., the extent to which they support the researchers' claims, illustrate ideas, illuminate experiences), their affective utility (e.g., how the evoke emotion and provoke response), and their linguistic composition (e.g., style, tone, rhythm, sound). Thus the voices of the researcher and the research participants are included in the written report, and both are evaluated for their capacity to communicate the findings clearly and reflect the underlying emotional experiences inherent in those findings, while holding the readers interest and attention.

In the context of studying rape, I believe attention to style and tone of academic writing is particularly important. Again, I perceive a marked mismatch between the dominant style of academic discourse and the often emotionally charged experience of surviving sexual assault. Consistent with Richardson's (1994) arguments, I contend that incorporating a stronger emotional focus in our writings will not jeopardize their quality but rather enhance them by creating vivid texts that close the gap between victims' experiences and the academic construction of rape. This does not mean that our work must read like sensationalized journalism, but it can be emotionally engaging, moving us as we write it and moving our audiences as they read it. If our writings can communicate in an emotional way how it feels to survive rape, I believe this is an important substantive contribution to the field.

We have created a place for rape at the table of scientific discourse. But this is not just any topic of inquiry—it comes with special baggage. Rather than pretending that it is not there, our field must come to terms with the emotions of rape. When we write about rape, we must discuss the emotional pain—to the survivors and to all secondary victims—that is caused by rape. There is much to be learned by feeling rape, by understanding the emotions of rape, and by embracing the emotionality of this topic. The emotional pain of rape is not a threat to "objectivity," nor is it necessarily a threat to the well-being of the researcher. Emotions can be an important resource for science, and the emotionality of rape is essential to its understanding.

Creating Balance—
Thinking and Feeling

The Possibilities for Emotionally Engaged Research

Throughout this book, I have argued that emotionality can have a useful function in social science research. Rejecting the notion that researchers' emotions may taint investigation, I believe that attuning to these affective components can be personally and professionally rewarding. My research team and I were deeply moved by what we heard from rape survivors (see chapter Three, "Feeling: The Emotions of Researching Rape"), and in chapter Four "From Feeling to Thinking: The Insights Feeling Rape Bring to Researching Rape," I examined how these feelings, both positive and negative, enhanced our substantive understanding of rape. In this final chapter, I return to some broader issues regarding the role of emotions in social science research. Rather than creating difference between thinking and feeling, I explore how the process and methods of social science research can balance the contributions of each source of knowledge. We can move away from the restrictive duality that hierarchically separates thinking and feeling, intellect and emotion. My experiences suggest that in some types of research, this duality is false to begin with, as thinking and feeling are not structurally separate and in fact co-occur in the research. Furthermore, reflective analysis of the researcher's emotions can provide theoretical insights.

I call this balanced approach "emotionally engaged research," which most simply means drawing upon feelings for scientific purposes and valuing and utilizing the kinds of knowledge that can be revealed through careful attention to the affective experiences of the researcher and the participants. Feelings are reconceptualized as a form of data to be analyzed as part of the scientific process. Emotionally engaged research is guided by an ethic of caring—caring for the research participants, caring for what becomes of a research project, and caring for one's self and one's research team. Throughout this chapter, I outline ideas and caveats for each of these three domains of caring. The nature of the relationship between the researcher and those researched is a well traveled subject in the ethics literatures in philosophy, psychology, sociology, and other disciplines (see Brabeck & Ting, 2000, for an overview). Consequently, my goal here is not to review these varied debates but instead to explore how emotionality may influence how we relate to our participants, how we think about the broader outcomes and products of our research, and how we interact with our fellow researchers. My thoughts on this topic are grounded in postpositivist epistemologies; and I argue for in-depth exploration into the multitude of factors that shape our understanding of the social world. I do not accept the dichotomy that attuning to emotionality in science sacrifices its quality. Being methodologically rigorous and being emotionally engaged do not have to be mutually exclusive.

I offer this perspective not as a prescriptive statement of how research *should* be but instead as a beginning framework for how it *could* be for some researchers. The procedures for creating high-quality research—quantitative or qualitative—are well defined in the academic literature and *should* remain the foundations of our work. In this chapter, I explore the underlying processes that accompany those steps and how social research *could* acknowledge emotionality in methods. Some of the choices researchers make are essentially nonnegotiable. The peer review process screens out work with serious theoretical and/or methodological problems, so it is critical that the fundamentals of sampling, assessment, analysis, and interpretation are respected. These components are "policed" by the larger scientific community and are judged for their quality, as well they *should* be.

Yet there are also more private choices researchers make regarding how they do their work. How will the researchers interact with the study's participants? What will be asked of or observed among the participants, and how will this be done? What will be offered to the participants? What will be reported from the findings and why? How these questions are answered, I believe, is negotiable and worthy of more reflection. However, it is important to acknowledge that there is also a fair amount of "policing" regarding these other aspects of research. Sociologist Shulamit Reinharz (1993) noted that these choice points become traps for piling on "extra requirements," setting the bar higher and higher, which inadvertently could be creating unrealistic standards and silencing some researchers. Heeding that call, my intent here is not to add another set of demands or standards that should now be "policed" but rather to provide ideas, support, and encouragement for how some social scientists could choose to do their work.

Just as it is critical to clarify the purpose behind my exploration of emotionally engaged research, it is similarly important to specify for whom this approach to research may be relevant. The role of emotions in research may not be a pertinent concern for all social scientists. When I said emotionality could be a helpful resource for *some* researchers, I truly meant that part about "some." My grasp of the diverse range of theories and topics of interest to social scientists is hardly broad enough to attempt generalized statements about how all researchers could be doing their work. Instead, I believe that my research on emotions and sexual assault may provide useful insight for those doing projects in *related* areas.

I define "related" in two primary ways. First, the substantive topic of this study was sexual assault, an emotionally charged social problem. I suspect that many of the emotional struggles we experienced in our work could also occur in research on other "difficult issues." In conducting this researching-the-researcher project, I found literatures on diverse topics to be quite helpful: other forms of violence against women (Huff, 1997; Iliffe & Steed, 2000); other forms of violence, trauma, and disaster (Amick McMullan, Kilpatrick, & Veronen, 1989; Beaton & Murphy, 1995; Motta, et al., 1997; Nelson & Wright, 1996; Rosenheck & Nathan, 1985); HIV/AIDS (Lather & Smithies, 1997); grief and mourning (Saunders, 1999); the Jewish Holocaust (Davidson, 1980; Feingold, 1995; Freyberg, 1980; Linden, 1993); state-sponsored violence/torture (Conroy, 2000); animal rights (Groves, 1995, 1997; Jasper & Nelkin, 1992); cancer and other potentially fatal health problems (Ellis, 1995; Rose, 1998); health care (DeCoster, 1997; Foner, 1994; Heimer & Stevens, 1997); and abortion and reproductive health care (Fitzpatrick & Wilson, 1999; Simonds, 1996). Thus the role of emotions in research may be particularly salient for those who study emotionally involved social issues. If an area of study may put the researcher in contact with people who have had or are currently experiencing psychological and/or physical health distress and pain, then it may be fruitful to examine how emotionality enters into such work. Although my thinking on emotionally engaged research is rooted in my own substantive focus on sexual violence against women, I believe there are generalizable themes in this work that apply to other emotionally difficult research topics.

Second, irrespective of the substantive focus of a study, researchers using interpretative methodologies may find useful parallels between their work and this researching-the-researcher project. Locating the self within qualitative research is a critical task (see Guba & Lincoln, 1994; Lincoln & Guba, 1985; see Pierce, 1995, for an example narrative), and to date, there has been less attention on how researchers' feelings influence the research process as compared to other personalogical factors (e.g., beliefs, values) (see Ellis, 1991a; Kleinman & Copp, 1993, for exceptions). Similarly, the feminist methodology literature (both qualitative and quantitative) has articulated how gender, race/ethnicity, age, and sexual orientation affect the ways in which research is defined and interpreted (Cannon, Higginbothan, & Leung, 1988; Collins, 1991; Cook & Fonow, 1990; Fonow & Cook, 1991; Hartsock, 1998; Mies, 1983, 1991; Nielsen, 1990). The role of emotions in research may be particularly relevant to qualitative and/or feminist methodologists. Moreover, recent debates on the subjectivity of social science research touch upon issues of emotionality (Acker, Barry, & Esseveld, 1983; Campbell & Wasco, 2000; Ellis, 1991a; Fonow & Cook, 1991; Gergen, 1985, 1994; Krieger, 1991). In my exploration of emotionally engaged research, I consider how investigators can emotionally connect with their research participants and research findings, regardless of the specific topic of study.

I suspect that researchers' emotions have shaped a great deal of what we know about the social world and how we know it. In her book, *On Becoming a Social Scientist* (1979), Shulamit Reinharz advocates for the "integration of person, problem, and method" (p. 369). She writes, "All projects should generate knowledge within the three components engaged in a research project: person, problem, and method. In this scheme, self-knowledge (person) is a necessary and publicly relevant product of social research" (p. 370). My goal here is to continue the development of the "person" aspect of Reinharz's model, namely the potential role for researchers' emotions. That not all researchers would want to define their work as "emotionally engaged" does not trouble me at all. Nor is it my mission to convince others that such a perspective is "right." Instead, my goal is to speak to those who already feel some traces of emotion in their work and to validate those feelings by building them into the larger research process. By articulating the ways in which emotions can be a resource for research, I hope to strike a balance between thinking and feeling, whereby both can be valued ingredients of knowledge.

Creating Balance: An Ethic of Caring in Research

The conceptual foundation for this approach to research is built upon an ethic of caring.[1] Within philosophy, and feminist philosophy in particular, the exact meaning (or meanings) of "caring" is a hotly debated topic in contemporary moral theory (see Bowden, 1997; Brabeck & Ting, 2000; Cole & Coultrap-McQuin, 1992; McMillan, 1982; Meyeroff, 1971; Noddings, 1984; Ruddick, 1980; Tronto, 1989). Without transgressing into these specific debates, I want to highlight common themes that may be useful to social science research practice. In her book, *Caring: A Feminine Approach to Ethics and Moral Education* (1984), philosopher Nel Noddings offers this definition of "caring," which provides a starting place for analysis:

> Care is a state of mental suffering or of engrossment: to care is to be in a burdened mental state, one of anxiety, fear, or solicitude about something or someone. Alternatively, one cares for something or someone if one has a regard for or inclination toward that something or someone . . . to care may mean to be charged with the protection, welfare, or maintenance of something or someone. (p. 9)

> [Caring] is born of the fundamental recognition of relatedness; that which connects me naturally to the other, reconnects me through the other to care for myself. As I care for others and am cared for by them, I become able to care for myself. (p. 49)

Similarly, in her essay, "Women and Caring" (1989), feminist philosopher Joan Tronto emphasizes the relational commitment as a critical element in caring:

> Caring implies some kind of on-going responsibility and commitment. . . . When a person or group cares about something or someone, we presume that they are willing to work, to sacrifice, to spend money, to show emotional concern, and to expend energy toward the object of care. . . . Caring involves responding to the particular, concrete, physical, spiritual, intellectual, psychic, and emotional needs of others. (pp. 173, 174)

From this view, caring involves an emotional connection and concern for a person, persons, or issue. That concern can bring some uncomfortable feelings—worry, anxiety, fear. But such potential negative affect is part of a dynamic system, a relationship where that concern can be rewarded by the investment in the well-being of another. Caring is a relationship whereby the welfare of one can be shaped by another, and vice versa. In other words, this commitment and connectedness can be mutually beneficial and supportive. To care is to invest oneself in an outcome for another. Caring involves learning what others need and responding to those needs in ways consistent with that knowing.

In the context of research, this conceptualization of caring may seem, at first glance, strange and even inappropriate. It certainly challenges traditional norms for research and the researcher-as-dispassionate-outside-observer model. What I think is useful about Noddings's and Tronto's writings is not their literal interpretations so much as their tone of compassion and connection. I don't read this as a mandate that researchers must develop deep emotional, personal attachments to research participants. Such a constrained view would have limited utility for several reasons, not the least of which is that there are many models of research in which an investigator never has contact with those being researched. Rather, my interpretation is much broader and focuses on the emotional investment researchers can make to the issues that they study and to the welfare of those who participate or are otherwise touched by their studies. An ethic of caring allows researchers to express their passion, their concern, their personal investment in what they study and for the people who are affected by what they study. Researchers do not have to become activists, quite the contrary. Rather, this view gives researchers the freedom to express their concern about an issue and commitment to people by gathering useful information for scientific investigation.

Caring involves attuning to the well-being of those affected by the research, and allowing that concern to guide the many decisions researchers make over the course of the project. An ethic of caring prompts researchers to learn about the emotional needs of their research participants, and regardless of whether they have direct interactions with these individuals, to create a research environment that can respond to those needs. Caring means thinking through what people will get out of participating in the research process, what they would gain, and what effect it would have on their lives. Caring also involves investing in the welfare of other members of the research team and for one's self. Research built from a foundation of caring balances the requirements of science with a personal concern for the well-being of all those impacted by a project. This does not mean that researchers must assume the ridiculously expansive burden of responsibility for every single thing that could come from their work. Rather, an ethic of caring prompts researchers to think about the impact of their work in ways more broadly defined than what is traditionally specified in research codes of ethics and institutional review boards (IRBs) (Rosnow et al., 1993; Sieber, 2000; Smith, 2000; Trickett, 1998). An ethic of caring focuses attention on the vast needs of the research population and expresses a commitment to learn and respond to those needs in the research setting.

Before going any further in this exploration of caring and emotionally engaged research, it is critical to stop and examine the potential or implied "gendered" nature of this construct. It has become almost impossible in academic discourse to talk about the role of emotions, caring, and ways of connecting with others without getting into the issue of whether these are uniquely female, feminine, or feminist traits. In fact, a colleague once asked me if I thought it was ironic that (in this book) I was raising these issues of emotions in research, "you know, with you being female and all." Underlying my colleague's question was the assumption that things like emotions and feelings are women's issues, concerns, domains, territory, etc. In fact, some academics have indeed claimed that these "emotional things" are inherently and uniquely female. Emotions are central to the "different voice" (Gilligan, 1982) and "women's ways of knowing" (Belenky et al., 1986) notions that have become lightning rods for criticism throughout academia. As such, it gets tricky trying to talk about these topics without running the risk of misinterpretation. What is clear is that many of the early writers who discussed an ethic of caring did claim female or feminine essentialism as a defining feature of the construct (see Brabeck & Ting, 2000). For example, in elaborating on her concept of caring, Noddings wrote:

> An ethic built on caring is, I think, characteristically and essentially feminine—which is not to say, of course, that it cannot be shared by men, any more than we should care to say that traditional moral systems cannot be embraced by women. But an ethic of caring arises, I believe, out of

our experiences as women, just as the traditional logical approach to ethical problems arises more obviously from masculine experience. (p. 8)

Noddings is not alone in her positioning of women as fundamental keepers of emotionality. For her book, *Has Feminism Changed Science?* (1999), historian of science Londa Schiebinger conducted an extensive review of diverse literatures to find multiple examples of this ideology. She summarizes:

> More recently the focus on culturally specific "feminine" characteristics has prompted claims that women have distinct "ways of knowing"— including "caring" (Nel Noddings), "holism" (Hilary Rose), and "maternal thinking" (Sara Ruddick)—which purportedly have been excluded from the practices of the dominant forms of science. Carol Gilligan maintained that women speak "in a different voice" when making moral judgements, and that they value context and community over abstract principles. Mary Belenky and her colleagues, in the influential book *Women's Ways of Knowing*, suggested that women use connected knowledge, contextual thinking, and collaborative discourse rather than "separate" knowledge that privileges impersonal and abstract rules and standards. (pp. 4–5)

Whether implied or directly stated, notions that there is a uniquely female voice or way of knowing, defined in large part by things like feelings and emotions, have been strongly criticized. As Schiebinger argues, such essentialist positions:

> tend[ed] to romanticize those values traditionally considered feminine . . . the celebrated "feminine" or "women's ways of knowing" usually represents little more than the flip side of culturally dominant practices." (p. 5)

> Efforts to refashion science by adding traditional feminine traits can be appealing: they create immediately life-affirming projects, alluring visions of how things could be different . . . [but] . . . [e]asy stereotypes concerning women and "feminine" qualities can prove needlessly divisive." (p. 7)

I agree with Schiebinger's analysis that defining certain traits, states, or attributes as uniquely female can be unproductively divisive. Perhaps more importantly, the empirical research suggests that such essentialism is not founded anyway. Although sex differences do crop up, past and current research findings suggest there is often more similarity across the genders than differences between them (Maccoby & Jacklin, 1974; West & Zimmerman, 1991; Williams, 1987). Mary Brabeck's (1996) research on gender morality, in particular, does not support the "different voice" of women nearly to the extent postulated by Gilligan. Caring and emotionality are not inherently, necessarily gendered. Because these are issues central to many women hardly means that they define women.

Returning to the concept of caring as a central element of emotionally engaged research, I do not assert that caring is essentially female, feminine, or feminist. Although there are founded criticisms of Noddings, Gilligan, Ruddick, and others, I don't believe it is necessary to toss out the entire construct of caring. Whether caring is essentially female has become such a dominating topic of discussion that moving beyond that issue to consider the role of caring in both genders has been hampered. My goal here is to pick up the general idea of caring, regardless of gender, and see how this notion may play out in the context of research roles. In a setting of research, caring is about the investment of personal concern for an issue and those impacted by research. Such care cannot possibly be the domain of only one gender. Furthermore, although these issues may be of particular interest to feminist researchers, an ethic of caring is not a uniquely defining feature of feminism in the academy. Feminist ideology may shape how a researcher expresses such caring, but that there would even be an expression of concern throughout the research process is what defines an ethic of caring. In the research relationship, the broader notions of relational care found in Noddings's and Tronto's work can stimulate interesting ideas for how researchers interact with their participants, how we attune to what becomes of our research, and how we connect with ourselves and other researchers.

Caring for the Research Participants

An emotionally engaged approach to social science is guided by an underlying ethic of caring, but how is that caring and concern manifested? One mechanism is building an emotional connection between the researcher and the research participants. This does not have to be limited to the specific instances where researchers and participants have face-to-face interactions (e.g., interviews, observations). In other words, an emotionally connected relationship can be established in a variety of ways, across diverse methods. The nature of the relationship between the researcher and those researched has been a central focus in the feminist methodology literature, which provides grounding for this exploration. The issues raised here are not particular to feminist research, as numerous books and articles have been written about how researchers should interact with their participants (e.g., Becker & Geer, 1957; Benney & Hughes, 1970; Dexter, 1956; Kahn & Cannell, 1957; Rosenthal, 1966; Rosenthal & Rosnow, 1969; Rubin & Rubin, 1995; Weiss, 1994). Yet these more traditional sources rarely touch upon the potential emotional connections in the research process, and by contrast, feminist scholars have identified these issues as critical factors in conducting research (Campbell & Wasco, 2000; Edwards, 1993;

Fonow & Cook, 1991; Reinharz, 1992). In her 1996 paper for the *Annual Review of Sociology*, Majorie DeVault provided a succinct summary of the general aims of feminist research:

> Feminists seek a science that minimizes harm and control in the research process. In response to the observation that researchers have often exploited or harmed women participants, and that scientific knowledge has sustained systematic oppression of women, feminist methodologists have searched for practices that will minimize harm to women and limit negative consequences (Nebraska Feminist Collective 1983, 1988). (p. 31)

More specifically, Shulamit Reinharz (1993) explains how this overarching mission of minimizing harm and limiting adverse effects has been interpreted and practiced in feminist scholarship:

> [T]he extent that part of the ideology of feminism is to transform the competitive and exploitative relations among women (and between women and men) into bonds of solidarity and mutuality, we expect mutual assistance and reciprocated understanding to be part of the researcher/subject relation. We assume that because relationships in general should be transformed, research relationships should be as well. (p. 73)

Transforming the research relationship has typically meant building a close, personal connection between a researcher and the participants, developed and maintained through face-to-face exchanges centered around data collection. Sociologist Ann Oakley wrote extensively on this issue in her classic paper, "Interviewing Women: A Contradiction in Terms" (1988). She argued that traditionally, a hierarchy has existed between the researcher and the researched: the researcher is the "all-knowing" expert, the participant is not; the researcher has access to all information about the study, its designs, and questions, the participant does not. This hierarchy does very little to facilitate trust, and in fact seriously undermines the building of an open relationship. Oakley summarized her concerns about the traditional interviewing model as such:

> Interviewers define the role of interviewees as subordinates; extracting information is more to be valued than yielding it; the convention of interviewer-interviewee hierarchy is a rationalization of inequality; what is good for interviewers is not necessarily good for interviewees. (p. 40)

In light of this critique, Oakley suggested creating nonhierarchical relationships between researchers and participants where both parties invest their personal identities by sharing experiences and information. Both the interviewer and interviewees are expected to ask and answer questions about the subjects at hand. Interviewing is no longer a one-way "interroga-tion" but a two-way dialogue. Interviewing could become a process where an emotional bond is formed between the researcher and the participant that transcends the specific context and setting of the study. In explaining her alternate approach to interviewing, Oakley wrote:

> [T]here were three principal reasons why I decided not to follow the text-book code of ethics with regard to interviewing women. First, I did not regard it as reasonable to adopt a purely exploitative attitude to intervie-wees as sources of data. My involvement in the women's movement in the early 1970s and the rebirth of feminism in an academic context has led me, along with many others, to re-assess society and sociology as mas-culine paradigms and to want to bring about change in the traditional cultural and academic treatment of women. . . .
>
> A second reason for departing from conventional interviewing ethics was that I regarded sociological research as an essential way of giving the sub-jective situation of women greater visibility not only in sociology, but, more importantly, in society, than it has traditionally had. Interviewing women was, then, a strategy for documenting women's own accounts of their lives. . . . Note that the formulation of the interviewer role has changed dramatically from being a data-collecting instrument for researchers to being a data-collecting instrument for those whose lives are being researched.
>
> A third reason . . . I had found, in my previous interviewing experiences, that an attitude of refusing to answer questions or offer any kind of per-sonal feedback was not helpful in terms of the traditional goal of pro-moting "rapport." A different role, that could be termed "no intimacy without reciprocity," seemed especially important in longitudinal in-depth interviewing. (pp. 48–49)

The end result of this approach to research, according to Oakley, is high-quality data that has been generated in an open and trusting environment. The researcher can "believe" the data because she/he has earned the legiti-mate trust of the research participants by demonstrating kindness, caring, and personal investment in the work. These conversations generate not only data but also an emotional connection that brings interviewers and interviewees closer together. In fact, Oakley mentioned how she has main-tained long-term relationships with some of the women who have partici-pated in her studies.

This model of emotional connection has become something of an implied standard for the "ideal" relationship between the researcher and the researched in feminist social science. Although Oakley never stated so directly, it can certainly be inferred from her essay that feminist scholars are "supposed" to become personally invested in their work and in the lives of their research participants. However, in more recent writings in the feminist methods literature, this implicit criterion for creating research relationships has drawn some criticism. For example, Shulamit Reinharz (1993) expresses concern that the kind of emotional connection Oakley described is unrealistic. In her address to the American Sociological Association, Reinharz (1993) relayed an interaction she had with a doctoral student who was reluctant to publish her completed dissertation because she (the student) believed that she had violated the principles of feminist research because she had not formed research relationships like those described by Oakley. Reinharz described:

> I have found that the "attempt to develop special relations" can slip into an "excessive demand." . . . This conversation [with the doctoral student] made me wonder if there were other feminist researchers burdened with excessive demands, exaggerated notions of bonding between researcher and subjects, and unrealistic expectations. (p. 72)

> It seems dangerous to require rapport in all feminist research, even all feminist interview research. Any creation of absolute standards seems to me to be fraught with epistemological and even ethical contradictions. . . . I believe that we can develop nonexploitative relations with the people involved in our research projects, without attempting to "achieve rapport" or intimacy with them. Relations of respect, shared information, openness and clarity of communication seem like reasonable substitute goals. (p. 74)

Reinharz argues that developing and maintaining close, personal, emotional rapport between a researcher and participant is not only an extremely difficult "extra" requirement to try to fulfill, but is also not always necessary or even desirable. Instead, something less hierarchical than "standard" methods may be more suitable and practical.

With regard to the relationship between the researcher and the researched, a dominant focus has been on the specific method of interviewing and what's "supposed" to happen in that setting. Reinharz's (1993) essay starts to nudge the field away from these prescriptive notions. Continuing in that vein, my view is that feminist scholarship has raised important issues regarding the nature of relationships in the research process; I concur with Reinharz's critiques regarding practicality, but my larger concern is that the idea of "emotional connection" has been too narrowly construed, focusing too heavily on the specific face-to-face personal attachments that can be formed in a research interview. Instead, I define "emotional connection" as the more general idea that a research setting is attuning to and respectful of participants' emotional needs. To me, "emotionally connected" means making decisions throughout the entire research process that acknowledge and respond to the affective needs of the research population. This broader conceptualization does not locate the point of data collection as the be-all-end-all critical juncture for establishing emotional connections, nor does it focus exclusively on the specific method of interviewing. An emotional relationship between an investigator and the participants can begin forming long before the specific juncture of data collection. The research environment—whatever it may be, a survey, an interview, an observation—can be created to be in tune with the emotional needs of the participants. The connection is not necessarily between an individual researcher and how he/she interpersonally engages with a particular participant. Such an individual level of analysis is problematic for several reasons, not the least of which is that it is entirely possible a researcher may not genuinely feel a positive emotional connection with a specific participant. Rather, I am defining the connection at a different level of analysis. The general research process has instead been designed to reflect an awareness of and response to feelings, concerns, and issues of importance to the participants. This shift in focus may also make it more feasible to address the critical issues raised by feminist scholars regarding research relationships without creating unduly restrictive "extra" demands.

To explore this broader interpretation of the emotional connection between researchers and participants, it may be helpful to examine these issues at two specific phases of the research process: project planning and data collection. First, before a study even begins, investigators can be building connections by making decisions from an emotionally engaged point of view. How? Through direct contact and communication with members of target populations, the researcher can begin to learn about their emotional needs. Volunteer work, community service, or other ways of stepping outside of the academic world and meeting potential participants can go a long way in developing a researcher's understanding of the feelings and concerns of their participants. What do these "potential participants" say? What are their concerns? What are their worries? I realize this verges on circular reasoning—well, wouldn't one need to do research to find out what those needs and concerns are? Not necessarily. At the risk of overgeneralizing, much of what I have learned about the emotional needs of rape survivors has come from my volunteer work at rape crisis centers. I have heard similar testimonials from colleagues who study other social issues—homelessness, HIV/AIDS, gang violence, school dropouts, disability services, etc. What I am suggesting here is that these non-research, real-world experiences can be immensely helpful in providing initial information about a potential research population. Similarly, talking with community service providers or other groups that have direct contact with a target population could also shed some light on these issues. From this emotional reconnaissance work, subsequent decisions regarding sampling, methods, analysis, and interpretation can be guided by an awareness of and commitment to making the research environment emotionally supportive and respectful.

Another source of background information regarding the emotional needs of research population is the academic literature. By necessity, researchers familiarize themselves with the literature prior to initiating new work. But rather than just summarizing, integrating, and critiquing existing findings, we can look for clues as to what may be the emotional needs of a population. *How* we read existing works and *what* we learn from them can be another perspective on understanding potential research populations. We can take what is already known and make new decisions guided by that information. For example, in my own area of research, to decide which sampling strategy may be more or less helpful in our particular project, my research team and I reviewed what has already been learned about rape survivors over the past 30 years of research. A variety of techniques have been successful in identifying samples of rape survivors, so what did we learn about victims in those studies, and what do those findings suggest for how we sample in the future? For example, if we now know that the psychological trauma of rape is at its peak distress one to three months postassault (see Koss, et al., 1994), what does that suggest for how and when we sample rape survivors in future research projects? Given that prior work suggests the emotional needs of this population are quite extensive in this time frame, what can be done to address those needs if one is planning research with recently victimized survivors? In this example, the literature findings clearly indicate that rape victims experience high levels of psychological distress for up to three months postassault. This is not only a substantiated research finding, it is also a clue as to how we can frame studies in ways that are emotionally sensitive. Some researchers may choose not to sample recent victims as a means of not adding to their distress. Others may choose to provide extensive community service referrals for these survivors. We can let prior findings in the literature shape not only what we will study in the future but also how we will go about studying those topics.

In gathering this background information about the potential emotional needs of a research population, it is important to recognize that there probably isn't one clear set of needs that are shared by all members of a target population. Individual differences are always present within a relatively homogenous group, and it may not even be the case that the potential research population even approximates a homogenous group. Diversity— be it racial/ethnic, gender, social class, age, sexual orientation, ability/ disability—shapes how individuals view and experience their social world, and as such, it is reasonable to assume that the emotional needs of one group may be quite different from another. By raising these issues, I am not suggesting that researchers address just the clearly identifiable concerns that are present for the majority. Rather, in this background work of getting to know a target population, we can be looking for general concerns that crop up across individuals of various backgrounds and be alert for the specific concerns of particular subgroups within a population.

Developing a diverse awareness of the emotional needs of a research population—through community service, the academic literature, or other means—is a beginning step toward creating these emotional connections. However, this awareness must be carried through to action by creating research environments that respond to the emotional needs of a research population. The data collection phase can be shaped and informed by prior emotional reconnaissance work. This process is not limited to methodologies where there is face-to-face interaction between the researcher and the participants. Rather, by construing of the variety of ways in which researchers collect data as "research environments," we can think more inclusively about how investigators set up and carry out their communications with their participants—be it in writing, such as in surveys, or orally and/or nonverbally, as in interviews or observations. Regardless of the specific tools of data collection—surveys, interviews, observations—the manner in which the investigator "interacts" with the participants reflects an awareness of and attempt to respond to their emotional needs. It is important to note that attuning to the affective needs of research participants does not require that researchers compromise their intellectual curiosity or sacrifice methodological rigor for the emotional good of the participants. At issue here is forming an emotional connection with participants by *how* researchers go about their craft. As sociologist Diana Russell (1982) summarizes her research on marital rape: "In designing my study . . . it was my intention to combine the most rigorous, scientifically sound methodology with a deep knowledge of and sensitivity to the issues of rape" (p. 28).[2] An emotional connection between researchers and the participants can be reflected in the overall process of conducting a study without endangering intellectual or methodological rigor.

To illustrate these points regarding the "hows" of data collection, it may be useful to examine an instance where researchers reflected their awareness of the emotional needs of a research population in different ways across different methods. In creating the Women and Violence Project, an interview study with rape survivors, my research team and I drew upon our prior experiences with victims. Several of us had noted in our volunteer work that survivors often become visibly upset when asked if and how they fought back or attempted to resist the rapist. It's a common question posed by police, prosecutors, doctors, and nurses. In the past, resistance was a necessary legal requirement, but that is no longer the case in most jurisdictions (Berger, Searles, & Neuman, 1988; Fischer, 1989). Asking about resistance can be useful in identifying a suspect (e.g., are the police looking for someone with scratch marks, cuts, bruises) and revealing what medical evidence may be present (e.g., skin samples underneath the victim's fingernails). However, our volunteer experiences suggested that victims may not understand or appreciate these reasons. When I have talked to survivors about this issue as a volunteer advocate, what I hear is that the question often hurts because it feels blaming—like she was supposed to fight back, or she was clearly not good at it, or she got what she deserved because she didn't. Again, not all survivors react this way; my point here is that my volunteer experiences suggested that this was an emotional concern for many survivors.

How to respond to that need in the research setting can take different forms and can vary depending on the methodology of a project. In the Women and Violence Project, my research team and I decided not even to ask about rape resistance in our interviews. We were certainly aware of the possibility that questions about resistance may be upsetting when posed by a police officer or doctor but may not be troublesome when asked by a researcher. On the other hand, we were also aware that it may be the questions themselves that are upsetting, regardless of who is asking them. But in the context of our work, such distinctions didn't really seem to be the point. Upon further reflection, we realized the topic of rape resistance really wasn't a central substantive concern for our project. The participants' answers to those questions—if asked—didn't figure into anything else we were exploring in this project. Therefore we chose to not ask about it. In other words, we were making a decision about the content of an interview based on our collective understandings of the emotional needs of our target population. In balancing our interests as researchers with the emotional well-being of the participants, we decided not to ask about potentially upsetting topics that were not substantively necessary. There were plenty of other places in the interview where we would be asking about upsetting information; therefore we wanted to minimize the potential distress by cutting out all things unnecessary to our central themes.

By contrast, psychologist Sarah Ullman has done a series of studies specifically on the topic of rape resistance and has done so in ways that reflect an emotional awareness of the potential sensitivity surrounding these issues. In some work, she analyzed existing police records where the subject of resistance had already been raised by law enforcement personnel (Ullman, 1998; Ullman & Knight, 1992, 1993, 1995). Therefore she was able to learn something about rape resistance without having to ask about it herself. In other studies, Ullman did directly inquire about resistance in self-report written surveys (Ullman, 1996a, b, c). However, she contextualized these questions through careful attention to what she wrote in the introduction to the survey and how she asked the specific questions in the survey itself. By letting women know why she was asking these questions— that the purpose of the survey was to learn about what happens in an actual rape or attempted rape and what that means for victims later on in life—Ullman could still ask about an emotionally upsetting topic, but could do so in an emotionally connected way. Responding to the emotional needs of a research population can take place in a variety of methods and does not mean avoiding sensitive issues. Rather, emotional connection is about reflecting an awareness of those concerns and direct proactive attempts to respond to them.

This example illustrates how emotional awareness can play out in two different research projects of different methodologies. Specifically, our concerns about how rape survivors might view questions regarding rape resistance strategies influenced what was asked, and if asked, how asked. Yet this issue of "how asked" is quite complex and requires further analysis. How can researchers interact with, communicate with, and relate to their research participants during data collection in ways that reflect an understanding of their emotional needs? Unfortunately, this issue has gone largely unexplored in survey research, but as noted previously, it has been a hot topic in interviewing. Sociologist Diane Vaughan (1986) notes that there is an implied relationship in research: "An invitation to be interviewed was an invitation to make secrets public to a stranger. The interview itself promised a relationship—one made intimate by the revelation of private thoughts and acts" (p. 197). If the Oakley model of close, personal, emotional connections between researchers and participants characterized by mutual disclosure, sharing, and building a relationship that can transcend the research environment is too restrictive or unrealistic, then what are some other options? Evaluation researcher Michael Quinn Patton provides a useful compromise in his book, *Qualitative Evaluation and Research Methods* (1990). He argues that in the process of gathering data, researchers should reflect "empathic neutrality":

> Upon first encountering the phrase "empathic neutrality," it may appear to be an oxymoron, combining contradictory ideas. Empathy, however, is a stance toward the people one encounters, while neutrality is a stance toward the findings. Neutrality can actually facilitate rapport and help build a relationship that supports empathy by disciplining the researcher to be nonjudgmental and open. Empathy communicates interest in and caring about people, while neutrality means being nonjudgmental about what people say and do during data collection. (p. 58)

Patton describes a "how" approach to research based on listening with concern and compassion but without judgment or evaluation. There is no expectation for a longer-term relationship; in the here and now of data collection, the researcher can reflect real, genuine interest and support for what someone has to say. Although Patton does not specifically address the issues of hierarchy within the research environment, it seems generally consistent with his approach that a researcher might answer a few questions posed by a participant or provide them with additional information. The focus would remain on the interviewee, not the interviewer, but the dialogue could reflect a more balanced, empathic exchange. The extent to which such discussions would verge on Patton's "neutrality" concept probably varies somewhat depending on the substantive focus of the research. For instance, sociologist Raquel Kennedy Bergen's (1993, 1996) work interviewing survivors of marital rape provides an excellent example of blending Patton's notions of empathic listening with some of the broader themes in the feminist methods literature:

> From the beginning of each interview, I tried to establish an interpersonal relationship rather than act in "an indifferent, disinterested, alienated [way] towards the 'research objects' as positivism requires" (Mies, 1983, p. 122). I immediately explained my counseling experience and my interest in marital rape. This seemed to place most of the women at ease because they realized that I was genuinely interested in helping marital rape survivors, not just using their experiences for exploitive purposes. To further identify with me, most of the women felt understandably inclined to ask me personal questions. I was commonly asked if I was married, whether I had been a victim of rape, and my personal reasons for doing the study. I tried to answer all of their questions and freely discussed my opinions about violence against women. Rather than biasing their responses, as many social scientists feel that sharing personal information does, I think this exchange of information was essential in establishing a relationship based on trust and mutual interaction. (pp. 207–208)

Bergen's work reflects her understanding of the emotional needs of this research population. Her prior volunteer work and the academic literature suggested that victims of rape, and particularly marital rape survivors, experience a great deal of distrust of others, which must be addressed prior to disclosure. By answering her participants' questions, Bergen was responding to those emotional needs and reflecting empathy for their difficult task of talking about sexual violence. In many respects, it seems perfectly reasonable that a participant in Bergen's study might want to know a bit more about the researcher prior to disclosing such personally painful and violating information. Bergen's point that some degree of mutual disclosure was necessary to move forward with the interview represents a pragmatic reinterpretation of Oakely's basic concepts. It is important to emphasize that building an emotional connection during data collection is predicated upon developing an understanding of the emotional needs of the participants in prior stages of the research. How researchers collect data can reflect their continued interest and commitment to the emotional well-being of their participants.

Caring for What Becomes of the Research

Emotionally engaged research focuses not only on how researchers build connections with their participants but also on what these people take away from their involvement in research projects. What did participating mean to them? What was the impact on them? What became of the research in their minds and lives? An ethic of caring in research prompts investigators to look at their projects from another point of view, that of the participants. Regardless of whether the research is specifically designed as an intervention project, the very act of participating in research is something of an intervention in its own right. What is normal and commonplace to researchers—the idea and inclination to tap into what people are thinking, feeling, or experiencing through structured activities—may very well be an unusual event to those participating. Over the course of my research, I have met countless women for whom "participating in research" was an important activity, something you might take a day off work for, something you'd dress carefully for, something that's a defining event. So what did this mean to them and what impact did it have on their lives? I am not suggesting that researchers are fully responsible for what becomes of a research study in the minds and lives of our participants. We cannot control how people view us or feel about us. Nevertheless, I believe it is important to consider what it might feel like to participate and ask what may be gained through involvement. Because we cannot control exactly what someone might experience in a research project does not mean that we cannot be mindful of what could happen and make efforts to generate positive outcomes.

The impact of participation, from the point of view of institutional ethical review boards, should be minimal—no harm, or very, very minimal harm; no guarantee of benefits for participation—and this has become the defining standard for social research (Rosnow, et al., 1993; Sales & Folkman, 2000). No promised benefits, though, is quite different from benefits that emerge anyway. Paying attention to the potential emotional needs of a research population and responding to them in data collection can create a setting in which participants will experience beneficial effects. Nursing scholars Sally Hutchinson, Margaret Wilson, and Holly Skodol Wilson (1994) argue that participating in qualitative interviews (in particular) can provide a helpful setting for participants to reflect upon and make meaning of their lives. The process of sharing these stories with an interested, engaged, and empathic researcher can be incredibly validating and beneficial. Hutchinson, Wilson, and Wilson analyzed the spontaneous, unsolicited comments research participants in their studies have made about what it meant to them to be involved in the study; this synthesis revealed seven potential benefits of participating in research interviews.

First, research can provide participants with a supportive setting for catharsis, which the researchers define as:

expressing personal feelings, thoughts, and problems. . . . When interviewed about sensitive and painful topics, participants have expressed feelings of relief that seem to come in part from having an engaged, accepting listener. . . . Certain situations such as teenage abortion, incest, and drug abuse engender secrets. Secrets are powerful and often shameful. Talking with a good listener defuses the power of the secret, thus providing some emotional relief. (p. 162)

Second, interviews can provide a medium for self-acknowledgment: "Interviews that provide opportunities to describe events validate these experiences, and as a result, the person's self-worth. The act of interviewing, with the rhythms of speaking, listening, and responding, promotes a connection between interviewer and participant. The interview gives the participant a voice" (p. 162). Third, participants may feel a sense of purpose: "participants describe feeling good about sharing information with researchers that may in turn be shared with other professionals or lay people through publications and presentations" (p. 163). The possibility that the information they are providing through their participation will do some good for someone else can be a rewarding experience. Fourth, interviews can develop interviewees' self-awareness: "participants describe gaining a new perspective about their situations. They contend that hearing themselves talk about something is different from thinking about it" (p. 163). Fifth: "telling one's story and really feeling heard can be empowering for participants" (p. 163). Sixth, the careful reflection and discussion of the experiences in one's life can be emotionally therapeutic: "interviews appear to be healing to many" (p. 163). Finally, participating in research can provide a voice for the disenfranchised: "in-depth research interviews can give a voice to the voiceless because researchers sometimes investigate questions that involve the dying, incest victims, and others who have never been allowed to tell their story" (p. 164).

Unfortunately, the benefits of participating in research have gone largely unexplored in survey research or other methodologies, making it difficult to evaluate if and how the positive outcomes Hutchinson, Wilson, and Wilson describe in interview studies may generalize to other forms of research. In a notable exception, Edward Walker, Elana Newman, Mary Koss, and David Bernstein (1997) examined these issues from a slightly different perspective by investigating whether participating in survey research was harmful or hurtful to women with histories of childhood and/or adult sexual victimization. In the context of a larger survey project that itself reflected an extensive awareness of the emotional needs of rape survivors, participants rated the degree to which completing such surveys was distressing. Although some reported it was upsetting to participate (namely those with higher symptomatic distress and trauma exposure), the majority indicated that it was not emotionally difficult to answer survey questions on these issues. Taken together with the Hutchinson, Wilson, and Wilson findings, this study suggests that when researching emotionally difficult topics, providing a supportive environment for recounting the experiences of one's life—either face-to-face in an interview or in the anonymous protection of a written survey—is typically not harmful and could even be emotionally rewarding and helpful.

What becomes of a research project not only includes how it is processed and interpreted by the participants, but also entails the choices researchers make regarding the dissemination of their findings—what is shared, what is released, and how such information is framed and contextualized. An ethic of caring prompts researchers to consider what may become of their work before it is released, making decisions about dissemination that balance the well-being of the research population with the interests of the investigator and the larger scientific community. The possibility of not reporting findings, reporting only some findings, or very carefully crafting particular findings for release may be an anathema to many researchers. Yet, such options, however unseemly, are the very kinds of hard choices investigators may need to consider. Within the field of community psychology, these final responsibilities of the researcher are a key focus. In their chapter in the *Handbook of Community Psychology* (2000) on ethics, David Snow, Katherine Grady, and Michele Goyette-Ewing write:

> Community psychologists may refuse to give feedback on their findings. At first glance, it would seem that such uses of research are likely to be considered unethical. Yet, in practice, situations are not always clear-cut; there may be ethically defensible reasons for any of these acts. For example, some community psychologists may refuse to divulge findings because of concerns over the uses to which the information may be put, particularly if they perceive the findings to be potentially harmful to themselves or the individuals involved. Other psychologists may believe that divulging all findings is the greater good, no matter what the immediate repercussions. A dilemma exists between choosing to reveal potentially damaging results and contributing to a long-standing knowledge base. (p. 912)

> We assume there is an obligation on the part of the community psychologist to make adequate use of sound theory and existing knowledge in designing community interventions and research studies. . . . This raises the need to attend to how work can be conducted and reported so as to provide new and useful evidence, while paying proper attention to minimizing potential risks to participants. (p. 914)

Snow, Grady, and Goyette-Ewing, as well as other community psychologists, are not advocating for the censorship of research findings. Rather, they suggest that researchers carefully reflect upon what they release to the academic community and other dissemination outlets in deference to the possibility that some results could harm or be used to harm the research participants or the population from which they were drawn. In the context of research on social issues, the notion that a complete release of all information is always the right thing to do because it is in the best interest of science is too simplistic. Drawing upon an ecological analogy, psychologist James Kelly (1968, 1970, 1986, 1988) argues that the research setting is a dynamic system—changes in one part can affect outcomes in another. As a result, there are often unanticipated consequences of social research—both positive and negative. The positive ones are typically viewed as fortuitous bonuses; the negative ones are reinterpreted as essentially blameless by-products of science. Therefore it is not realistic to believe that researchers simply release their findings into the value-free vacuum of science, where there are examined, handled, and picked over without any implication. As other audiences work through the results of a study, there is always the possibility that, irrespective of a researcher's intentions, the outcomes for the participants and other members of their social groups could be hurtful.

Snow's, Grady's, and Goyette-Ewing's and Kelly's writings suggest that researchers may choose to limit or otherwise select what they release from their research project. Whereas there is always some editing (for it is impossible to publish or otherwise disseminate all findings), rather than letting the process of selection be guided by the practical concerns and needs of the researcher, instead let the process be guided by the researchers' concerns for the emotional well-being of the participants. The shelved results do not need to remain shelved forever; follow-up work may help illuminate the original findings, placing them in a different context that would minimize the risk of harm. Again, mindful of Reinharz's (1993) concerns regarding "excessive demands," my sense is that many researchers may already be making these behind-the-scenes decisions with an eye, or rather, a heart, toward the well-being of their research populations. By more clearly and openly articulating the processes underlying research, we can develop a more complete picture of how knowledge is socially constructed.

Caring for Oneself and the Research Team

Throughout this book, I have emphasized what I see as the benefits of bringing emotion into the research process. Whenever I get too rosy a glow about this, I make myself remember—honestly—what our work really felt like on a regular day-to-day basis. As I examined in chapter Three ("Feeling: The Emotions of Researching Rape"), it often didn't feel great. The intellectual benefits were by no means immediate, nor did they provide the same satisfaction to all members of our research team. It was costly—emotionally expensive—to engage in this work. Consequently, mitigating these effects becomes an integral part of an emotionally engaged approach to social research. In other words, an ethic of caring involves how a researcher relates with her/his research team, as well as how one cares for one's own well-being. In this final section, I examine self-care strategies and organizational supports for research teams involved in emotionally difficult work. My approach to these issues has been greatly shaped by my volunteer experiences in rape crisis centers, which have been training staff and volunteers to work with survivors of violence for over 30 years.[3] In addition, I have found the academic literature on compassion fatigue/vicarious traumatization to be immensely helpful in planning preventive strategies. Psychologists Karen Saakvitne's and Laurie Pearlman's practical guide for trauma work, *Transforming the Pain: A Workbook on Vicarious Traumatization* (1996), is an invaluable resource of assessment tools and activities for combating the ill-effects of regular exposure to the suffering of others. Although Saakvitne's and Pearlman's work developed from their specific focus on trauma therapy with survivors of sexual abuse, their strategies for comprehensive self-care and support are applicable not only to clinical practice but also to emotionally engaged research.

Saakvitne's and Pearlman's approach to addressing vicarious traumatization emphasizes three key factors, all of which are relevant for research teams doing work on emotionally difficult topics. First, the researcher/practitioner must develop his or her sense of awareness, which is: "[b]eing attuned to one's needs, limits, emotions, and resources. Heed all levels of awareness and sources of information, cognitive, intuitive, and somatic. Practice mindfulness and acceptance" (p. 76). Second, one must work toward balance: "[m]aintaining balance among activities, especially work, play, and rest. Inner balance allows attention to all aspects of oneself" (p. 76). Finally, awareness and balance can foster connection: "[c]onnections to oneself, to others, and to something larger. Communication is part of the connection and breaks the silence of unacknowledged pain. These connections offset isolation and increase validation and hope" (p. 76). These three components should be addressed within three fundamental domains of one's life: professional, organizational, and personal. Saakvitne's and Pearlman's clinical recommendations acknowledge what one may be experiencing in difficult work and encourage one to seek reprieve through involvement in other activities, which is sound advice for those researching emotionally difficult topics. Whether the work at hand is providing therapy or conducting research, the exposure to painful material can become burdensome without counterefforts. Activities that heighten awareness, provide structure for respite, and develop a psychological sense of community may be effective preventive strategies for research teams.

In applying these general principles to the research setting, projects where the primary investigator(s) is leading a team of other research assistants, employees, volunteers, etc. in emotionally charged work, training and supervision activities can incorporate both substantive instruction on the research tasks and ways of addressing the emotions of the research team. Careful selection of team members is a critical first step. Although some researchers choose not to involve undergraduate assistants in work of this kind, my experience suggests that academic status is not nearly as important as emotional maturity and self-awareness. The volunteer programs in rape crisis centers and domestic violence shelters heavily draw upon college populations, and consulting with local programs can provide useful training models for these groups. In addition, several research and intervention projects have successfully trained undergraduate students as interviewers, community advocates, and para-professionals (Davidson et al., 1990; Mitchell et al., 1985; Sullivan, 1991; Sullivan et al., 1992). In the selection process, it may be helpful to explore applicants' reasons for their interest in this work and assess the degree to which those factors may be compatible or incompatible with the broader philosophies of the research team. For instance, in trauma work, it is not uncommon that those who have experienced such violence may want to volunteer or otherwise become involved in these issues. Some rape crisis centers and domestic violence shelters have policies that do not allow survivors in their volunteer program, but it is more typical to discuss with survivor applicants where they are in their own healing process and to make case-by-case determinations as to whether the candidate may be ready for the work at hand (Campbell 1996, 1998b). In these initial screenings and interviews, it is also important that researchers share what they know regarding the possible risks—personally and professionally—of joining the research team. Providing information regarding the potential impact on one's self, one's personal relationships, and one's physical health can help applicants evaluate for themselves whether such work is appropriate for them. Example stories and narratives, such as those described in this book as well as in Saakvitne and Pearlman's workbook, can make these ideas less abstract. However, it can be difficult to convey fully what this kind of work can mean to those who have not experienced it. As Saakvitne and Pearlman noted regarding trauma therapy, "Having chosen these careers, we will never again be the same. Few of us entered into the field fully understanding this truth" (p. 17). Yet, it also important to acknowledge that not all people who are exposed to emotionally difficult material experience it as distressing. Thus, the researcher should note the variety of reactions research team members could encounter in their work on a project.

In addition to gauging the emotional maturity of prospective research assistants, I believe it is also important to attune to the diversity of the research team, especially in regards to race/ethnicity and social class. Researchers have noted the benefit of matching researchers and participants on demographic characteristics (e.g., Russell, 1982), but my experience suggests there are other benefits to embracing diversity as well. Over the course of this researching-the-researcher project, as well as in prior studies, I have observed that women of varying races/ethnicities draw upon different sets of coping strategies. As I will explore shortly, group discussion and support can buffer the ill-effects of this kind of work, and it may be helpful to have a variety of strategies shared among the group. In particular, the African-American, Latina, and Native American women with whom I have worked have shared stories of how their religious faith and extended families provide them with support in general and in the specific instance of doing emotionally difficult work. For others, this kind of disclosure may suggest new ideas for garnering support as well as developing a deeper understanding of one's coworkers. Similarly, I have observed that women of different social-class backgrounds have vastly different experiences of conducting community-based interviewing. What is a "scary" neighborhood to some does not register as problematic for others. These brief examples illustrate how such differences can provide a useful focal point for exploring the sociocultural contexts of stress.

Creating a sense of group identity, cohesion, and support can be an effective preventive strategy once a team is assembled and going about its work. In many rape crisis centers and domestic violence shelters, it is not uncommon to have mandatory staff/volunteer meetings (weekly, biweekly, sometimes monthly) both to discuss specific tasks of the day-to-day operations but also to share and vent emotional experiences. Nursing researcher Mary Pickett and her team similarly note the utility of group "debriefing" to prevent compassion fatigue in research teams (Pickett, et al., 1994; see also Munroe, et al., 1995). Based on Jeffrey Mitchell's and George Everly's (1995) model, the Critical Incident Stress Debriefing (CISD) process, Pickett and colleagues. suggest five domains for group discussion: 1) ventilation of feelings; 2) assessment of stress response intensity; 3) discussion of stress response symptoms; 4) provision of support and information; and 5) referrals and resources for additional support and information. In such meetings, it is important that team leaders also disclose some of their own personal concerns and worries to normalize such reactions and create a setting supportive of open reflection and dialogue. It is not necessary nor even appropriate for the group leaders, or any other member of the team for that matter, to reveal everything that is on their minds. Sometimes, being in a supportive group while nurturing private feelings can provide solace. Saakvitne's and Pearlman's workbook provides numerous group activities to stimulate discussion and reflection around the five components in the CISD model.

In addition to regular discussion regarding the nature of the research project itself, it may also be helpful to engage in group activities unrelated to the substantive focus at hand; (e.g., attending movies, book readings, shopping, craft activities, cooking classes, and so on can provide a mental and emotional break from the research work). For example, one of the research teams I worked on in graduate school had a project lending library—we brought in some of our favorite popular, fiction novels to share with others on the team. On another, we kept a running list of books and movies that contained images, characters, and story lines that make reference to violence against women so we would know what to avoid if we wanted to escape from the topic or what to see if we wanted to take a look at popular press renderings of the issue. I have also held arts-and-crafts parties and other get-togethers for members of my project teams. Such group activities do not need to be overly regular events, which could inadvertently put pressure on team members to attend when what may be most helpful is to have a break from being around the people who remind you of difficult work. But incorporating fun, humorous events into the research schedule can provide a useful emotional break for everyone. In addition, sharing ideas for personal private self-care—yoga, massage, favorite forms of exercise, involvement in religious groups/communities of faith—may suggest new ideas for team members.

In the specific research tasks of a project, scheduling breaks and alternating activities can provide helpful organizational support. For instance, when working with undergraduate research assistants, flexibility around midterms and finals can alleviate some of their stress and support their longer-term commitment to the project. Similar kinds of scheduling rotations can benefit other members of the team as well. As individuals become more self-aware regarding what they need for themselves to do the work at hand, it can pay off in the long run to individually tailor work plans and schedules. In the various interviewing projects I have done, I have found that some interviewers prefer to do several interviews in a row, followed by a longer break, whereas others prefer more of a day-on, day-off schedule. Such flexibility demonstrates at an organizational level the project's collective commitment to self-care and support. In the instances where I have limited time off or restricted schedules due to deadlines and time pressures, I have always regretted it later on. Although team members pressed on with their activities, the additional time spent in individual and group support to mitigate this stress was no time savings at all. Variety in the kinds of research tasks may also provide the break needed from particularly difficult jobs. Switching off interviewing, for example, to do coding, xeroxing, library searching, community contacts, and so on can make training more extensive but may ultimately benefit the personal and professional development of the members of the research team.

Clearly defining the "end" of a project or individuals' participation in the project is a final supportive strategy researchers can offer their teams. To the primary investigator, the project may very well never have an ending point;

it's more of a continuous flow of ideas and studies connected in a larger program of research. Such ongoing fluidity may be quite normal for those in research careers, but may not be the case for the undergraduate or graduate students, volunteers, or other employees in a project. Therefore, setting specific schedules with completion dates can provide comforting clarity. In wrapping up a project, providing opportunities for emotional closure—a final release, reflection, integration of what has been learned and witnessed over time—are vital. In my work, I have done group writing projects and individual exit interviews which became part of the impetus and data sources for this book. Saakvinte and Pearlman described exercises which may serve as useful closing activities, such as the Toxic Waste Dump, in which group members "dump" specific experiences, images, and so on in writing, in pictures, or in silence into a center, collective pile to be symbolically thrown away,[4] and Reclaiming Life and Laughter, in which group members bring a symbol that represents health and well-being or collaborate in activities that represent the healthy sustaining and supporting of life.

For the primary researcher, providing these kinds of supports for a team can be personally rewarding as well, allowing the giving and receiving of support simultaneously. However, some investigators may not work within a team setting, and even for those that do, there are some stresses and supports that cannot be addressed within the research group. Self-care must be something that the primary researcher not only preaches but practices as well. All of the specific strategies described above for research teams apply equally to the primary investigator. In team settings, this is particularly important to combat the additional stress of looking out for the welfare of the other members of the group. For those who do not work in such settings, self-care is critical to alleviate the social isolation of the work. A supportive personal life—partners, husbands, wives, friends—can buffer many ill effects, but it is important not to overburden these supports with the emotional ventilation that is often necessary in this kind of work. Saakvitne and Pearlman emphasize that outside professional assistance, such as therapy, counseling, support groups, or vicarious traumatization workshops, can be invaluable support to practitioners, and by extension, researchers who work on emotionally difficult topics.

In addition to these personal self-care strategies for the primary researchers, several forms of organizational support can be instrumental for addressing the stresses that cannot be absorbed by a research team, no matter how close and committed, or by friends and family. Doing emotionally engaged research on emotionally difficult topics can sometimes be at odds with the norms and expectations of academic research settings. Many of the suggestions presented in this chapter for building emotional connections between researchers and participants and for the training and support of research teams can be labor-intensive. The time-lines for project completion can be quite long and are typically longer than many laboratory-based studies. Furthermore, there can be considerable emotional downtime, where one needs to place some distance between one's self and the material collected in the project. For instance, the combination of the highly detailed nature of transcription work or narrative coding and the emotional baggage of the content of that transcription can thwart speedy data analysis. In many universities, colleges, and research institutes, there is often considerable pressure to analyze and release findings quickly to keep the research literature current. Furthermore, job promotions and reviews are typically based, in part, on the amount of work produced. Logging multiple years on a single project could be self-defeating in some work settings. Making special concessions in job requirements for "those kinds" of researchers and their projects is hardly necessary nor even really needed. Organizational flexibility regarding other job tasks, such as teaching, service, and grant administration responsibilities, may provide useful support to mitigate these time crunches.

These time-line challenges are in many respects one manifestation of a more global issue regarding organizational support for emotionally engaged research: developing a climate that reflects understanding of and appreciation for this kind of work. Perhaps one of the most helpful things is also one of the hardest to achieve: an awareness by one's professional colleagues of the emotional impact of this kind of work. I recall the incredible frustration I felt when one of my colleagues once told me that he had never really thought about what it meant, really, that I was studying rape. Wow, does that mean you actually talk to rape victims? Isn't that depressing? While I was, and still am, aware of the fact that many people study the topic of sexual assault, and do so in many ways, and that some do not talk with victims or experience depression from their work, I was struck by the ignorance of my colleague's question. I mean "ignorance" in the true sense of the word— unaware, not knowing. From his worldview, within his kind of research, such possibilities were outside the realm of possibility. That's not what research is, to him. Days later, apparently because he was still curious about what I do, he asked to read something I was working on. At the time "what I was working on" was the preface of this book. It was a much rougher draft, devoid of many of the details in the survivor's story (as I was still discussing with her what would/would not be okay to reveal), so I passed it along. Two days later, he came back to my office and said, "I had no idea."

As mentioned throughout this book, one of my goals in this researching-the-researcher project was to make "I had no idea" a less-common response. My aim has been to raise awareness about how it can be for some researchers. Developing a broader awareness of what this kind of work may entail requires open conversations between those who "don't," those who "do," and those in between. When I have had these discussions, I have valued the supportive curiosity of my colleagues. In particular, senior colleagues can play a major role in supporting this kind of work through sharing their own experiences and offering their encouragement and commitment to educating others regarding the emotional investment that can be required for some research approaches. That they are "senior" usually affords an unusually attentive audience. Developing supportive colleagues, both within one's home institution as well as in the larger research community, at all ranks and levels of social power, requires ongoing dialogue. Organizing discussions at conferences, workshops, on online chat groups and listservs, and in the academic professional literature can provide a structure for education and support.

Closing Thoughts on Creating Balance

The emotions of researching emotionally difficult topics are often overlooked in academic discourse. Yet, the emotionally engaged researcher bears witness to the pain, suffering, humiliation, and indignity of others over and over again. Traditional models of social science have strongly emphasized the *thinking* aspects of inquiry, shunning the *feeling* components in fear of biasing the research. I think it's fair to ask whether these traditional notions were developed with any kind of awareness of the emotionality inherent in social issues research. Throughout this book, I have argued that emotions are not to be avoided or excised from academic writing; they are an integral part of research, worthy of reflection because they can bring greater intellectual clarity to the phenomenon of interest. Emotions are an important resource, not necessarily a source of bias. It seems unnecessary to restrict or devalue some forms of information available to researchers. Attuning to emotionality in research provides no guarantee of new insight or better-quality data, but I do wonder what more we could learn about the social world if we stepped outside our heads from time to time.

The Development, Process, and Methodology of the Researching-the-Researcher Study

One of the key difficulties in writing this book was sorting the main story plot from the subplots. I wrote a couple of different versions of this book, each with different information in the foreground and background. I ultimately decided to place the material on the development and methodology of this project in an appendix, not because it was of secondary importance but because it deserved its own separate place. The story behind the story seemed useful to tell because it illuminates the challenges of researching researchers' emotions. This story must be put in its own context, so in this appendix I first explore the events and experiences that led me to do this project. My previous community volunteer work and studies influenced how I approached the Women and Violence Project and consequently how I conducted this researching-the-researcher project. With that background, I then describe how this study of our emotions unfolded.

In this discussion, I highlight several of the conflicts that arose in this work. Issues of confidentiality are particularly critical when studying researchers' emotions, which can be made even more challenging by the power differentials that often exist within research teams. I wasn't just the person who was analyzing highly sensitive, emotional data; I had other roles and relationships with my "research participants"—employer, advisor, dissertation chair, master's chair, preliminary exam grader, letter of recommendation writer, and so on. Throughout the project I tried to create a setting of open exchange and dialogue, free from worry of retribution. Nevertheless, I am fully aware that I can say that and do what I think helps create that, but whether others believe and trust that is an entirely different thing. The extent to which people could and would challenge my decisions and interpretations regarding this project must be evaluated in

light of this context. Moreover, when I didn't communicate clearly with
the research team, what were mistakes of omission from my perspective
may have been interpreted as mistakes of commission in view of these
power differences. The normal challenges of analyzing qualitative data and
locating the voice of the researcher within those data were made even more
difficult by the nature of the material analyzed in this project.

Finally, I describe the methodology used for analyzing these data. I was
trained as a quantitative psychologist, but over the past five years, I have
been integrating qualitative methodologies into my work. In addition, my
collaborations on other research projects with "purely" qualitative scholars
(sociologists) has been enhanced by familiarity and practice with narrative
data. Therefore, in this researching-the-researcher project, working with
textual data was not novel to me, but that the data themselves were from
myself and members of our research team undoubtedly complicated matters. I used open coding and axial coding (see Strauss & Corbin, 1990) to
analyze the data; however, some of the most highly detailed coding could
not be presented in this book because it might have jeopardized confidentiality. As a result, the final analysis and findings reported in this book
reflect more general themes that emerged in the data. It is not the case that
I reported only points of agreement and similarity; differences in opinions
and experiences are indeed reflected and explained. My goal was to balance
the rigor of the method with respecting the privacy of our research team.

The Development of a Research Ethic

This study was not my first in-depth experience with rape. I have been a
volunteer rape victim advocate for nearly ten years, beginning as a sopho-
more in college, through graduate school, and continuing into my current
position as faculty. Throughout these years, I have worked with approximately 200 rape survivors in varied capacities: as a crisis intervention counselor, medical advocate, legal advocate, and counselor. Of these jobs, I
prefer medical advocacy and have logged most of my volunteer hours in
hospital emergency rooms. Seeking medical care can be a harrowing experiences for rape survivors: disrobing in front of the hospital staff, turning
over their clothes to police as evidence, enduring a lengthy pelvic exam (to
check for injuries and to obtain semen samples), and submitting to other
evidence collection (combing pubic hair, scraping under fingernails). In the
midst of this, nurses come and go taking blood (pregnancy, STD screening)
and bringing medications (morning-after pill, antibiotics). This medical
care is typically provided in a hospital ER, which, as a trauma-focused setting, can be quite frenetic. The job of the medical advocate is to explain
these medical procedures and help victims through them by restoring their
sense of control. If victims want the advocate to be present for the medical

exam, the advocate will stay in the room to provide support. If victims are treated in an inappropriate or insensitive manner, the advocate speaks up on their behalf.

You see some extraordinary things in this kind of work. I have seen doctors and nurses perform these tasks with incredible skill and humanity. But I have seen inexperienced doctors bumble through the exam, making it take twice as long as it should (which is already twice as long as a regular pelvic exam). I've seen doctors use victims' abdomens as a book rest, propping the instruction materials up on their bodies. I've seen police officers demand to stand behind the doctor so they can watch the pelvic exam, which by law they do not have the right to do. I have had more "I want to talk with you outside in the hallway" conversations with hospital staff and police than I care to think about. I have learned not to be surprised by rape because it can, and does, happen to anyone. I've learned not to be surprised by the injustices leveled against rape victims by social system personnel through their victim-blaming behaviors. It's not that I am unaffected by what I've seen; I'm just rarely surprised by it.

These experiences as an advocate conditioned me to the realities of rape, and they provide the backbone for my research on sexual assault. The rape crisis centers I have worked with taught me not only how to assist victims but also how to train others to work with rape survivors. To become a rape victim advocate, a volunteer must complete a 40-hour training program, which requires mastering an enormous amount of information about rape, medicine, and the law. It also incites a good deal of soul-searching, as you must find a way within yourself to work with something so painful. But if you make it through this training, you're well prepared to walk right into the chaos of rape and be of help to survivors.

The training at rape crisis centers is comprehensive, covering myths and facts about sexual assault and violence against women, the role of culture and media in violence, the psychological impact of rape (Rape Trauma Syndrome), crisis counseling techniques, advocacy strategies, the physical health effects of rape, the medical exam procedures, and the process of criminal prosecution.[1] To cover this material, a variety of learning formats are used: readings (academic articles, essays, poems), lectures, question-and-answer sessions, field trips, and perhaps most importantly, role plays. With other volunteers and rape crisis center staff, advocates-in-training have to practice their skills. Someone plays the role of rape survivor, another the doctor, another the police officer, and the new advocate practices what to say, how to say it, what to do. The role plays are then discussed in the group to provide positive support and suggestions for improvement. The center's staff drill the advocates-in-training: What would you do in this situation, that situation? The new advocates barrage the staff with endless "what if" questions: What if this happens, that happens? An advocate must successfully proceed through a series of increasingly challenging role plays before she is allowed to sign up for a shift of working with rape survivors. Once a volunteer completes training, advocates working with survivors usually attend weekly or monthly staff meetings to share their experiences, vent, and garner support. The primary purpose of these meetings is for advocates to learn how to take care of themselves when doing this kind of work, and to provide support to fellow advocates. The message was very clear: this is hard work, and being a good advocate to the survivor means that you are being good to yourself.

Rape crisis centers' training and self-care ethic made an indelible impression on me. I was taught, and taught well, by center staff that those who work with rape victims must know a great deal about rape, because one of the most important things they offer victims is information that normalizes and contextualizes their experiences. It is a job that will bring you very, very close to the pain of rape. To help the survivor get through that pain, you have to travel into it to guide her out of it. Day in and day out, shift after shift, the misery that is rape will seep into you. But I also learned that you can do this work if you are equally attentive to your own reactions and emotions. Support from others who know what you are going through can provide the necessary buffers. If the training model used by rape crisis centers could prepare volunteers for this kind of work, I figured it could certainly train research interviewers. Although the tasks are obviously quite different, an interviewer, like an advocate, will learn about very frightening events and will have to learn how to respond appropriately. For my first major research project on rape, I developed a training program for research interviewers based upon how I had been trained as an advocate.

I suppose that it's not surprising that my first major research project on rape (my dissertation) involved interviewing rape victim advocates (see Campbell, 1998a). I wanted to know how rape victims were being treated by the legal, medical, and mental health systems throughout the country. As I saw it, there were three ways I could explore this research question. One would be to interview system personnel. However, I had done my masters research on police responses to date rape, and had learned how difficult it can be to gain the trust of system personnel. In addition, from my experiences as an advocate, I knew that system workers often saw things differently from victims. More often than not, police, detectives, doctors, and nurses thought they were being helpful, but as an advocate, I heard from victims that they felt revictimized by their contact with system personnel. Interviewing system personnel would tell me what they thought they had done, but I suspected that would be different from what was perceived by victims. What I really wanted to understand was victims' perspectives, how they experienced these contacts. That left two other options: interview the victims themselves, or make the case that interviewing advocates would be a valid proxy source of information. I knew, as an advocate, that if asked about what happened in my most recent case, I could tell you very specific details about the assault and the community response to that victim. I was often privy to information police, detectives, doctors, and nurses never received—how victims felt about their contact.

After a small pilot study where I empirically verified that advocates could indeed provide reliable and valid information, I interviewed, along with a team of ten staff, 168 rape victim advocates throughout the country. First, I started small by conducting 30 interviews myself to work the bugs out of the interview. Then I asked three undergraduates if they would become project interviewers. My choice of research assistants was very deliberate: I handpicked these women from the statistics and research methods courses I was teaching. They had impressed me with maturity, intelligence, ambition, warmth, and attention to detail, so I asked them if they would like to join my newly formed research team. All three readily agreed.[2] I developed a training model similar to what I had known at my rape crisis centers. In the years since I had first gone through advocate training, I had participated in teaching new advocates to develop my skills as an instructor. I used the same readings, lectures, question-and-answer sessions, and field trips with my interviewers as I had with new advocates. Instead of role-playing how to respond to an advocacy case, we role-played the interview. We went through the interview question by question, discussed what it meant, and considered possible answers. We then practiced by interviewing each other and providing feedback. My doctoral advisor did not tell me anything about the style in which the interviewers should be trained, so I trained them as I felt was appropriate. We read Ann Oakley's (1988) piece on interviewing women, and used it as a general guide to develop our style. Following Oakley's lead, we decided that it would be okay to show some emotion during the interview, to talk and respond to the interviewee, to encourage them to ask us questions, and to answer those questions. The interview could be an opportunity for discussion and dialogue. We wanted this research project to provide a safe, supportive, and respectful environment for sharing information.

After completing a 40-hour interviewing program, the four of us (myself and three newly trained interviewers) embarked on more interviews. We met weekly to discuss our interviews. Even hearing about rape from a secondary source was still incredibly difficult. In our weekly meetings, we attended to the business end of interviewing (e.g., coding), but also, much as in my weekly meetings at the rape crisis center, we also processed how it felt to be hearing about rape. Support and self-care were built into our research meetings. After a semester and a half, we had 60 interviews completed, and I needed at least 110 more. We needed more help. So I recruited another group of interviewers, again specifically selected from the courses I was teaching. Along with my three experienced interviewers, I trained our new recruits in a manner similar to how I trained the original three. We interviewed, we met weekly, we processed our feelings. Over the course of another semester, this team of ten finished the project, interviewing 168 rape victim advocates.

The impact of hearing about victims' experiences with the legal, medical, and mental health systems stirred many emotions within all of us, mostly anger. We were incredibly angry about what we were hearing—victims contacting HIV from the rape; victims attempting suicide because all other coping had failed; victims being treated poorly by hospitals; doctors who were not trained to perform the rape exam, but muddled through it anyway; police officers who accused victims of lying and refused to take their reports; prosecutors refusing to prosecute because the victim wouldn't make a "good witness." At the end of the project, we decided that we would each write an essay about what these experiences meant to us—how we were affected by what we learned, how we felt about it, how it changed us. We would share these essays with each other in a bound collection for each of us to keep as a reminder of what we had done. These essays are moving, painful, and upsetting to read, but I treasure them. As their trainer, supervisor, and instructor, I started to feel incredibly guilty about putting my students through this process. They wrote about not being able to sleep, not being able to feel safe out at night, about looking at their own boyfriends with nervous suspicion. But their essays also expressed their gratitude for learning about the world in which they live, their personal development as women, and their desire to continue helping victims of violence. They felt well trained, well educated, and well supported. It was useful pain. They felt stronger as women than they ever had before in their lives. To this day, I still feel bad about the lost sleep and the sickening feeling in their stomachs, but I don't feel I could have prevented those experiences. Unfortunately, this is what it means to research rape in this manner. The work will impact the researchers emotionally.

The Process of Researching Researchers

I felt very lucky at the end of my dissertation project to have gotten myself and ten others through that process with only "useful pain." Because I was never told how to train the interviewers or what style of interviewing to use, I did what I felt was right. I believed that the training curriculum developed by rape crisis centers would be appropriate and that feminist interviewing techniques would elicit richer, more complete information. It is only in retrospect that I realize I made so many critical research decisions based upon my emotions and values, which had been shaped by the feminist antirape movement. The fact that these decisions were considered good decisions by my doctoral committee, student interviewers, and the advocates who participated in my research gave me confidence to guide my work by my emotional ethic. But I was emotionally spent. I had no interest in being emotionally engaged, at least for a while.

Two years later, I felt ready to interview rape survivors about their post-assault community experiences. I started the Women and Violence Project in my second year in a tenure-track faculty position. My grant from NIMH was a small award relative to what I wanted to accomplish, but it did support salaries for two graduate students and provide funds to reimburse rape survivors for their time and travel expenses. In my dissertation study, I was hearing only about cases where women had the assistance of a rape victim advocate, a specially trained assistant who knew the ropes. I couldn't shake off my concern for what happens to all the women who have contact with police, detectives, prosecutors, and doctors without the assistance of an advocate. Although my training as a social scientist made me consider the possibility that perhaps advocates were not all that helpful to victims, I personally did not believe that was the case. An advocate cannot prevent every mishap, but most can prevent a great deal of confusion and stress. Although there can be strained relations between advocates and hospital and law enforcement personnel, in general most system workers appreciate what advocates do. Advocates spare other community agency personnel the pain of close contact with rape. I suspected that I had not seen or heard the worst. I knew there was more to be unearthed about the problems women face after they have been raped.

I felt ready, personally and professionally, to interview rape victims and to train others to interview victims as well. As with my previous project, I started out small. The design of the study, its sampling plan, interview protocol, and interviewing plans were developed by a team consisting of myself, four graduate students, and two undergrads (again selected from courses I had taught). The planning group was primarily, though not exclusively, white women, all well educated, but from different social-class backgrounds. We spent a semester developing the plan and forming our overarching goal: to provide a safe, supportive environment for rape survivors to talk about their experiences. We wanted to do no harm to these women because more than enough had already been done to them. We weren't trying to be therapists, but we wanted to create a supportive space for survivors to talk about the assault without judgment or evaluation. By listening to and witnessing women's stories, we believed that we could create a research study that was healing. With every decision, we literally asked ourselves if that choice could be potentially upsetting, hurtful, or distressing to rape victims. We asked ourselves how we could make participating in this project a positive, empowering experience. I suspect that our reasons behind this shared value were different. For some, it was a reflection of a deeper commitment to feminism; for others, it was the specific influence of the feminist methodology literature and believing that research should be in the service to women; for others, especially those who had been or were rape victim advocates, it was an extension of that advocacy work; for others who were rape survivors, it was an opportunity to give something back by helping other women; for still others, it was as simple as being a good person to another person.

Once we had the interview and sampling procedures in place, our core research team identified and trained a group of interviewers. We trained them much as I had the interviewers in my dissertation project, teaching them Rape 101, Community Systems 101, Interviewing 101, and using role plays. Two issues were far more salient in this training: because we were interviewing rape survivors in locations and neighborhoods throughout the city, we spent a great deal of time discussing how to respond to victims in distress and how to protect our physical safety. Although I knew there was no way I could prepare the interviewers for every possible scenario, our "what if" discussions went on for weeks. The bottom-line message I emphasized over and over again was that if they were in a situation with a survivor and they weren't sure exactly how to respond, they should do what they thought was the good, human thing to do: don't worry about being a perfect researcher, be a good person. Ask the survivor what she wants to do, and do accordingly. If she wants to stop, stop. If she wants to go on, go on. It's about reinstating control—the survivor must have control over what she will and will not answer. If the interviewers found themselves in a situation where they felt their physical safety was in danger, get out. No interview was worth their safety. Given these instructions, I had some concern that the interviewers would come back with partial interviews and unusable data. This was not the case. The interviews came back complete and no one's safety was endangered. For some of the women we interviewed, none of the questions posed difficulty, and interviews were completed relatively quickly (about 90 minutes). For others, it was much tougher, and interviewers needed to move at their own pace. We obtained complete, valid, reliable interviews, but it sometimes took five hours. That's the pace that felt comfortable to the survivor, so that's what we respected. And the interviews took their toll on us.

We met weekly to discuss cases, share emotional experiences, and support each other. In fact, we ended up having two weekly meetings: one just to address the business of the project (recruiting, staffing, financial matters) and one just about interviewing. Even for a well-trained, streetwise group, interviewing was still very painful, and we had a lot to talk about. It was never lost on us that we were studying rape as women, never lost on us that we were studying it in a major urban area in which we also lived, never lost on us that we were asking about the comprehensive effects of rape, so we would hear about its devastation throughout women's lives. We were there to understand, in as much detail as we felt was respectful to the survivor, everything that was hurtful and healing postassault. We heard stories of incredible strength and resilience, and we really treasured those because we heard others that kept us from sleeping, made us cry in staff meetings, and made us scream at the male partners in our lives in displaced anger.

As time wore one, we rotated people on and off the interviewing schedule because there were weeks when each interviewer just could not hear one more story. Some interviewers were proactive and asked not to be scheduled, and I always honored these requests. On occasion, I pulled interviewers from the schedule even if they didn't ask when I thought they needed a break. We were running on empty at the end. In retrospect, I should have trained an addditional group of interviewers, but I thought that the time expense of training more students wasn't justified because our end goal of completing a hundred interviews was well in sight. But we did cross our finish line, completed our interviews, and had a big party. No one was physically harmed, but we were all emotionally spent.

Throughout the Women and Violence Project, I kept detailed field notes documenting processes such as group conflicts, struggles, and tensions; instances of group cohesion and bonding; details from survivors' stories that moved us; my emotions and the impact this study was having on my life and my relationships with my partner, students, and colleagues; and my observations of how the team was also emotionally responding to this work. I collected information about all of these topics from day one. So in some respects the researching-the-researcher study also started at the very beginning of the project, with side-by-side data collection with the main research study.

However, it wasn't until the project had been under way for two months that I saw these field notes as research. My motivations for writing them were much simpler. I was incredibly lonely doing this project. I didn't feel a lot of support from my colleagues. They weren't hostile to my research by any means; they just wouldn't ask about it. I assumed, I think correctly, that they really didn't want to hear the details of what I was learning and what I was going through. I did talk with team members and was open about my own experiences, but I edited and selected what I revealed. I did not feel it was appropriate to disclose everything on my mind because my role on the project was quite different from anyone else's. The proverbial buck stopped with me. I had administrative oversight on all aspects of the project. It was a sobering responsibility, and I took it very seriously. I always had a lot on my mind. The field notes provided a constructive medium for documenting the activities of project and reflecting on my experiences. They were a medium for me to talk to myself, to get what was in me out of me. I told the research team that I was keeping field notes, although it is important to note that some members do not recall that to be the case. My recollection, and what is recorded in my field notes, is that I did tell the group I was doing this, but that I didn't talk about it regularly or extensively. This makes sense in light of the fact that I viewed them to some extent as a personal space to record what was happening.

I started viewing my field notes as both a method of self-conversation and formal data collection because some members of the research team encouraged me to write something about how it feels to study rape. One of the undergraduate interviewers once asked me if I was planning to analyze these field notes. My reply was that I'd probably write an essay about all of this somewhere down the road. She remarked: "That's gonna be a damn long essay because there's a lot going on." When I logged that quote in my field notes, it struck a chord with me. She was right. I read back through the first two months of notes and realized that I had more material than I knew what to do with. These experiences deserved a formal analysis. An essay could capture some of what we experienced, but it would not be the appropriate medium for telling the entire story. At our next interviewing meeting, I broached the topic of a more formal study of our experiences and that I wanted to analyze my field notes as data. There were no objections, but some curiosity about how I would go about this task. After this meeting, an interviewer said to me: "The survivors we interview entrust their stories to us to tell the world what rape is like. In the same way, we trust our experiences of doing that study with you to tell the world what it's like to research rape."

My field notes are only one source of data for this research project. In addition, at the end of the main study, after all of the interviews were completed, I conducted individual, one-on-one exit interviews with members of the research team. I knew from my dissertation study how important it was to provide closure and have some mechanism for reflection that brought an emotional end to the work. In that project, we decided to each write essays about our experiences and share them in a collected volume. I didn't think that medium would work with this group. We had learned the power of listening to and witnessing people's stories. It seemed to me that a better way to provide closure would be for each of us to have the opportunity to tell our stories. About two weeks before the end of the project, I raised this subject with the group and proposed this idea for exit interviews. I would interview each of them, and during those conversations, each would have an opportunity to interview me as well. My story would also be captured, spread throughout all of their interviews. They were supportive of this venture because for many, a formal opportunity to vent and reflect was much needed.

Because providing closure was my primary goal, I did not immediately think of these interviews as another data source. When it did occur to me, I was somewhat ambivalent about using these narratives. Again, it was my conversations with some of the research team members that made me see things in a different light; these narratives did belong in the bigger story of our work, provided, of course, that their confidentiality as interviewees would be respected. In preparation for these staff interviews, I submitted and received approval from my university's institutional review board for this new phase of research. It is important to note that at the time the interviews were conducted and consent forms reviewed and signed, I did not know I would be writing a book about this project. I did know I would be analyzing these data for research purposes, which was noted in the consent form,[3] but I had not yet decided what medium I would select to tell this story. There were no expressed objections or concerns at the time of the interviews regarding how this information would be used or where and in what form it would be disseminated, but that certainly changed as the process unfolded.

After I completed the interviews, I realized that I needed the space and freedom that comes with writing a book to be able to capture this story. Although it is far more common in psychology to write journal articles, this work didn't seem to fit that mold. I applied for and received a fellowship from my university to develop this book manuscript. The award provided a release from all teaching and service responsibilities for a full academic year, which is a critical contextual factor that seemed to have inadvertently complicated matters. I wasn't around my department as much and I had less interaction with team members. The core research team (i.e., myself, the graduate students, and one to two of the undergraduate assistants) continued to meet regularly to plan analyses of the survivors' interview data, but beyond that, I was away from my office working on this project. It is only in hindsight that I realize how much that physical distance contributed to some communication difficulties. We didn't talk much about this work because I wasn't around much for such conversations to happen. From time to time, I would talk about what I was doing, what I was finding, what I was thinking about with some but not all members of the team, and I showed some of them copies of the book prospectus or draft chapters for their feedback. Beyond that, I kept my work on this project separate and private. I was concerned about protecting confidentiality, which partially kept me quiet, but the bigger reason was that it was daunting work to sift through these experiences to try to tell a coherent story. I had undertaken something much bigger and far more complicated than I realized.

In retrospect, a lot of conflict could have been avoided if I had been more communicative about this project. In light of the power differences between myself and the others, I suspect they may have been reluctant to ask about what I was doing or challenge it. It was probably naïve on my part to have assumed that people would feel comfortable raising these issues with me. My experiences throughout the project were that members would challenge me, would question me, and that I valued and supported that kind of dialogue. But then again, I was still their employer or advisor or teacher or some other role with power over them. An example of this problematic dynamic emerged in the communication surrounding the coding of the data. I felt that I needed help with this task—another perspective on the data. I wanted someone to look through the data with me to see if we agreed on the overarching themes in the field notes and interviews. I could not ask any of the members of the research team to do this task because it would have involved seeing all of the transcripts, and they could have very easily identified who was whom. I was viewing the entire pile of data and I needed someone else to look at it too and help me make sense of it. I asked one of the rape victim advocates I knew at a suburban rape crisis center to help me. She did not know anyone on the research team and had not been affiliated with this work in any way. Still very concerned with protecting the confidentiality of the data, I gave her edited copies of my field notes and the interview transcripts. I read over all of the materials and cut out all names, all references to names, and any information or stories that I believed revealed any possible identifying information. I was seeking macrolevel feedback from her—what did she see as the dominant themes in the data? We met several times to discuss the materials, which yielded agreement on some very broad issues. I needed her perspective on what I was beginning to see as the primary story line in the data: the research team experienced a variety of emotions, many of them difficult and negative (though not exclusively); these emotions were difficult to cope with and affected many areas of their personal and professional lives; but such feelings brought them closer to understanding violence against women and its pervasiveness in our culture. After agreeing on that central thesis, she returned the materials and did not participate further in the analysis. The more detailed coding was performed solely by me. (See details of coding later on in this appendix.)

The communication around these issues must not have been completely clear. Some members of team later told me that I never told them I would be working with a second coder. They expressed that this made them angry and it felt hurtful to have this information shared with others. The consent form specified that the data would be analyzed for research purposes, but it did not specify exactly how this process would unfold. My recollection was that I did tell them that I was going to do this; some team members maintain that I did not have this conversation with them. Their perspective was that I should have informed them *exactly* how I would be working with these data. That I said I would be analyzing the data for research purposes was not enough for them. One member of the team decided to withdraw her data from the analyses; she remained involved in other ways by providing feedback on drafts of this manuscript. Whether or not my actions would be considered acceptable by the larger research community was not the point (from their point of view); some members indicated that they felt my actions were unacceptable to them. I have discussed these issues at length with members of the team, apologized for the poor communication, and acknowledged that my actions in this instance (regardless of their intent) were hurtful to some people.

That my relationships with these women survived these incidents is meaningful to me personally and instructive to me professionally. For some members of the team, their concerns about confidentiality were tempered when they realized that their words and identity would be protected but mine would not be. Unlike other research, I was not going to be the silent absent researcher. My experiences would be right there with everyone else's, though my identity was out in the open. I would not be analyzing them, reflecting on them, silently and separately. My words and experiences were right there, too. As one interviewer said to me as we discussed her data, "I'm okay with this because your guts will be out there the same as ours. The only difference is you can protect our identities and confidentiality. You can't protect your own."

These experiences also reflect another difficult aspect of researching researchers' emotions. This was an emergent project, unfolding as it happened, with decisions being made along the way. I don't believe this is necessarily problematic. I agree with Howard Becker in his book, *Tricks of the Trade: How to Think about Your Research while You're Doing It* (1998), that if researchers waited until we had everything figured out, we'd miss a lot of good research opportunities. On the other hand, this project highlights the critical need for open communication in emerging work. If a project is steeped within a feminist ideology, such dialogue is particularly critical and highly valued, and as such, I think missteps, even those unintentional and accidental, can hurt, because there exists the ideal that these things *shouldn't* happen.

In reflecting on this experience of researching myself and my research team, I echo many of the suggestions Frances Grossman and her colleagues (1999) raised for feminist research on emotional topics. A project leader needs to be very self-aware and -reflective throughout the project. Decisions must be continually reviewed and rereviewed as projects evolve over time. Up-front discussions regarding power relationships within a team setting are particularly important; whereas it may not be possible to dramatically alter that dynamic, not addressing those issues won't make them not be there. In addition, I believe it is necessary to acknowledge the underlying irony that for all the interest and attention to emotions and concern for other's feelings, it can be really, really difficult actually to talk about them. It's easier to talk around them, refer to them in abstract ways, state that they are important, but actually to talk about what you're feeling is harder to do. Acknowledging that may be an effective way to start the conversation. As Grossman summarizes, "This means being clearly aware that emphasizing subjectivity of the researchers and sharing those self-reflections can greatly enhance the richness of the research, but it will also lead to increased tensions around longings for greater intimacy and a more egalitarian structure of decision making" (pp. 132–133). Whether such processes actually do unfold in an egalitarian way, I suspect, may be not quite as important as whether there is clear communication about whether the group is actually aiming for that goal or not. A misfire of shared power and participation in an expectation of hierarchy will probably not be nearly as problematic as less equity when there were expectations for more.

The Methodology of Data Analysis

Turning to the specific design and methods, this researching-the-researcher project used a collective case study design whereby a number of cases were studied to understand a general condition, phenomenon, or population (Stake, 1994; Yin, 1994). The small number of individual cases are selected because "it is believed that understanding them will lead to better under-standing, perhaps better theorizing, about a still larger collection of cases" (Stake, 1994). Field notes were collected on all aspects of the research project and included observations of the entire Women and Violence Project staff, which consisted of the core research group who participated in all tasks of the project (seven); the recruitment team, whose only task was to work through-out the community to invite rape survivors to participate in our project (three); and the interview team, whose only task was to interview the rape sur-vivors (five). Of this group of 15 women, one was faculty (myself), four were graduate students in the social sciences, and ten were upper-level undergradu-ates majoring in psychology or related fields. Six of these women were white, four were African American, two were Latina (Mexican American), and three were of mixed race. All of the core research staff and interviewers participated in the staff interviews at the end of the project (12) (one faculty, four graduate students, seven undergraduate students; six white women, three African-American women, three women of mixed race); data were analyzed and reported from 11 interviews. Most of the staff interviews took two hours to complete. All interviews were tape-recorded in their entirety and were tran-scribed verbatim by myself and a professional transcriber.

I followed the approaches of Matthew Miles and Michael Huberman (1994) and Anselm Strauss and Juliet Corbin (1990) to analyze the field notes and interview transcripts. Analysis unfolded in three stages: data reduction, data display, and data interpretation. First, Huberman and Miles (1994) defined data reduction thus: "the potential universe of data is reduced in an anticipatory way as the researcher chooses a conceptual framework, research questions, cases, and instruments" (p. 429). To that end, each day of field notes and each interview transcript was open-coded, which is defined by Strauss and Corbin as:

The process of breaking down, examining, comparing, conceptualizing, and categorizing data. . . . Open coding is the part of analysis that pertains specifically to the naming and categorizing of phenomena through close examination of the data. . . . During open coding the data are broken down into discrete parts, closely examined, compared for similarities and differences, and questions are asked about the phenomena as reflected in the data. (pp. 61–62)

This process reduces the entire set of textual data into smaller sections of coded text that can be examined more closely. It is a within-case analytic strategy, identifying the specific themes in each individual's set of data. As mentioned previously, a second coder worked with me in the initial tasks of data reduction. She is an African-American women who has ten years of experience as a rape victim advocate and an advanced degree in social work, but had not worked on this project. The coder and I independently read all of the textual data and generated lists of key constructs that should be coded. We met to review and discuss those lists and jointly developed a final set of constructs for coding. In addition, we cowrote a manual to guide us in performing the open-coding task. Using color-coded pens and pencils, we independently marked sections of the text that pertained to our constructs of interest: 1) emotions experienced (emotions coded: anger, fear, pain, confusion, loss, hurt, sadness, worry, guilt, hope, happiness); 2) coping resources and strategies (coping mechanisms coded: cognitive, behavioral, affective); and 3) knowledge gained through the emotional and coping experiences of participating in this research (knowledge coded: information for self regarding own history of violence, information for self regarding pervasiveness of violence against women, information for self regarding impact of violence against women, information shared with others in participant's life regarding violence against women).

After we had each completed open-coding all of the data, we met to compare analyses. We had substantial agreement in coding coping and knowledge gained, that is, there were no instances where one of us marked text for a construct and the other did not, we agreed on what construct each section of marked text represented, but we often varied in how much of the text we highlighted (I tended to highlight the contextual information around the instance, and she tended to highlight only the specific sentence(s) that most directly captured the construct of interest). In creating the final open-coded analyses, we reflected both systems for marking text; a color-coded bracket marked the start of a section (my approach) and highlighting marked the specific sentences that most directly exemplified the construct (her approach). We had more disagreement with respect to coding the emotions reflected in the text. Through our discussions, we realized we had created too many categories that became extremely difficult to differentiate; we therefore decided to collapse the number of emotions coded into five inclusive categories (loss, pain, fear, anger, hope). We worked together to conduct the final open-coding on the emotions experienced. At the conclusion of open-coding, we discussed what we each saw of the overarching story line in these data. With this agreed-upon basic framework, I continued the remainder of the analyses alone.

To complete the data-reduction phase, I then used axial coding to examine the specific contexts of each open-coded instance of emotion, coping, and knowledge. Strauss and Corbin (1990) define axial coding as:

> A set of procedures whereby data are put back together in new ways after open coding, by making connections between categories. This is done by utilizing a coding paradigm involving conditions, context, action/interactional strategies and consequences. (p. 96)

With respect to coding emotions experienced, the axial codes reflected several factors, including intensity of emotion, indication of change over time (in kind or intensity of emotion), spillover of that emotion into personal or professional life, and contextual triggers for the emotion. It appeared that many of the settings that triggered emotionality were directly linked to specific stories from the rape survivor interviews. Thus, for emotions triggered by stories, I then developed a new set of codes for those stories to reflect the type of rape experienced, perceived similarity between the interviewer and survivor, postassault community response, and postassault response from the survivor's informal support networks. The open codes for coping were axial-coded to differentiate between personal coping responses and organization responses. For example, I differentiated between instances of cognitive coping—reinterpreting an event to make it more consistent with existing schema—that a participant had developed and implemented on her own (personal) and those cognitive reinterpretations that came about through group discussion at research group meetings (organizational). Finally, the axial coding for knowledge gained focused on identifying the specific contexts that contributed to each instance of knowing. The primary differentiation was whether a section of text referred back to a specific story or rape survivor with whom the participant had interacted, or whether the text reflected a more global integration of experiences across specific cases.

In the second and third phases of data analysis, I shifted focus from within-case analyses to across-case analyses to explore the similarities and differences among the participants' experiences. Huberman and Miles (1994) call this second phase "data display," which is "an organized, compressed assembly of information that permits conclusion drawing and/or action taking . . . the researcher typically needs to see a reduced set of data as a basis for thinking about its meanings" (p. 429). Data can be displayed through diagrams, vignettes, summaries, and matrices. Data interpretation emphasizes "drawing meaning from displayed data" (p. 424). In my work on this project, data display and data interpretation were not distinct and unfolded essentially at the same time.

For data display, I initially started summarizing information into matrices that tried to capture the interconnections between feeling, coping, and knowledge (with their associated codes and subcodes), but this task proved unwieldy and unhelpful. At this stage of the analysis, I was even more focused on how to protect the confidentiality of the data. I found Nancy Whittier's book, *Feminist Generations* (1995), a helpful resource in trying to resolve these issues. In reporting her work with radical women's movement organizations, Whittier protected confidentiality by identifying respondents through their organizational affiliations or other roles; she did not use their real names or assign pseudonyms. She writes:

> I promised the women I interviewed that their identities would remain confidential and that I would not use quotations in a way that would allow the speaker to be identified, even by other members of the Columbus women's movement. . . . In some cases this has meant giving less than complete background information about particular quotations or giving only general information about speakers. (Footnote: In a few cases, it has been impossible to make the sources of a comment unrecognizable to other members of the Columbus women's movement. I have minimized such cases and have removed any potentially damaging or sensitive material from recognizable quotations.) (p. 11)

As in Whittier's work, I realized that some text, if quoted or explained in this book, would be readily identifiable to the other members of the team (but not to the public at large). We would know who said those textual examples because we had common knowledge of certain cases and experiences. Following Whittier's model, I limited the number of these instances and checked with the originators of such text to see if they were comfortable with including them in this book. I further realized that there were many other instances that would not be identifiable to either members of the team or the public at large; but, with further a cross-case analysis, I would be uncovering lots of contextual details that would make that example identifiable to the team. I wanted to find a way to compare across cases, but to do so in a way that did not increase the number of instances that were identifiable by other members of the team.

As a result, I then moved into data displays that emphasized textual summaries and vignettes. I developed a series of summaries that linked information regarding emotion, coping, and knowledge that were similar in their underlying themes, and then created parallel summaries that exemplified different relationships. Most notably, the across-case analyses revealed that for many of the participants in this project, specific stories triggered specific emotional reactions that then snowballed into a larger set of discomforting emotions that spilled over into everyday life as the project progressed. Through personal and organizational affective coping, these members of the team began to reinterpret the problem of rape at a larger macrolevel of analysis. However, a different pathway emerged for others who did not experience negative emotions as a result of specific interviews or the accumulation of stories. Through cognitive reinterpretation of those events, their understanding of rape emphasized the individual resiliency of women in the face of a larger culture of violence. These vignettes then guided the organization of the book and the specific content to be included within each chapter.

For data interpretation, it is necessary to assess credibility—the degree to which the coding and interpretation of the across-case comparisons are meaningful representations of the data. Credibility can be ascertained in different ways and at different stages of the research process. For example, one approach is member checking, where research findings are shared with the original participants for comment and reflection (Altheide & Johnson, 1994). As mentioned previously, drafts of this book were shared with members of the research team. I asked the participants to look at their specific quoted text as well as consider the broader interpretative themes in the chapters. I told them that I would fix any errors and address serious misinterpretations or omissions, but not all differences in opinion would be resolved by rewriting.

Another approach to assessing credibility is proposed by Virginia Oleson (1994), who recommends that researchers describe how a problem emerged, how different sources of data were triangulated, and how the researcher conducted herself/himself with the participants. Such information is critical to the reader for evaluating the credibility and accuracy of the work. Following Oleson's (1994) model, I explained in the prior sections of this appendix the experiences that led to this project and specific details as to how it unfolded. My primary goal in writing this appendix was to share with the reader the development, process, and methodology of this project. Through sharing this story within the story of how and why I researched our emotional experiences, my goal is to contribute to this growing field of interest in researchers' emotions and their role in the scientific process.

The Researching-the-Researcher Interview Protocol

Introduction and Overview

I wanted to start off today by providing you with some information about the general purpose of this interview. I will be talking with all interviewers from the Women and Violence Project to provide everyone an opportunity to talk, reflect, vent about their experiences interviewing rape survivors. It's been a very long year. We've heard from so many survivors and so many stories that are both heartwrenching and uplifting. To provide some closure to this year of interviewing, I wanted to talk with everyone about what this experience has been like for them.

Our interview today is what is called "semistructured," which is like having a somewhat structured discussion or conversation. I have a series of questions to ask you, which are grouped into three major themes. First, I'd like to start out by talking about the one interview that was most salient to you—the one that really stuck with you, for whatever reason. Then I'd like to talk more generally; thinking about all the interviews you've done, I'd like to discuss how you believe rape survivors are treated by community agencies and social systems. Finally, I'd like to talk about how participating in these interviews has affected you—what emotions you experienced and how you coped with those feelings throughout the year.

If you have questions for me as we go along, please ask them. Since I can't interview myself, my interview about my experiences will be conducted by all of you as we talk.

Everything we discuss today is private; your name will not be connected to anything you say. I will not disclose to anyone else on the team what we talk about today. As we're going through the interview, if there are any questions or topics that you do not want to discuss, just say so, and I will move on to the next section. You do not have to answer all of the questions in this interview.

When I originally thought about doing these interviews, I viewed them simply as a chance for us to talk about what it was like to do this project. I had no research plans for these interviews. But in developing this interview, it occurred to me that it would be interesting to share with other researchers what we have learned and how we have coped throughout this project.

But to do so, I would need everyone's consent to allow these interviews to be considered as data collection. To maintain everyone's confidentiality, I would be the only person on the team who would view, code, and analyze these data. If you are open to have our discussions today included as a data source for this project, I would like to tape-record our discussion. Your name is not on this interview, and it would not be on the tape or the transcription of the tape. Is this OK with you? [If yes, proceed with consent form.]

Section 1: Salient Interview

You've been interviewing for several months now; you've met lots of women, heard lots of stories. I'd like to start off our discussion today by asking you to think back over the interviews you've done and to focus on the ONE interview that really stands out in your mind—the interview that is most salient to you in your memory.

This interview may be the one that stands out because it was really good, really bad, really painful to hear, really got under your skin, or whatever. But, it's the interview that was most salient to you—the one you will think of, the one you will remember later on when you think about your involvement in this project. Tell me about the interview.

Probes:

What happened in the rape?
Was the Women and Violence interview the first time the survivor had disclosed?
How similar was this woman to you?
How similar was her situation to your own life experiences?
If the survivor had system contact, what happened in each contact?
When did this interview occur? How much interviewing experience did you have?
Why is this interview most salient to you?
What did you learn or walk away with from this experience?
How did this interview affect you?
How did this interview affect subsequent interviews?
How did you cope with what you heard in this interview?

Section 2: Expert Beliefs about System Response

Over the course of these interviews, you've heard a lot about how social systems, such as the legal system and medical system, respond to rape survivors.

1. Drawing upon these stories, how would you summarize how community systems respond to rape victims? If you had to explain to someone who was unfamiliar with how rape victims are treated by social systems, what would you say to them? How would you characterize the community response to rape?

Probes:

Any differences in how different survivors are treated?
Any differences across systems in how they respond?
What, if anything, do you think influences how social systems respond to victims?
What was the WORST thing you heard that happened to a survivor in system contact?
What was the BEST thing you heard that happened to a survivor in system contact?
Upon what cases or experiences are you drawing to form these conclusions?
Why do you characterize the community response to rape in the way you do?

2. Based on this understanding and perspective of this issue, what would you say to a rape survivor who was trying to decide whether to contact the police? The ER? A counselor? A member of a religious community?

3. What do you see as the "take-home" lesson for women?

4. Goddess forbid, but if you were to be sexually assaulted in the near future, would this experience interviewing survivors about their system contact influence you own choice about reporting? In what way?

5. What do you think should be done to improve how rape survivors are treated by community agencies?

6. What would you like to see done with the data we collected to improve how rape survivors are treated by community agencies?

Section 3: Impact on Selves

In this next section of the interview, I'd like to talk about how conducting these interviews affected you personally.

How did participating in this project and interviewing rape survivors affect you?

Probes:

What emotions did you experience?
Which emotion was the predominant one?
Were there any changes over time in what emotions you experienced and if so, how strongly?
What strategies did you use to cope with these emotions and experiences?
How helpful were the other team members in supporting you in this work?
Did this project affect your health in any way?
Did this project affect your interpersonal relationships in any way?
How did this affect your beliefs about rape? Men? Safety? Justice?
How did this affect your beliefs about sexism? Racism? Classism? Hetero-sexism?
Did your reaction to participating in this project surprise you in any way?
What impacted you the most that you didn't expect?

Section 4: Closing

A few final closing questions and reflections:

1. What was it like doing this? What, if anything, do you wish had happened differently?

2. If you could travel back through time and write yourself a note that would alert you to something important about this experience, something you should have known before getting started on interviewing, and you could place that note to yourself in that big training manual that I distributed way back at the beginning of the project—what would that note say?

Preface

1. Throughout this book, the focus is female rape survivors; hence I use female pronouns throughout.

2. Throughout this chapter, and entire book, font style denotes the type of text quoted. Excerpts from published works are in Stone Serif font; narrative data from my field notes and staff interviews are in Stone Sans font.

Chapter 1

1. Several psychologists have demonstrated that attitudes have both cognitive and affective elements (see Ajzen, 1988; Petty & Cacioppo, 1981 for general issues; see Katz, 1960; Smith, Brunner, & White, 1956 for specific work on cognitive dimensions; see Breckler & Wiggins, 1989; Zanna & Rempel, 1988 for specific work on affective components). Yet, in the debates about the role of the researcher in the scientific process, psychologists have conceptualized attitudes as primarily cognitive influences.

2. I am admittedly painting in very broad strokes, as there has been growing interest within certain areas of psychology concerning the role of values in research (see Gergen, 1985). For example, the field of community psychology has a long-standing interest in how researchers' values affect their work (Kelly, 1986, 1988; Rappaport, 1977; Trickett, 1984, 1996). Julian Rappaport (1977) argued that what is problematic about most psychological research isn't that it is biased, but rather that the values and beliefs of the researcher are not articulated and remain hidden from view. See also Chris Argyris's paper "Some Unintended Consequences of Rigorous Research" (1968), which raises questions about how social and emotional distance and the need for "rigor" can interfere with researchers' capacity to understand their phenomenon of interest.

3. In raising this question, I acknowledge the writings of feminist-standpoint theorists such as Patricia Hill Collins (1991) and Nancy Hartsock (1998), who have articulated thoughtful theoretical models for the simultaneous analysis of gender, race/ethnicity, and social class.

4. See Campbell, Sefl, Wasco, and Ahrens (2001) for more details regarding the sampling methodology.

Chapter 2

1. This effect has been found in women. But in rape prevention studies with men, Dianne Berg and her colleagues found that increasing empathy with rape victims actually increases rape myth acceptance and propensity to commit assaults (Berg, Lonsway, & Fitzgerald, 1999).

Chapter 4

1. The interview for this researching-the-researcher project is provided in Appendix B. It is important to note that the order in which the sections of the interview were covered varied somewhat across interview depending on the tone and flow of the conversation. Regardless of the exact order in which I asked the members of the team to reflect upon what they learned about rape through this project, their tone usually shifted—for the positive—and it seemed to be a relief to be talking about rape in academic terms once again.

2. These arguments are shaped by conversations with research team members, but they do not necessarily represent the opinions of all team members. My analysis draws out the implications of the kinds of questions and comments team members started to raise at the end of the project.

3. This estimate is based upon a review of the literature I conducted with a research assistant in 1999. The studies selected for review were obtained by searching the PSYCH-INFO database from 1976 to 1998 with the following search command: (rape or sexual assault or rape victim) not child. This search was limited to include only journal articles in English based on human populations in the United States. Four general types of published reports were *excluded* from this review: 1) analysis of official crime databases; 2) analysis of police records; 3) analysis of mental health center records or rape crisis center records; and 4) analysis of courtroom transcripts, observations of trials, or observations of prosecutors. These procedures yielded a total of 217 articles for review that surveyed/interviewed rape victim samples and/or secondary victims. We then coded these articles for their primary topical focus and level of analysis (see Campbell & Johnson [1997] for a summary of the methods to check reliability of coding) (in this review kappa = .89). Results revealed that 5 percent of these articles examined either: 1) how rape affects family, friends, partners, and/or helping professionals; or 2) how community-level factors contribute to the traumatic effects of rape.

4. With respect to these issues, I am far less interested in the specifics of who said what, and far more interested in what is broadly communicated in the vast academic literature on sexual violence against women. My goal is to examine more closely what is implicitly communicated in this literature.

5. Gillian Iliffee and Lyndall Steed (2000) uncovered nearly identical findings in samples of domestic violence shelter staff and volunteers.

6. The Figely/Joinson approach is conceptually quite similar to the work of Pearlman and Saakvitne in that both research teams emphasize the normative aspects of this trauma and its connections to empathic engagement. These approaches are different in that Pearlman's and Saakvithne's psychodynamic orientation places more emphasis on the transformative impact of this kind of work.

7. See also Peggy Thoits's (1985, 1986, 1990, 1996) recent work expanding these concepts, which she terms "emotional deviance"; her work places emphasis on how individuals cope with emotion work.

8. Recent work has also substantiated a link between women's employment outside the home and emotion work within the family life (Wharton & Erickson, 1995).

9. Most current statutes note that rapists and victims can be either male or female; thus the actors are defined insofar as to state that anyone can be a victim or assailant.

10. It is important to distinguish between what eventually gets published in the academic literature and the behind-the-scenes processes that generated that work. Based just on what is published, I am left wondering about the emotional accuracy of much research, but I suspect there's more that has been edited out, for whatever reason. In other words, I think it is quite probable that in collecting data about sexual assault, many researchers have indeed seen and felt what rape really does to women's lives, but those emotional sources of information get downplayed in the public sharing of research findings.

11. Specializations and subspecializations: e.g., prevalence estimates, psychological health impact, physical health impact, social support, rape myths, therapeutic interventions, community response; journals: e.g., *Journal of Interpersonal Violence*, *Violence & Victims*, and *Violence against Women*; publishers: e.g., Routledge, Sage, APA.

12. These four studies include: 1) the Violence against Women Survey (Tjaden & Thoennes, 1998, 2000); 2) the National College Health Risk Behavior Survey (Brenner, McMahon, Warren, & Douglas, 1999); 3) the U.S. Naval Recruit Survey (Merrill, Newell, Milner, Koss, Hervig, Gold, Rosswork, & Thronton, 1998); and 4) the Crime in the Ivory Tower Survey (Fisher, Sloan, Cullen, & Lu, 1998).

13. This RFP was found at http://www.ncjrs.org/txtfiles1/nij/s1000424.txt.

Chapter 5

1. I do not use the phrase "ethic of caring" in the same way in which it was originally proposed by Carol Gilligan in her classic book, *In a Different Voice* (1982). The differences between my conceptualization of caring and other writers' approaches will be outlined later on in this chapter.

2. My awareness of this quote came from reading Shulamit Reinharz's book *Feminist Methods in Social Research*, where it is cited on page 76 of her chapter on feminist survey research.

3. I examine the interrelationships between my volunteer experiences as a rape victim advocate, my research in the Women and Violence Project, and this researching-the-researcher project in more depth in appendix A.

4. Saakvitne and Pearlman cite Guzzino and Taxis (1995) as the original creators of the Toxic Dump exercise.

Appendix A

1. My awareness of how rape crisis centers are structured and function comes not only from my experience as a volunteer at three different centers but also from a nationwide study I conducted on these topics (see Campbell, 1996, 1998b; Campbell, Baker, & Mazurek, 1998; Campbell & Martin, 2001; see also Jones, 1997).

2. I worried about the dynamics of this arrangement. Would these students feel comfortable saying no? What kind of power does a teacher hold over her students? I talked about these concerns with my doctoral advisor, who suggested, jokingly, that maybe I was reading a bit too much feminist theory. He told me to be clear and honest with these students: explain the risks, explain the benefits, explain how you plan to train them and how you plan to support them, give them the right to take breaks when it gets too hard, and give them the right to withdraw from interviewing.

3. Specifically, the consent form read, "I consent to have my confidential interview content analyzed for research purposes." The participant then initialed that statement.

Acker, J., Barry, K., & Esseveld, J. (1983). Objectivity and truth: Problems in doing feminist research. *Women's Studies International Forum, 6*, 423–435.

Ahrens, C. E., & Campbell, R. (2000). Assisting rape victims as they recover from rape: The impact on friends. *Journal of Interpersonal Violence, 15*, 959–986.

Ajzen, I. (1988). *Attitudes, personality, and behavior.* Chicago: Dorsey Press.

Aldridge, M. (1994). Unlimited liability: Emotional labour in nursing and social work. *Journal of Advanced Nursing, 20*, 722.

Alexander, J. G., de Chesnay, M., Marshall, E., Campbell, A. R., Johnson, S., & Wright, R. (1989). Parallel reactions in rape victims and rape researchers. *Violence & Victims, 4*, 57–62.

Altheide, D. L., & Johnson, J. M. (1994). Criteria for assessing interpretive validity in qualitative research. In N. K. Denzin & Y. S. Lincoln (Eds.), *Handbook of qualitative research* (pp. 485–499). Thousand Oaks, CA: Sage.

American Psychiatric Association (1994). *Diagnostic and statistical manual of mental disorders: DSM IV.* Washington, DC: Author.

Amick-McMullan, A., Kilpatrick, D. G., & Veronen, L. J. (1989). Family survivors of homicide victims: A behavioral analysis. *The Behavior Therapist, 12*, 75–79.

Amir, M. (1971). *Patterns in forcible rape.* Chicago: University of Chicago Press.

Argyris, C. (1968). Some unintended consequences of rigorous research. *Psychological Bulletin, 70*, 185–197.

Astin, M. C. (1997). Traumatic therapy: How helping rape victims affects me as a therapist. *Women and Therapy, 20*, 101–109.

Bachar, K. J., & Koss, M. P. (2001). From prevalence to prevention: Closing the gap between what we know about rape and what we do. In C. M. Renzetti, J. L. Edleson, & R. K. Bergen (Eds.), *Sourcebook on violence against women* (pp. 117–142). Thousand Oaks, CA: Sage.

Bachman, R., & Saltzman, L. E. (1995). Violence against women: Estimates from the redesigned survey. Bureau of Justice Statistics Special Report: National Crime Victimization Survey. U.S. Department of Justice, Office of Justice Programs.

Barkus, R. (1997). Partners of survivors of abuse: A men's therapy group. *Psychotherapy, 34*, 316–323.

Barnett, M. A., Tetreault, P. A., Esper, J. A., & Bristow, A. R. (1986). Similarity and empathy: The experience of rape. *Journal of Social Psychology, 126*, 47–49.

Barnett, M. A., Tetreault, P. A., & Masbad, I. (1987). Empathy with a rape victim: The role of similarity of experience. *Violence & Victims, 2,* 255–262.

Beaton, R. D., & Murphy, S. A. (1995). Working with people in crisis: Research implications. In C. R. Figley (Ed.), *Compassion fatigue: Coping with secondary traumatic stress disorder in those who treat the traumatized.* New York: Brunner/Mazel.

Becker, H. S. (1998). *Tricks of the trade: How to think about your research while you're doing it.* Chicago: University of Chicago Press.

Becker, H. S., & Geer, B. (1957). Participant observation and interviewing: A comparison? *Human Organization, 16,* 28–32.

Becker, J., Skinner, L., Abel, G., Howell, J., & Bruce, K. (1982). The effects of sexual assault on rape and attempted rape victims. *Victimology, 7,* 106–113.

Beebe, D. K. (1991). Emergency management of the adult female rape victim. *American Family Physician, 43,* 2041–2046.

Belenky, M. F., Clinchy, B. M., Goldberger, N. R., & Tarule, J. M. (1986). *Women's ways of knowing: The development of self, voice, and mind.* New York: Basic Books.

Benney, M., & Hughes, E. C. (1970). Of sociology and the interview. In N. K. Denzin (Ed.), *Sociological methods: A source book.* London: Butterworth.

Berg, D. R., Lonsway, K. A., & Fitzgerald, L. F. (1999). Rape prevention education for men: The effectiveness of empathy induction techniques. *Journal of College Student Development, 40,* 219–234.

Bergen, R. K. (1996). *Wife rape: Understanding the response of survivors and service providers.* Thousand Oaks, CA: Sage.

Bergen, R. K. (1993). Interviewing survivors of marital rape: Doing feminist research on sensitive topics. In C. M. Renzetti & R. M. Lee (Eds.), *Researching sensitive topics* (pp. 197–211). Newbury Park, CA: Sage.

Berger, R. J., Searles, P., & Neuman, W. L. (1988). The dimensions of rape reform legislation. *Law and Society Review, 22,* 329–357.

Bowden, P. (1997). *Caring: Gender-sensitive ethics.* London: Routledge.

Brabeck, M. M. (1996). The moral self, values and circles of belonging. In K. F. Wyche & F. J. Crosby (Eds.), *Women's ethnicities: Journeys through psychology* (pp. 145–165). Boulder, CO: Westview Press.

Brabeck, M. M., & Ting, K. (2000). Feminist ethics: Lenses for examining ethical psychological practice. In M. M. Brabeck (Ed.), *Practicing feminist ethics in psychology* (pp. 17–35). Washington DC: American Psychological Association.

Brady, J. L., Guy, J. D., Poelstra, P. L., & Brokaw, B. F. (1999). Vicarious traumatization, spirituality, and the treatment of sexual abuse survivors: A national study of women psychotherapists. *Professional Psychology Research and Practice, 30,* 386–393.

Breckler, S. J., & Wiggins, E. C. (1989). On defining attitudes and attitude theory: Once more with feeling. In A. R. Pratkanis, S. J. Breckler, & A. G. Greenwald (Eds.), *Attitude structure and function* (pp. 407–427). Hillsdale, NJ: Erlbaum.

Brenner, N. D., McMahon, P. M., Warren, C. W., & Douglas, K. A. (1999). Forced sexual intercourse and associated health-risk behaviors among female college students in the United States. *Journal of Consulting and Clinical Psychology, 67,* 252–259.

Brown, L. S. (1994). *Subversive dialogues: Theory in feminist therapy.* New York: Basic Books.

Brownmiller, S. (1975). *Against our will: Men, women, and rape.* New York: Bantam.

Buchwald, E., Fletcher, P., & Roth, M. (1993). *Transforming a rape culture.* Minneapolis: Milweed Press.

Burt, M. R., & Katz, B. L. (1988). Coping strategies and recovery from rape. *Annals of the New York Academy of Sciences, 528,* 345–358.

Calhoun, C. (1989). Subjectivity and emotion. *Philosophical Forum, 20,* 195–210.

Calhoun, K., Atkeson, B., & Resick, P. (1982). A longitudinal examination of fear reactions in victims of rape. *Journal of Counseling Psychology, 29,*655–661.

Campbell, D. T., & Stanley, J. C. (1963). *Experimental and quasi-experimental designs for research*. New York: Houghton Mifflin.

Campbell, R. (1998a). The community response to rape: Victims' experiences with the legal, medical, and mental health systems. *American Journal of Community Psychology, 26*, 355–379.

Campbell, R. (1998b). Unpublished field notes: Interviews with forty rape crisis centers in Michigan. Chicago: University of Illinois at Chicago.

Campbell, R. (1996). Unpublished field notes: Interviews with 168 rape crisis centers across the country. East Lansing, MI: Michigan State University.

Campbell, R., Baker, C. K., & Mazurek, T. (1998). Remaining radical? Organizational predictors of rape crisis centers' social change initiatives. *American Journal of Community Psychology, 26*, 465–491.

Campbell, R., & Bybee, D. (1997). Emergency medical services for rape victims: Detecting the cracks in service delivery. *Women's Health, 3*, 75–101.

Campbell, R., & Johnson, C. R. (1997). Police officers' perceptions of rape: Is there consistency between state law and individual beliefs? *Journal of Interpersonal Violence, 12*, 255–274.

Campbell, R., & Martin, P. Y. (2001). Services for sexual assault survivors: The role of rape crisis centers. In C. Renzetti, J. Edleson, & R. Bergen (Eds.), *Sourcebook on violence against women* (pp. 227–241). Thousand Oaks, CA: Sage.

Campbell, R., & Raja, S. (1999). The secondary victimization of rape victims: Insights from mental health professionals who treat survivors of violence. *Violence & Victims, 14*, 261–275.

Campbell, R., Sefl, T., Barnes, H. E., Ahrens, C. E., Wasco, S. M., & Zaragoza-Diesfeld, Y. (1999). Community services for rape survivors: Enhancing psychological well-being or increasing trauma? *Journal of Consulting and Clinical Psychology, 67*, 847–858.

Campbell, R., Sefl, T., Wasco, S. M., & Ahrens, C. E. (2001). Doing community research without a community: Creating safe space for rape survivors. Manuscript submitted for publication.

Campbell, R., & Wasco, S. M. (2000). Feminist approaches to social science: Epistemological and methodological tenets. *American Journal of Community Psychology, 28*, 773–791.

Campbell, R., Wasco, S. M., Ahrens, C. E., Sefl, T., & Barnes, H. E. (2001). Preventing the "second rape:" Rape survivors' experiences with community service providers. *Journal of Interpersonal Violence, 16*, 1239–1259.

Cannon, L. W., Higginbothan, E., & Leung, M. L. A. (1988). Race and class bias in qualitative research on women. *Gender & Society, 2*, 449–462.

Charmaz, K., & Mitchell, R. G. (1997). The myth of silent authorship: Self, substance, and style in ethnographic writing. In R. Hertz (Ed.), *Reflexivity and voice* (pp. 193–215). Thousand Oaks, CA: Sage.

Chrestman, K. R. (1995). Secondary exposure to trauma and self-reported distress among therapists. In B.H. Stamm (Ed.), *Secondary traumatic stress: Self-care issues for clinicians, researchers, and educators* (pp. 29–36). Lutherville, MD: Sidran Press.

Cluss, P. A., Boughton, J., Frank, E., Stewart, B. D., & West, D. (1983). The rape victim: Psychological correlates of participation on the legal process. *Criminal Justice and Behavior, 10*, 342–357.

Cohen, L., & Roth, S. (1987). The psychological aftermath of rape: Long-term effects and individual differences in recovery. *Journal of Social and Clinical Psychology, 5*, 525–534.

Cole, E. B., & Coultrap-McQuin, S. (1992). *Exploration in feminist ethics: Theory and practice*. Bloomington, IN: Indiana University Press.

Collins, P. H. (1991). *Black feminist thought: Knowledge, consciousness, and the politics of empowerment*. New York: Routledge.

Cone, J. D., & Foster, S. L. (1993). *Dissertations and theses from start to finish: Psychology and related fields*. Washington, DC: American Psychological Association.

Conroy, J. (2000). *Unspeakable acts, ordinary people: The dynamics of torture*. New York: Knopf.

Cook, J. A., & Fonow, M. M. (1990). Knowledge and women's interests: Issues of epistemology and methodology in feminist sociological research. In J. M. Nielsen (Ed.), *Feminist research methods: Exemplary readings in the social sciences* (pp. 69–93). Boulder, CO: Westview Press.

Cronbach, L. (1975). Beyond the two disciplines of scientific psychology. *American Psychologist, 30*, 116–127.

Davidson, S. (1980). The clinical effects of massive psychic trauma in families of Holocaust survivors. *Journal of Marital and Family Therapy, 6*, 11-21.

Davidson, W. S., Redner, R., Amdur, R. L., & Mitchell, C. M. (1990). *Alternative treatment for troubled youth: The case of diversion from the justice system*. New York: Plenum.

Davies, C., & Rosser, J. (1986). Gendered jobs in the health service: A problem for the labour process analysis. In D. Knight & H. Wilmott (Eds.), *Gender and the Labour Process*. Hampshire: Gower.

Davis, R., Taylor, B., & Bench, S. (1995). Impact of sexual and nonsexual assault on secondary victims. *Violence & Victims, 10*, 73–84.

Day, K. (1994). Conceptualizing women's fear of sexual assault on campus: A review of causes and recommendations for change. *Environment and Behavior, 26*, 742–765.

DeCoster, V. A. (1997). Physician treatment of patient emotions: An application of the sociology of emotion. *Social Perspectives on Emotion, 4*, 151–177.

Denzin, N. K. (1990). On understanding emotion: The interpretive-cultural agenda. In T. D. Kemper (Ed.), *Research agendas in the sociology of emotions* (pp. 85–116). Buffalo, NY: State University of New York Press.

DeVault, M. L. (1997). Personal writing in social research: Issues of production and interpretation. In R. Hertz (Ed.), *Reflexivity and voice* (pp. 216–228). Thousand Oaks, CA: Sage.

DeVault, M. L. (1996). Talking back to sociology: Distinctive contributions of feminist methodology. *Annual Review of Sociology, 22*, 29–50.

Dexter, L. A. (1956). Role relationships and conceptions of neutrality in interviewing. *American Journal of Sociology, 62*, 153–157.

Drout, C. E., & Gaertner, S. L. (1994). Gender differences in reactions to female victims. *Social Behavior and Personality, 22*, 267–278.

Dunn, L. (1991). Research alert! Qualitative research may be hazardous to your health! *Qualitative Health Research, 1*, 388–392.

Dutton, M. A., & Rubinstein, F. L. (1995). Working with people with PTSD: Research implications. In C. R. Figley (Ed.), *Compassion fatigue: Coping with secondary traumatic stress disorder in those who treat the traumatized* (pp. 82–100). Bristol, PA: Brunner/Mazel.

Eberth, L. D. (1989). The psychological impact of rape crisis counseling on volunteer counselors. Unpublished dissertation: The Wright Institute.

Edwards, R. (1993). An education in interviewing: Placing the researchers and the research. In C. M. Renzetti & R. M. Lee (Eds.), *Researching sensitive topics* (pp. 181–196). Newbury Park, CA: Sage.

Ekman, P., & Davidson, R. J. (Eds.) (1994). *The nature of emotion: Fundamental questions*. New York: Oxford University Press.

Ellis, C. (forthcoming). "There are survivors": Telling a story of sudden death. *Sociological Quarterly*.

Ellis, C. (1995). *Final negotiations: A story of love, loss, and chronic illness*. Philadelphia: Temple University Press.

Ellis, C. (1991a). Emotional sociology. *Studies in Symbolic Interaction, 12*, 123–145.

Ellis, C. (1991b). Sociological introspection and emotional experience. *Studies in Symbolic Interaction, 14,* 23–50.

Ellis, C., Kiesinger, C. E., & Tillmann-Healy, L. M. (1997). Interactive interviewing: Talking about emotional experience. In R. Hertz (Ed.), *Reflexivity and voice* (pp. 119–149). Thousand Oaks, CA: Sage.

Ellis, E., Atkeson, B., & Calhoun, K. (1981). An assessment of long-term reaction to rape. *Journal of Abnormal Psychology, 90,*263–266.

Feingold, H. L. (1995). *Bearing witness: How America and its Jews responded to the Holocaust.* Syracuse, NY: Syracuse University Press.

Figley, C. R. (1995a). Compassion fatigue as secondary traumatic stress disorder: An overview. In C. R. Figley (Ed.), *Compassion fatigue: Coping with secondary traumatic stress disorder in those who treat the traumatized* (pp. 1–20). Bristol, PA: Brunner/ Mazel.

Figley, C. R. (1995b). Compassion fatigue: Toward a new understanding of the costs of caring. In B. H. Stamm (Ed.), *Secondary traumatic stress: Self-care issues for clinicians, researchers, and educators* (pp. 3–28). Lutherville, MD: Sidran Press.

Fischer, K. (1989). Defining the boundaries of admissible expert testimony on rape trauma syndrome. *University of Illinois Law Review, 1989,* 691–734.

Fisher, B. S., Sloan, J. J., Cullen, F. T., & Lu, C. (1998). Crime in the ivory tower: The level and sources of student victimization. *Criminology, 36,* 671–710.

Fitzpatrick, K. M., & Wilson, M. (1999). Exposure to violence and posttraumatic stress symptomatology among abortion clinic workers. *Journal of Traumatic Stress, 12,* 227–242.

Foa, E. B., Rothbaum, B. O., Riggs, D. S., & Murdock, T. B. (1991). Treatment of post traumatic stress disorder in rape victims: A comparison between cognitive-behavioral approaches and counseling. *Journal of Consulting and Clinical Psychology, 59,* 715–723.

Foa, E. B., Steketee, G., & Olasov, B. (1989). Behavioral/cognitive conceptualization of post-traumatic stress disorder. *Behavior Therapy, 20,* 155–176.

Foner, N. (1994). *The caregiving dilemma: Work in an American nursing home.* Berkeley, CA: University of California Press.

Fonow, M. M., & Cook, J. A. (1991). Back to the future: A look at the second wave of feminist epistemology and methodology. In M. M. Fonow & J. A. Cook (Eds.), *Beyond methodology: Feminist scholarship as lived research* (pp. 1–15). Bloomington, IN: Indiana University Press.

Francisco, P. W. (1999). *Telling: A memoir of rape and recovery.* New York: Harper Collins.

Frank, E., Anderson, B., Stewart, B. D., Dancu, C., Hughes, C., & West, D. (1988). Efficacy of cognitive behavioral therapy and systematic desensitization in the treatment of the rape victim. *Behavior Therapy, 19,* 403–420.

Frank, E., & Stewart, B. D. (1984). Depressive symptoms in rape victims: A revisit. *Journal of Affective Disorders, 7,* 77–85.

Frazier, P. A., & Haney, B. (1996). Sexual assault cases in the legal system: Police, prosecutor, and victim perspectives. *Law and Human Behavior, 20,* 607–628.

Freyberg, J. T. (1980). Difficulties in separation-individuation as experienced by offspring of Nazi Holocaust survivors. *American Journal of Orthopsychiatry, 50,* 87–95.

Friedman, N. L. (1990). Conventional covert ethnographic research by a worker. In R. G. Burgess (Ed.), *Studies in qualitative methodology* (pp. 99–120), Greenwich, CT: JAI Press.

Frohmann, L. (1991). Discrediting victims' allegations of sexual assault: Prosecutorial accounts of case rejections. *Social Problems, 38,* 213–226.

Gergen, K. J. (1994). *Realities and relationships: Soundings in social construction.* Cambridge, MA: Harvard University Press.

Gergen, K. J. (1985). The social constructionist movement in modern psychology. *American Psychologist, 40,* 266–275.

Giddens, A. (1993). *New rules of sociological method: A positive critique of interpretative studies.* Stanford, CA: Stanford University Press.

Gilbert, K. R. (2001). Introduction: Why are we interested in emotions? In K. R. Gilbert (Ed.), *The emotional nature of qualitative research* (pp. 3–15). Boca Raton, FL: CRC Press.

Gilligan, C. (1982). *In a different voice: Psychological theory and women's development*. Cambridge, MA: Harvard University Press.

Golding, J. M. (1994). Sexual assault history and physical health in randomly selected Los Angeles women. *Health Psychology, 13*, 130–138.

Goodman, L. A., Koss, M. P., & Russo, N. F. (1993a). Violence against women: Physical and mental health effects. Part I: Research findings. *Applied and Preventive Psychology, 2*, 79–89.

Goodman, L. A., Koss, M. P., & Russo, N. F. (1993b). Violence against women: Mental health effects. Part II: Conceptualizations of posttraumatic stress. *Applied and Preventive Psychology, 2*, 123–130.

Gordon, M. T., & Riger, S. (1989). *The female fear: The social costs of rape*. New York: The Free Press.

Grossman, F. K., Kruger, L., & Moore, R. P. (1999). Reflections on a feminist research project. *Psychology of Women Quarterly, 23*, 117–135.

Groves, J. M. (1997). *Hearts and minds: The controversy over laboratory animals*. Philadelphia: Temple University Press.

Groves, J. M. (1995). Learning to feel: The neglected sociology of social movements. *Sociological Review, 43*, 435–461.

Guba, E. G., & Lincoln, Y. S. (1994). Competing paradigms in qualitative research. In N. K. Denzin & Y. S. Lincoln (Eds.), *Handbook of qualitative research* (pp. 105–117). Thousand Oaks, CA: Sage.

Guzzino, M. H., & Taxis, C. (1995). Leading experiential vicarious trauma groups for professionals. *Treating Abuse Today, 4*, 27–31.

Habermas, J. (1971). *Knowledge and human interests*. Boston: Beacon Press.

Habermas, J. (1967). *On the logic of the social sciences*. Cambridge, MA: MIT Press.

Hartman, C. R. (1995). The nurse-patient relationship and victims of violence. *Scholarly Inquiry for Nursing Practice, 9*, 175–192.

Hartsock, N. (1998). *The feminist standpoint revisited and other essays*. Boulder, CO: Westview.

Heimer, C. A., & Stevens, M. L. (1997). Caring for the organization: Social workers as frontline risk managers in neonatal intensive care units. *Work and Occupations, 24*, 133–163.

Herman, J. L. (1992). *Trauma and recovery*. New York: Basic Books.

Hippensteele, S. K. (1997). Activist research and social narratives: Dialectics of power, privilege, and institutional change. In M. D. Schwartz (Ed.), *Researching sexual violence against women: Methodological and personal perspectives* (pp. 86–100). Thousand Oaks, CA: Sage.

Hochschild, A. R. (1983). *The managed heart: Commercialization of human feeling*. Berkeley, CA: University of California Press.

Hochschild, A. R. (1979). Emotion work, feeling rules, and social structure. *American Journal of Sociology, 85*, 551–575.

Hochschild, A. R. (1975). The sociology of feeling and emotion: Selected possibilities. In M. Millman & R. Kanter (Eds.), *Another voice* (pp. 280–307). Garden City, NY: Anchor.

Holmstrom, L., & Burgess, A. (1979). Rape: The husband's and boyfriend's initial reactions. *The Family Coordinator, 28*, 321–326.

Howarth, W. (1990). Oliver Sacks: The ecology of writing science. *Modern Language Studies 20*, 103–120.

Huberman, A. M., & Miles, M. B. (1994). Data management and analysis methods. In N. K. Denzin & Y. S. Lincoln (Eds.), *Handbook of qualitative research* (pp. 428–444). Thousand Oaks, CA: Sage.

Huff, J. K. (1997). The sexual harassment of researchers by research subjects: Lessons from the field. In M. D. Schwartz (Ed.), *Researching sexual violence against women: Methodological and personal perspectives* (pp. 115–127). Thousand Oaks, CA: Sage.

Hunter, A. (1990). *The rhetoric of social research: Understood and believed.* New Brunswick, NJ: Rutgers University Press.

Hutchinson, S. A., Wilson, M. E., Wilson, H. S. (1994). Benefits of participating in research interviews. *IMAGE: Journal of Nursing Scholarship, 26,* 161–164.

Iliffee, G., & Steed, L. G. (2000). Exploring the counselor's experience of working with perpetrators and survivors of domestic violence. *Journal of Interpersonal Violence, 15,* 393–412.

Jaggar, A. (1989). Love and knowledge: Emotion in feminist epistemology. In A. Jaggar & S. R. Bordo (Eds.), *Gender/body/knowledge* (pp. 145–171). New Brunswick, NJ: Rutgers University Press.

James, N. (1992). Care = organizational + physical labor + emotional labor. *Sociology of Health and Illness, 14,* 488–509.

James, N. (1989). Emotional labor: Skill and work in the social regulation of feelings. *Sociological Review, 37,* 15–47.

Janoff-Bulman, R. (1992). *Shattered assumptions: Towards a new psychology of trauma.* New York: The Free Press.

Janoff-Bulman, R. (1989). Assumptive worlds and the stress of traumatic events: Applications of schema construct. *Social Cognition, 7,* 113–136.

Janoff-Bulman, R. (1982). Esteem and control bases of blame: "Adaptive" strategies for victims versus observers. *Journal of Personality, 50,* 180–192.

Janoff-Bulman, R., & Frieze, I. H. (1983). A theoretical perspective for understanding reactions to victimization. *Journal of Social Issues, 39,* 1–17.

Jasper, J. M., & Nelkin, D. (1992). *The animal rights crusade: The growth of a moral protest.* New York: The Free Press.

Jayaratne, T. E., & Stewart, A. J. (1991). Quantitative and qualitative methods in social sciences: Current feminist issues and practical strategies. In M. M. Fonow & J. A. Cook (Eds.), *Beyond methodology: Feminist scholarship as lived research* (pp. 85–106). Bloomington, IN: Indiana University Press.

Joinson, C. (1992). Coping with compassion fatigue. *Nursing, 22,* 116–122.

Jones, L. C. (1997). Both friend and stranger: How crisis volunteers build and manage unpersonal relationships with clients. *Social Perspectives on Emotion, 4,* 125–148.

Kahn, R. L., & Cannell, L. F. (1957). *The dynamics of interviewing.* New York: Wiley.

Kalven, J. (1999). *Working with available light: A family's world after violence.* New York: Norton.

Kanin, E. J. (1957). Male aggression in dating-courtship relations. *American Journal of Sociology, 63,* 197–204.

Kassam-Adams, N. (1995). The risks of treating sexual trauma: Stress and secondary trauma in psychotherapists. In B. H. Stamm (Ed.), *Secondary traumatic stress: Self-care issues for clinicians, researchers, and educators* (pp. 37–48). Lutherville, MD: Sidran Press.

Katz, D. (1960). The functional approach to the study of attitudes. *Public Opinion Quarterly, 24,* 163–204.

Kelly, J. G. (1988). *A guide to conducting prevention research in the community.* New York: Haworth Press.

Kelly, J. G. (1986). Context and process: An ecological view of the interdependence of practice and research. *American Journal of Community Psychology, 14,* 581–589.

Kelly, J. G. (1970). Antidotes for arrogance: Training for a community psychology. *American Psychologist, 25,* 524–531.

Kelly, J. G. (1968). Towards an ecological conception of preventive interventions. In J. W. Carter, Jr. (Ed.), *Research contributions from psychology to community mental health* (pp. 75–99). New York: Behavioral Publications.

Kelly, L. (1988). *Surviving sexual violence*. Minneapolis: University of Minnesota Press.

Kemper, T. D. (1990). Themes and variations in the sociology of emotions. In T. D. Kemper (Ed.), *Research agendas in the sociology of emotions* (pp. 3–23). Buffalo, NY: State University of New York Press.

Kemper, T. D. (1981). Social constructionist and positivist approaches to the sociology of emotions. *American Journal of Sociology, 87*, 336–362.

Kemper, T. D. (1978). *A social interaction theory of emotions*. New York: Wiley.

Kilpatrick, D., Resick, P., & Veronen, L. (1981). Effects of a rape experience: A longitudinal study. *Journal of Social Issues, 37*, 109–122.

Kilpatrick, D., Saunders, B., Veronen, L., Best, C., & Judith, V. (1987). Criminal victimization: Lifetime prevalence, reporting to police and psychological impact. *Crime and Delinquency, 33*, 479–489.

Kimerling, R., & Calhoun, K. S. (1994). Somatic symptoms, social support, and treatment seeking among sexual assault victims. *Journal of Consulting and Clinical Psychology, 62*, 333–340.

Kimmel, E. B., & Crawford, M. (2000). *Innovations in feminist psychological research*. New York: Cambridge University Press.

Kleinman, S. (1997). Essaying the personal: Making sociological stories stick. *Qualitative Sociology, 20*, 553–564.

Kleinman, S., & Copp, M. A. (1993). *Emotions and fieldwork*. Newbury Park, CA: Sage.

Koss, M. P. (1999, August). Rape research in the year 2000 and beyond. Paper presented at the American Psychological Association Conference, Boston, MA.

Koss, M. P. (1993). Rape: Scope, impact, interventions, and public policy responses. *American Psychologist, 48*, 1062–1069.

Koss, M. P., Gidycz, C. A., & Wisniewski, N. (1987). The scope of rape: Incidence and prevalence of sexual aggression and victimization in a national sample of higher education students. *Journal of Consulting and Clinical Psychology, 55*, 162–170.

Koss, M. P., Goodman, L. A., Browne, A., Fitzgerald, L. F., Keita, G. P., & Russo, N. F. (1994). *No safe haven: Male violence against women at home, at work, and in the community*. Washington, DC: American Psychological Association.

Koss, M. P., & Harvey, M. R. (1991). *The rape victim: Clinical and community interventions* (second edition). Newbury Park, CA: Sage.

Koss, M. P., Woodruff, W. J., & Koss, P. G. (1991). Criminal victimization among primary care medical patients: Prevalence, incidence, and physician usage. *Behavioral Sciences and the Law, 9*, 85–96.

Krieger, S. (1991). *Social science and the self: Personal essays on an art form*. New Brunswick, NJ: Rutgers University Press.

Kuhn, T. S. (1970). *The structure of scientific revolutions* (2nd ed.). Chicago: University of Chicago Press.

Lather, P., & Smithies, C. (1997). *Troubling the angels: Women living with HIV/AIDS*. Boulder, CO: Westview Press.

Lerner, M., & Miller, D. (1978). Just world research and the attribution process: Looking back and ahead. *Psychological Bulletin, 85*, 1030–1051.

Lincoln, Y. S., & Guba, E. G. (1985). *Naturalistic inquiry*. Newbury Park, CA: Sage.

Linden, R. R. (1993). *Making stories, making selves: Feminist reflections on the Holocaust*. Columbus, OH: Ohio State University Press.

Lira, L. R., Koss, M. P., & Russo, N. F. (1999). Mexican American women's definitions of rape and sexual abuse. *Hispanic Journal of Behavioral Sciences, 21*, 236–265.

Lofland, J., & Lofland, L. H. (1995). *Analyzing social settings: A guide to qualitative observation and analysis* (3rd ed.). New York: Wadsworth.

Lonsway, K. A. (1996). Preventing acquaintance rape through education: What do we know? *Psychology of Women Quarterly, 20*, 229–265.

Lord, C. G., Ross, L., & Lepper, M. R. (1979). Biased assimilation and attitude polarization: The effects of prior theories on subsequently considered evidence. *Journal of Personality and Social Psychology, 37*, 2098–2109.

Maccoby, E. E., & Jacklin, C. N. (1974). *The psychology of sex differences*. Stanford, CA: Stanford University Press.

MacKinnon, C. A. (1987). *Feminism unmodified: Discourses on life and law*. Cambridge, MA: Harvard University Press.

Madigan, L., & Gamble, N. (1991). *The second rape: Society's continued betrayal of the victim*. New York: Lexington Books.

Martin, P. Y., & Powell, M. R. (1994). Accounting for the "second assault": Legal organizations' framing of rape victims. *Law and Social Inquiry, 19*, 853–890.

Matoesian, G. M. (1993). *Reproducing rape: Domination through talk in the courtroom*. Chicago: The University of Chicago Press.

Mattley, C. (1997). Field research with phone sex workers: Managing the researcher's emotions. In M.D. Schwartz (Ed.), *Researching sexual violence against women: Methodological and personal perspectives* (pp. 101–114). Thousand Oaks, CA: Sage.

McCann, I. L., & Pearlman, L. A. (1993). Vicarious traumatization: The emotional costs of working with survivors. *Treating Abuse Today, 3*, 28–31.

McCann, I. L., & Pearlman, L. A. (1990a). Vicarious traumatization: A framework for understanding the psychological effects of working with victims. *Journal of Traumatic Stress, 3*, 131–149.

McCann, I. L., & Pearlman, L. A. (1990b). *Psychological trauma and the adult survivor: Theory, therapy, and transformation*. New York: Brunner/Mazel.

McMillan, C. (1982). *Women, reason, and nature: Some philosophical problems with feminism*. Princeton, NJ: Princeton University Press.

Merrill, L. L., Newell, C. E., Milner, J. S., Koss, M. P., Hervig, L. K., Gold, S. R., Rosswork, S. G., & Thornton, S. R. (1998). Prevalence of premilitary adult sexual victimization and aggression in a Navy recruit sample. *Military Medicine, 163*, 209–212.

Meyeroff, M. (1971). *On caring*. New York: Harper & Row.

Mies, M. (1991). Women's research or feminist research? The debate surrounding feminist science and methodology. In M. M. Fonow & J. A. Cook (Eds.), *Beyond methodology: Feminist scholarship as lived research* (pp. 60–84). Bloomington, IN: Indiana University Press.

Mies, M. (1983). Toward a methodology for feminist research. In G. Bowles & R. Duelli Klein (Eds.), *Theories of women's studies* (pp. 117–139). London: Routledge & Kegan Paul.

Miles, M.B., & Huberman, A. M. (1994). *Qualitative data analysis*. Thousand Oaks, CA: Sage.

Mitchell, C. M., Davidson, W. S., Redner, R., Blakely, C., & Emshoff, J. G. (1985). Non-professional counselors: Revisiting selection and impact issues. *American Journal of Community Psychology, 13*, 203–220.

Mitchell, J. T., & Everly, G. S. (1995). The critical incident stress debriefing (CISD) and the prevention of work-related traumatic stress among high risk occupational groups. In G. S. Everly & J. M. Lating (Eds.), *Psychotraumatology: Key papers and core concepts in post-traumatic stress* (pp. 267–280). New York: Plenum.

Montada, L., & Lerner, M. J. (1998). Responses to victimization and belief in a just world. New York: Plenum.

Moran-Ellis, J. (1996). Close to home: The experience of researching child sexual abuse. In M. Hester, L. Kelly, & J. Radford (Eds.), *Women, violence, and male power* (pp. 176–187). Buckingham: Open University Press.

Motta, R. W., Joseph, J. M., Rose, R. D., Suozzi, J. M., & Leiderman, L. J. (1997). Secondary trauma: Assessing inter-generational transmission of war experiences with a modified stroop procedure. *Journal of Clinical Psychology, 53*, 895–903.

Munroe, J. F., Shay, J., Fisher, L., Makary, C., Rappaport, K., & Zimering, R. (1995). Preventing compassion fatigue: A team treatment model. In C. R. Figley (Ed.), *Compassion fatigue: Coping with secondary traumatic stress disorder in those who treat the traumatized* (pp. 209–231). Bristol, PA: Brunner/Mazel.

Murphy, S. M. (1990). Rape, sexually transmitted diseases and human immunodeficiency virus infection. *International Journal of STD and AIDS, 1,* 79–82.

Naples, N. A. (1996). Feminist participatory research and empowerment: Going public as survivors of childhood sexual abuse. In H. Gottfried (Ed.), *Feminism and social change: Bridging theory and practice* (pp. 160–183). Urbana, IL: University of Illinois Press.

National Victim Center (1992). *Rape in American: A report to the nation.* Arlington, VA: Author.

Nelson, B. S., & Wright, D. W. (1996). Understanding and treating post–traumatic stress disorder symptoms in female partners of veterans with PTSD. *Journal of Marital and Family Therapy, 22,* 455–467.

Nielsen, J. M. (1990). *Feminist research methods: Exemplary readings in the social sciences.* Boulder, CO: Westview Press.

Noddings, N. (1984). *Caring: A feminine approach to ethics and moral education.* Berkeley, CA: University of California Press.

Oakley, A. (1988). Interviewing women: A contradiction in terms. In H. Roberts (Ed.), *Doing feminist research* (pp. 30–61). New York: Routledge.

O'Brien, M. (1994). The managed heart revisited: Health and social control. *Sociological Review, 42,* 393–413.

Oleson, V. (1994). Feminisms and models of qualitative research. In N. K. Denzin & Y. S. Lincoln (Eds.), *Handbook of qualitative research* (pp. 158–174). Thousand Oaks, CA: Sage.

Ortony, A., Clore, G. L., & Collins, A. (1988). *The cognitive structure of emotions.* New York: Cambridge University Press.

Parrot, A. (1991). Medical community response to acquaintance rape: Recommendations. In L. Bechhofer & A. Parrot (Eds.), *Acquaintance rape: The hidden victim* (pp. 304–316). New York: Wiley.

Patton, M. Q. (1990). *Qualitative evaluation and research methods* (2nd ed.). Newbury Park, CA: Sage.

Pearlman, L. A., & Maclan, P. S. (1995). Vicarious traumatizations: An empirical study of the effects of trauma work on trauma therapists. *Professional Psychology: Research and Practice, 26,* 558–565.

Pearlman, L. A., & Saakvitne, K. W. (1995a). Treating therapists with vicarious traumatization and secondary traumatic stress disorders. In C. R. Figley (Ed.), *Compassion fatigue: Coping with secondary traumatic stress disorder in those who treat the traumatized* (pp. 150–177). Bristol, PA: Brunner/Mazel.

Pearlman, L. A., & Saakvitne, K. W. (1995b). *Trauma and the therapist: Countertransference and vicarious traumatization in psychotherapy with incest survivors.* New York: Norton.

Perloff, L. S. (1983). Perceptions of vulnerability to victimization. *Journal of Social Issues, 39,* 41–61.

Petty, R. E., & Cacioppo, J. T. (1981). *Attitudes and persuasion: Classic and contemporary approaches.* Dubuque, IA: Brown Company Publishers.

Pickett, M., Brennan, A. M., Greenberg, H. S., Licht, L., & Wornell, J. D. (1994). Use of debriefing techniques to prevent compassion fatigue in research teams. *Nursing Research, 43,* 250–252.

Pierce, J. L. (1995). *Gender trials: Emotional lives in contemporary law firms.* Berkeley, CA: University of California Press.

Raine, N. V. (1998). *After silence: Rape and my journey back.* New York: Crown.

Rappaport, J. (1977). *Community psychology: Values, research, and action.* New York: Holt, Rinehart, and Winston.

Reinharz, S. (1993). Neglected voices and excessive demands in feminist research. *Qualitative Sociology, 16*, 69–76.

Reinharz, S. (1992). *Feminist methods in social research*. New York: Oxford University Press.

Reinharz, S. (1979). *On becoming a social scientist*. San Francisco: Jossey–Bass.

Remer, R., & Elliott, J. (1988a). Characteristics of secondary victims of sexual assault. *International Journal of Family Psychiatry, 9*, 373–387.

Remer, R., & Elliott, J. (1988b). Management of secondary victims of sexual assault. *International Journal of Family Psychiatry, 9*, 389–401.

Resick, P. A. (1993). The psychological impact of rape. *Journal of Interpersonal Violence*, 223–255.

Resick, P. A., & Schnicke, M. K. (1992). Cognitive processing therapy for sexual assault victims. *Journal of Consulting and Clinical Psychology, 60*, 748–756.

Richardson, L. (1994). Writing: A method of inquiry. In N. K. Denzin & Y. S. Lincoln (Eds.), *Handbook of qualitative research* (pp. 516–529). Thousand Oaks, CA: Sage.

Rogers, J. K. (1995). Just a temp: Experience and structure of alienation in temporary clerical employment. *Work and Occupations, 22*, 137–166.

Ronai, C. R., & Ellis, C. (1989). Turn-ons for money: Interactional strategies of the table dancer. *Journal of Contemporary Ethnography, 18*, 271–298.

Rose, K. E. (1998). Perceptions related to time in a qualitative study of informal careers of terminally ill cancer patients. *Journal of Clinical Nursing, 7*, 343–350.

Rosenheck, R., & Nathan, P. (1985). Secondary traumatization in children of Vietnam veterans. *Hospital and Community Psychiatry, 36*, 538–539.

Rosenthal, R. (1966). *Experimenter effects in behavioral research*. New York: Appleton-Century Crofts.

Rosenthal, R., & Rosnow, R. L. (1969). *Artifact in behavioral research*. New York: Wiley.

Rosnow, R. L., Rotheram-Borus, M. R., Ceci, S. J., Blanck, P. D., & Koocher, G. P (1993). The Institutional Review Board as a mirror of scientific and ethical standards. *American Psychologist, 48*, 821–826.

Rothbaum, B. O. (1997). A controlled study of eye movement desensitization and reprocessing in the treatment of posttraumatic stress disordered sexual assault victims. *Bulletin of the Menninger Clinic, 61*, 317–334.

Rothman, B. K. (1986a). Reflections: On hard work. *Qualitative Sociology, 9*, 48–53.

Rothman, B. K. (1986b). *The tentative pregnancy: How amniocentesis changes the experience of motherhood*. New York: Norton.

Rubin, H. J., & Rubin, I. S. (1995). *Qualitative interviewing: The art of hearing data*. Thousand Oaks, CA: Sage.

Ruddick, S. (1980). Maternal thinking. *Feminist Studies, 6*, 342–367.

Russell, D. E. H. (1982). *Rape in marriage*. New York: Macmillian.

Saakvitne, K. W., & Pearlman, L. A. (1996). *Transforming the pain: A workbook on vicarious traumatization for helping professionals who work with traumatized clients*. New York: Norton.

Sales, B. D., & Folkman, S. (2000). *Ethics in research with human participants*. Washington, DC: American Psychological Association.

Sandelowski, M. (1994). The use of quotes in qualitative research. *Research in Nursing and Health, 17*, 479–482.

Sarason, S. B. (1974). *The psychological sense of community: Prospects for a community psychology*. San Francisco: Jossey-Bass.

Saunders, C. M. (1999). *Grief, the mourning after: Dealing with adult bereavement*. New York: Wiley.

Schachter, S., & Singer, J. E. (1962). Cognitive, social, and physiological determinants of emotional state. *Psychological Review, 69*, 379–399.

Schauben, L. J., & Frazier, P. A. (1995). Vicarious trauma: The effects on female counselors of working with sexual violence survivors. *Psychology of Women Quarterly, 19*, 49–64.

Schechter, S. (1982). *Women and male violence*. Boston: South End Press.

Schiebinger, L. (1999). *Has feminism changed science?* Cambridge, MA: Harvard University Press.

Schwartz, M. D. (1997). Emotion in researching violence against women. In M. D. Schwartz (Ed.), *Researching sexual violence against women: Methodological and personal perspectives* (pp. 71–73). Thousand Oaks, CA: Sage.

Searles, P., & Berger, R. J. (1987). The current status of rape reform legislation: An examination of state statutes. *Women's Rights Law Reporter, 10,* 25–40.

Sebold, A. (1999). *Lucky.* New York: Simon & Schuster.

Shaver, K. G. (1975). *An introduction to attribution processes.* Cambridge, MA: Winthrop.

Shaver, K. G. (1970). Defensive attribution: Effects of severity and relevance on the responsibility assigned for an accident. *Journal of Personality and Social Psychology, 14,* 101–113.

Shott, S. (1979). Emotion and social life: A symbolic interactionist analysis. *American Journal of Sociology, 84,* 1317–1334.

Sieber, J. E. (2000). Planning research: Basic ethical decision-making. In B. D. Sales & S. Folkman (Eds.), *Ethics in research with human participants* (pp. 13–26). Washington, DC: American Psychological Association.

Siegel, J. M., Golding, J. M., Stein, J. A., & Burnam, M. A. (1990). Reactions to sexual assault: A community study. *Journal of Interpersonal Violence, 5,* 229–246.

Simonds, W. (1996). *Abortion at work: Ideology and practice in a feminist clinic.* New Brunswick, NJ: Rutgers University Press.

Singer, J. A. (1995). Putting emotion in context: Its place within individual and social narratives. *Journal of Narrative and Life History, 5,* 255–267.

Sloan, L. M. (1995). Revictimization by polygraph: The practice of polygraphing survivors of sexual assault. *Medicine and Law, 14,* 255–267.

Small, E. (1995). Valuing the unseen emotional labor of nursing. *Nursing Times, 91,* 40–41.

Smith, A. C., & Kleinman, S. (1989). Managing emotions in medical school: Students' contracts with the living and the dead. *Social Psychology Quarterly, 52,* 56–69.

Smith, M. B. (2000). Moral foundations in research with human participants. In B. D. Sales & S. Folkman (Eds.), *Ethics in research with human participants* (pp. 3–10). Washington DC: American Psychological Association.

Smith, M. B., Brunner, J., & White, R. W. (1956). *Opinions and personality.* New York: Wiley.

Smith, P. (1992). *The emotional labour of nursing.* Basingstoke: MacMillan.

Smith, P. (1991). The nursing process: Raising the profile of emotional care in nurse training. *Journal of Advanced Nursing, 16,* 74–81.

Smith, P. (1989). Nurses' emotional labor. *Nursing Time, 85,* 47; 49–51.

Snow, D. L., Grady, K., & Goyette-Ewing, M. (2000). A perspective on ethical issues in community psychology. In J. Rappaport & E. Seidman (Eds.), *Handbook of community psychology* (pp. 897–917). New York: Plenum.

Spencer, C. C. (1987). Sexual assault: The second victimization. In L. L. Crites & W. L. Hepperle (Eds.), *Women, the courts, and equality* (pp. 54–73). Newbury Park, CA: Sage.

Spohn, C. & Horney, J. (1992). *Rape law reform: A grassroots revolution and its impact.* New York: Plenum Press.

Staden, H. S. (1998). Alertness to the needs of others: A study of the emotional labour of caring. *Journal of Advanced Nursing, 27,* 147–156.

Stake, R. E. (1994). Case studies. In N. K. Denzin & Y. S. Lincoln (Eds.), *Handbook of qualitative research* (pp. 236–247). Thousand Oaks, CA: Sage.

Stanko, E. A. (1997). "I second that emotion": Reflections on feminism, emotionality, and research on sexual violence. In M. D. Schwartz (Ed.), *Researching sexual violence against women: Methodological and personal perspectives* (pp. 74–85). Thousand Oaks, CA: Sage.

Stanko, E. A. (1993). Ordinary fear: Women, violence, and personal safety. In P. Bart, & E. G. Moran (Eds.), *Violence against women: The bloody footprints* (pp. 155–164). Newbury Park, CA: Sage.

Stanko, E. A. (1992). The case of fearful women: Gender, personal safety, and fear of crime. *Women & Criminal Justice, 4,* 117–135.

Steketee, G., & Foa, E. (1987). Rape victims: Post-traumatic stress responses and their treatment: A review of the literature. *Journal of Anxiety Disorders, 1,* 69–86.

Strauss, A., & Corbin, J. (1990). *Basics of qualitative research: Grounded theory procedures and techniques.* Newbury Park, CA: Sage.

Sullivan, C. M., Tan, C., Basta, J., Rumptz, M., & Davidson, W. S. (1992). An advocacy intervention for women with abusive partners: Initial evaluation. *American Journal of Community Psychology, 20,* 309–332.

Sullivan, C. M. (1991). The provision of advocacy services to women leaving abusive partners: An exploratory study. *Journal of Interpersonal Violence, 6,* 41–54.

Thoits, P. A. (1996). Managing the emotions of others. *Symbolic Interaction, 19,* 85–109.

Thoits, P. A. (1990). Emotional deviance: Research agendas. In T. D. Kemper (Ed.), *Research agendas in the sociology of emotions* (pp. 180–203). Buffalo, NY: State University of New York Press.

Thoits, P. A. (1986). Social support as coping assistance. *Journal of Consulting and Clinical Psychology, 54,* 416–423.

Thoits, P. A. (1985). Self-labeling processes in mental illness: The role of emotional deviance. *American Journal of Sociology, 92,* 221–249.

Tjaden, P. A., & Thoennes, N. (2000). Prevalence and consequences of male-to-female intimate violence as measured by the National Violence against Women Survey. *Violence against Women, 6,* 142–161.

Tjaden, P. & Thoennes, N. (1998). *Prevalence, incidence, and consequences of violence against women: Findings from the National Violence against Women Survey.* Washington DC: U.S. Department of Justice, National Institute of Justice.

Tolich, M. B. (1993). Alienating and liberating emotions at work: Supermarket clerks' performance of customer service. *Journal of Contemporary Ethnography, 22,* 361–381.

Trickett, E. J. (1998). Toward a framework for defining and resolving ethical issues in the protection of communities involved in primary prevention projects. *Ethics & Behavior, 8,* 321–337.

Trickett, E. J. (1996). A future for community psychology: The contexts of diversity and the diversity of contexts. *American Journal of Community Psychology, 24,* 209–234.

Trickett, E. J. (1984). Towards a distinctive community psychology: An ecological metaphor for training and the conduct of research. *American Journal of Community Psychology, 12,* 261–279.

Tronto, J. C. (1989). Women and caring: What can feminists learn about morality from caring? In A. Jaggar & S. R. Bordo (Eds.), *Gender/body/knowledge* (pp. 172–187). New Brunswick, NJ: Rutgers University Press.

Tyra, P. A. (1979). Volunteer rape counselors: Selected characteristics—empathy, attribution of responsibility, and rape counselor syndrome. Unpublished dissertation: Boston University School of Education.

Ullman, S. E. (1998). Does offender violence escalate when rape victims fight back? *Journal of Interpersonal Violence, 13,* 179–192.

Ullman, S. E. (1997). Review and critique of empirical studies of rape avoidance. *Criminal Justice and Behavior, 24,* 177–204.

Ullman, S. E. (1996a). Do social reactions to sexual assault victims vary by support provider? *Violence & Victims, 11,* 143–156.

Ullman, S. E. (1996b). Social reactions, coping strategies, and self-blame attributions in adjustment to sexual assault. *Psychology of Women Quarterly, 20,* 505–526.

Ullman, S. E. (1996c). Correlates and consequences of adult sexual assault disclosure. *Journal of Interpersonal Violence, 11,* 554–571.

Ullman, S. E., & Knight, R. A. (1995). Women's resistance strategies to different rapist types. *Criminal Justice & Behavior, 22,* 263–283.

Ullman, S. E., & Knight, R. A. (1993). The efficacy of women's resistance strategies in rape situations. *Psychology of Women Quarterly, 17*, 23–38.

Ullman, S.E., & Knight, R.A. (1992). Fighting back: Women's resistance to rape. *Journal of Interpersonal Violence, 7*, 31–43.

Vaughan, D. (1986). *Uncoupling: Turning points in intimate relationships.* New York: Oxford University Press.

Veronen, L. J., Saunders, B. E., & Resnick, H. S. (1989). Initial and long-term reactions of partners of sexual assault victims. Paper presented at the 97th Annual Convention of the American Psychological Association, New Orleans.

Walker, E. A., Newman, E., Koss, M., & Bernstein, D. (1997). Does the study of victimization revictimize the victims? *General Hospital Psychiatry, 19*, 403–410.

Wasco, S. M. (2000). Conceptualizing the harm done by rape: Applications of trauma theory to experiences of sexual assault. Manuscript submitted for publication.

Wasco, S. M., & Campbell, R. (in press) Emotional reactions of rape victim advocates: A multiple case study of anger and fear. *Psychology of Women Quarterly.*

Weaver, T. L., & Clum, G. A. (1995). Psychological distress associated with interpersonal violence: A meta-analysis. *Clinical Psychology Review, 15*, 115–140.

Weber, M. (1949). *Methodology of the social sciences.* New York: The Free Press.

Weber, M. (1947). *The theory of social and economic organization.* New York: The Free Press.

Weiss, R. S. (1994). *Learning from strangers: The art and method of qualitative interview studies.* New York: The Free Press.

West, C., & Zimmerman, D. H. (1991). Doing gender. In J. Lorber & S. A. Farrell (Eds.), *The social construction of gender* (pp. 13–37). Newbury Park, CA: Sage.

Wharton, A. S., & Erickson, R. J. (1995). The consequences of caring: Exploring the links between women's jobs and family emotion work. *Sociological Quarterly, 36*, 273–296.

Whittier, N. (1995). *Feminist generations: The persistence of the radical women's movement.* Philadelphia: Temple University Press.

Wichroski, M. A. (1994). The secretary: Invisible labor in the workworld of women. *Human Organization, 53*, 33–41.

Wilkins, R. (1993). Taking it personally: A note on emotion and autobiography. *Sociology, 27*, 93–100.

Williams, J. E. (1984). Secondary victimization: Confronting public attitudes about rape. *Victimology, 9*, 66–81.

Williams, J. H. (1987). *Psychology of women: Behavior in a biosocial context.* New York: Norton.

Wilson, T. D., DePaulo, B. M., Mook, D. G., & Klaaren, K. J. (1993). Scientists' evaluations of research: The biasing effects of the importance of the topic. *Psychological Science, 4*, 322–325.

Wyche, K. F., & Rice, J. K. (1997). Feminist therapy: From dialogue to tenets. In J. Worell & N. G. Johnson (Eds.), *Shaping the future of feminist psychology: Education, research and practice* (pp. 57–71). Washington, DC: American Psychological Association.

Yin, R. K. (1994). *Case study research: Design and methods* (2nd ed.). Thousand Oaks, CA: Sage.

Zanna, M., & Rempel, J. K. (1988). Attitudes: A new look at an old concept. In D. Bar-Tal & A. W. Kruglanski (Eds.), *The social psychology of attitudes* (pp. 315–334). New York: Cambridge University Press.

Author Index

191

Subject Index